WORLD POLITICS SIMULATIONS IN A GLOBAL INFORMATION AGE

This comprehensive guide explains how to create simulations of international relations for the purposes of both teaching and research. The use of web-based social networks allows for simulations not only among students on the same campus but also among participants literally around the globe.

Hemda Ben-Yehuda, Luba Levin-Banchik, and Chanan Naveh offer as a model their hallmark "World Politics Simulation Project," which involves participants in teams representing various states, nonstate actors, and media organizations embroiled in an international political crisis. Following the trajectory of a simulation, they describe theory, implementation, and analysis. Starting with a typology of simulations, they present a framework for selecting the most suitable kind of simulation in a given teaching situation, based on academic setting, goals, costs, and other practical considerations. The authors then provide step-by-step instructions for creating simulations on cyber platforms, particularly Facebook, complete with schedules, guidelines, sample forms, teaching tips, and student exercises. Throughout the simulation, and during the postsimulation analysis, they explain how to reinforce students' learning and foster critical thinking, creativity, teamwork, and other essential skills. The authors conclude with suggestions for using the data gathered during a simulation for scholarly research.

Instructors in both introductory and advanced courses in political science, international relations, media, history, and area studies, as well as leaders of professional training programs in the civil and military service and media organizations, will find this guide invaluable.

Hemda Ben-Yehuda, Department of Political Studies at Bar-Ilan University, Ramat-Gan, Israel.

Luba Levin-Banchik, Department of Political Studies at Bar-Ilan University, Ramat-Gan, Israel.

Chanan Naveh, School of Communication at Sapir College, Sha'ar Hanegev, Israel.

D1710101

World Politics Simulations in a Global Information Age

HEMDA BEN-YEHUDA, LUBA LEVIN-BANCHIK, AND CHANAN NAVEH

University of Michigan Press
Ann Arbor

Published in the United States of America by the
University of Michigan Press
Manufactured in the United States of America
♾ Printed on acid-free paper

2018   2017   2016   2015   4   3   2   1

A CIP catalog record for this book is available from the British Library.

Library of Congress Cataloging-in-Publication Data

Ben-Yehuda, Hemda, 1954–
    World politics simulations in a global information age / Hemda
Ben-Yehuda, Luba Levin-Banchik, and Chanan Naveh.
        pages   cm
    Includes bibliographical references and index.
    ISBN 978-0-472-07276-7 (hardcover : alk. paper) — ISBN
978-0-472-05276-9 (pbk. : alk. paper) — ISBN 978-0-472-12129-8
(ebook)
    1. International relations—Simulation methods.   2. International
relations—Study and teaching.   I. Levin-Banchik, Luba.   II. Naveh,
Chanan.   III. Title.

JZ1327.B46   2015
327.101'1—dc23
                                        2015020812

CONTENTS

PREFACE

Why have students read about Munich 1938, the Cuban Missile Crisis, the First Palestinian Intifada, or the 2014 confrontation over Crimea, when they can re-create them? This book introduces simulations, conducted in the classroom and on social networks, as innovative, informative, and fun tools for teaching and studying world politics in the 21st century. It is a handbook for educators that explains how to integrate cyber elements into face-to-face simulations and how to preserve the human touch in cyber simulations involving participants who may never meet in person.

The simulations addressed in the book bring together at the negotiating table teams that represent states, non-state actors, and media organs. This interplay between political and media actors enhances the understanding of the complexities of world politics, illuminates multicultural perspectives, and guides students to adopt an analytical and open-minded approach to theory and data.

In the global information age, simulations are a subset of hybrid learning, which complements the most valuable aspects of traditional teaching methods with high-tech resources. Hybrid learning has been proven useful as a way to advance in-depth learning along with analytical capabilities that prepare students for professionalism in academe and beyond. Simulations coupled with cyber tools constitute an effective educational method that provides students with an exciting learning experience that stays with them long after the semester ends.

This book focuses on three kinds of simulation experiences: face-to-face, which involve human participants interacting in a common physical environment; cyber, which involve human participants interacting in a common virtual environment, like social networks with designated Facebook groups as computer-generated "rooms"; and hybrid, which integrate at least two simulation rounds, one face-to-face and the other cyber. Educators can determine which type of simulation is appropriate for their particular courses and then use this book as a step-by-step guide on how to run simulations, with cyber platforms as a supplementary or a major element. Either way, the process will reinforce gradual learning for long-term retention of knowledge and allow students to practice and develop important skills such as critical thinking, creativity, persistence, empathy, and coping during periods of solitary study and teamwork.

The book consists of four parts: Theory, Implementation, Analysis, and Conclusion. It discusses (1) the state of the art on world politics simulations; (2) the types of simulations from which to select a suitable version for a particular course; (3) the facilities required and setup constraints to consider as one prepares for a simulation in an academic setting; (4) a selection of assignments to include as part of the simulation and considerations to take into account for grading participants; (5) the use of simulations to facilitate teaching of different topics, such as theory, methodology, case studies, and area studies; (6) the importance of analysis as an ongoing process during and after the simulation, with feedback, debriefing, and assessment that create a comprehensive overview of the interactive experience; and (7) conclusions on the wide spectrum of tools and simulation designs available and an examination of how the choices we make today are likely to impact the future of simulations in the digital age.

Part I, on theory, consists of three chapters. Chapter 1 outlines simulations as a new mode of study within the hybrid learning field. It reviews the goals for using simulations and provides a framework for the analysis of simulation attributes. The chapter explains why the four framework components of platforms, boundaries, interactions, and study efficiency are useful building blocks for analyzing simulations and how their detailed attributes can be used in planning new simulations. Chapter 2 takes a close look at the academic setting, focusing on course subjects, on-campus vs. online teaching styles, course duration, class type, and cooperation with other educators. It then explains how your specific academic setting affects your options in planning simulations. Chapter 3 offers a new typology of world politics simulations, which can serve as a practical toolbox with which to characterize simulations and plan new ones. The typology is then applied to a variety of simulations reported in academic publications with an emphasis on the 21st century, an era when the Web 2.0 and social networks emerged. The chapter addresses the costs of teaching with simulations and shows how to minimize them in face-to-face and cyber exercises.

Part II, on implementation, consists of three chapters. This part of the book takes you by the hand and leads you through every step of the simulation process. Chapter 4 lays out the essentials of how to create and run a simulation. It starts with a description of the preparations for the event and points to ways you can enhance face-to-face and cyber simulations by using online tools, creating assignments, planning the schedule carefully, and integrating authentic theatrical formats into scenarios. Chapter 5 continues with procedures for the policy formation process within teams, and chapter 6 focuses on the mechanisms for world politics interactions among teams. Unless mentioned otherwise, the same guidelines in these chapters apply to the simulations on campus and in fully online courses.

All three implementation chapters adopt a dual outlook: yours, as an educator, and that of your students. Even as you develop your simulation-related plans and activities to convey the concepts you want to teach and methods for assessing student mastery, you must also consider how things look from a student's point of view. Each chapter contains concise instructions for participants in order to get your students ready to step into the shoes of political and media characters and begin to fulfill their roles in the simulation from the start.

Part III, on analysis, consists of four chapters that form an overview of the entire learning cycle within a simulation project. Chapter 7 addresses feedback, debriefing, and assessment and discusses the overlap among them. The next three chapters deal with each of these concepts in-depth. Chapter 8 looks at feedback, chapter 9 focuses on debriefing, and chapter 10 illuminates assessment. All of them include an in-depth analysis of the various choices for focus, method, and schedule, so you can choose how to best implement the full simulation overview within the parameters specific to your resources and constraints. Chapters 8 and 9 involve activities of educators and students, so each one ends with summary instructions for participants.

In **part IV**, chapter 11 offers a closing discussion on current trends in world politics simulations and possible future interactions. With a macro look at hybrid learning by simulations, it revisits the evolutionary path of simulations till the present, evaluates the contributions of hybrid tools, and suggests insights for future modifications. It also highlights challenges that we have faced in our own simulations, describes solutions we have adopted, and illustrates how ongoing communication with our students and colleagues led to novel ideas for the conduct and appraisal of simulations in a global information age.

Together, the four parts of the book present the core attributes of a simulation project from its drawing board stage, through the learning cycle, to the assessment of students and of the simulation as a whole. All parts embrace theoretical and practical topics, consider options to choose from, discuss costs, and offer tips on how to avoid pitfalls. Illustrative examples from our simulation experiences add detail and contextual substance to operational guidelines for setting up a simulation plan and performing specific procedures for policy formation, world politics activity, feedback, debriefing, and assessment.

If you are familiar with the theoretical underpinnings of simulations as an essential pedagogical tool, you may choose to skip directly to the practical chapters in parts II and III. Novices, however, may want to begin with the theoretical discussion in part I to fully grasp what this rich field of simulations offers educators and students and why such exercises should be an essential part of hybrid learning in the 21st century.

Students live in an increasingly digital world; why not meet them there? While many aspects of traditional teaching retain pride of place, simulations will complement them by allowing your students to engage in active learning, giving you innovative ways to improve their learning efficiency and digital tools with which to enhance the appeal of your class. It is a brave new world, but with this book in hand you can navigate through the wealth of available choices for making an exciting and productive simulation project the highlight of the semester.

ACKNOWLEDGMENTS

This book is a product of cooperation among colleagues. Its main ideas developed gradually over the years of our joint work, from early attempts to break the routine of traditional teaching by use of simulations, to the present, when simulations have become an integral part of our courses and academic projects. From one simulation to another, year after year, we seek ways to enhance learning and make simulations an appealing and efficient teaching tool.

Over time, we have collaborated with many outstanding teachers, inspiring partners, and motivated students, all of whom contributed greatly to our way of thinking about and practicing simulations. We deeply appreciate the generous support provided by our home institutions, Bar-Ilan University and Sapir College. We also want to thank Meirav Mishali-Ram, our associate at Bar-Ilan University, with whom we first tested our idea of Facebook as a platform for simulations.

We owe our International Studies Association (ISA) colleagues, especially Andrea Gerlak, the Director of Academic Development, and Nikolaos Biziouras, Section President of the Active Learning in International Affairs (ALIAS), a debt of gratitude for giving us the chance to try out innovative practices at ISA conferences and to improve implementation procedures. We also want to thank Laurie Zittrain Eisenberg and Mary Jane Parmentier, who took part in our simulation project for ISA scholars and became our keen partners in running several cross-continental simulations for Israeli and American students.

Many of our dedicated students played a vital role in the refinement of the World Politics Simulation Project. We are especially indebted to Guy Zohar, who has been deeply involved in our simulations, first as a participant and later as the crucial cyber administrator overseeing all web-related issues for encounters in Israel, at the ISA conferences, and among academic institutions in Israel and the United States. Whatever wisdom is collected here reflects the insights and contributions of the many individuals whom we thanked above. Any missteps or errors are solely of our own devising.

We would like to extend our deep appreciation and thanks to Melody Herr for the continued enthusiastic support of our project from its genesis stage, and to Kevin Rennells and the dedicated staff at the University of Michigan Press for their commitment to our manuscript. Without their help, the book would not have reached its present state.

Most of all, we owe a tribute to our families. They followed us from one simulation to another and worked hard to keep straight which stunning political events were occurring in the real world and which were confined to our simulated universes. Their unconditional support and ongoing encouragement made this book possible.

Hemda Ben-Yehuda
Luba Levin-Banchik
Chanan Naveh
July 2014

LIST OF FIGURES

LIST OF TABLES

DETAILED TABLE OF CONTENTS

PART I

Theory

CHAPTER 1

Simulations in Hybrid Learning

The study of world politics in the global information age requires proper tools that fit the era. The main purpose of this chapter is to show how simulations are integrated into hybrid learning as an efficient educational method. *Hybrid learning* has become a common practice that brings together traditional and modern technology-based teaching procedures to achieve in-depth learning.[1] Simulations are offered herein as an innovative subset of hybrid learning that involves a rich and rewarding mix of solitary and interactive knowledge acquisition. Simply put, simulations of world politics are processes in which participants representing political or media actors interact with one another according to a fiction or nonfiction story to advance their goals and policies. We extend this definition to simulations as political systems later in the chapter.

This book is designed for 21st-century educators and students who are rapidly internalizing the benefits of hybrid learning during individual preparation of assignments and research, multimedia assisted lectures, class discussions, simulation rounds, feedback, and debriefing. It focuses on face-to-face and cyber simulations on social networks designed for digital natives who are nowadays the typical students in institutions of higher education. The idea of hybrid learning with simulations takes into account that the introduction of Web 2.0 platforms into classes is unequal: some use it frequently and in all aspects of learning, others don't. So the book offers adaptation techniques and motivational inducements for newcomers, late adaptors, and experienced devotees. As such, it is made to fit the coming generation of college educators and students, offering a new, exciting, and effective mode of teaching.

Along with the introduction of simulations as an innovative tool, we highlight the roles and contributions of the virtual environment as an indispensable part of solitary and collective learning. So we offer this manuscript to educators who have used simulations for years, as well as for ones that want to try out this new way of teaching.

Throughout the book we refer to three simulation genres discussed in-depth in chapter 3: (1) **face-to-face**, which involve human participants interacting in a common physical environment like a classroom, a lecture hall, or a conference lounge; (2) **cyber**, which involve human participants interacting on a common virtual environment like social networks with designated Facebook groups as their computer-generated "rooms"; and (3) **hybrid**, which integrate at least two rounds within a single simulation, one face-to-face and the other cyber.

Experienced faculty who run face-to-face simulations will find many ideas and practical tools on how to add cyber elements to various parts of the learning process, with or without the simulations on social networks.[2] Newcomers will find a detailed scheme on how to integrate various types of simulations into the teaching plan and practical advice on how to conduct the simulation from A to Z.

In academe, teaching styles differ, some remain traditional on-campus ones, others apply hybrid learning tools in class, provide supplementary materials on distance learning platforms, or teach fully online courses. In addition to class and office meetings, students often communicate with faculty and peers via e-mail, conduct research on the web, and integrate digital resources into their study assignments.

Chapter 3 demonstrates that simulation types also

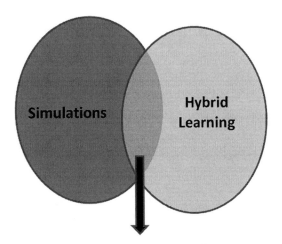

Hybrid Learning with Simulations

Fig. 1.1. Simulations and hybrid learning

vary greatly. Some of them involve face-to-face interactions with no resort to web platforms or digital resources while others are cyber ones that are run on advanced web platforms. Figure 1.1 illustrates the area of overlap between hybrid learning and simulations.

Not all simulations are part of hybrid learning as some of them only involve short ad-hoc role-play exercises in class with no resort to online features. Similarly, not all hybrid learning practices integrate simulations, so many fully distance-learning classes use web platforms for remote access with no integration of simulations in their curriculum.

This book is about the intersection zone. It is designed to show that the application of simulations in hybrid learning can encompass a wide variety of choices, with a different emphasis on traditional and virtual elements in teaching and in simulation modes, detailed in the second part of the book on implementation. It is the joint impact of simulations integrated in a hybrid learning cycle that produces the gains we highlight in the third part of the book on analysis and in the fourth part of the book on the projections for the use of simulations in the coming years.

The variants at the intersecting zone of simulations and hybrid learning are many, open to modification and adjustment. At one end of the spectrum you may choose to run a traditional face-to-face simulation, but integrate some hybrid learning tools into lectures and online student assignments to enrich and liven up the process. At the other end, alongside on-campus classes or distance learning, you may run several cyber simulation rounds and conclude them with an international conference, conducted face-to-face or by a video conference that brings

together participants from afar. Regardless of your particular choice, the overlap of simulations and hybrid learning means that simulations become an integral part of a comprehensive learning cycle described below.

We regard simulations as an effective way to teach world politics. The idea of extending the learning process to virtual environments captures the main thrust of the book. Social networks and other free Web 2.0 platforms, with Facebook in particular, are our starting point for describing how to run simulations. Google+, WhatsApp, or Edmodo, as an educational forum, various e-mail services, and designated websites are also useful for the same purpose. But ample room should be left for the incorporation of an infinite range of innovations that are likely to take place in the future. Whenever we refer to cyber simulations on Facebook, we actually mean any social network or suitable alternative platform that is available and popular. With the appearance of new digital tools and resources you can easily add them to the modular structure of this manuscript, to fit your learning environment.[3]

Many simulations build on a real or fictional crisis scenarios within an ongoing conflict. The crisis embodies dramatic and rapidly unfolding events that are related to a much broader conflict reality. This type of scenario makes it easy for the students to assimilate in time and space to a particular well-defined role and to learn what they are about to play. Indeed, most of our examples relate to conflict situations in the Middle East and more specifically to the Arab-Israel conflict.[4] But simulation scenarios can be applied to other geographic regions and acute phases in nonconflict situations. They may include negotiations among states and nonstate actors on integration processes, the formation of an alliance or its policies, and a decision-making process with choices that touch upon culture, values, and moral dilemmas related to human rights, welfare, the environment, or the creation of new international regimes. Simulations can focus on current or past cases, by reliance on historical documents supplemented by fictional material created for the purpose of the simulation. Scenarios can also build on science fiction narratives, like George Orwell's *1984, The Lord of the Rings, The Matrix,* or *Star Wars.*[5]

Some international crises evolve without violence, while others escalate to war. While war simulations are common in military training, the primary focus of this book is on simulations of diplomacy and media. At the core of the exercise is a policy formation process and its implementation in world politics, in a peaceful or conflict setting. Diplomacy may be triggered by a war scare, acts of violence, civil war, terror, or even full-scale war.

All these may be part of the scenario, marking the onset of a simulation. But policy formation within teams and world politics interactions among teams include the consideration and exchange of various political, diplomatic, economic, and military threats and promises, short of violence and war. This means that although a wide range of foreign policy tools can be used, the simulation is not a war game or a strategic fight between armies. So, in the Gulf nuclear simulation, described in the appendix, a brief and limited missile exchange between Israel and Iran was followed by intensive negotiations to work out a settlement for "the day after," which was the main concern of all participants. As we explain in chapter 5 on simulation rules, any resort to violence requires the consent of the educator who runs the simulation. Therefore, diplomacy, in a cooperative or coercive context, along with economic and public diplomacy moves, can be coupled with limited violence only if a team gets the educator's permission to go ahead with their plan for a well-defined political purpose. This fundamental simulation rule ensures the diplomatic nature of the world politics simulations we use and describe in this book.

In what follows, we first present the rationale for using simulations in hybrid learning with an emphasis on the basic goals you can attain by this mode of teaching. Next we offer a conceptual framework that is designed as a toolbox of four concise elements and many detailed attributes that characterize all simulations. The framework designates platforms, boundaries, interactions, and study efficiency as the core building blocks of simulations, designed to guide the discussion on goal promotion in simulations. The analysis shows that many goals can be met by face-to-face or cyber simulations and highlights the wealth of options for choice when you plan your simulation. It also indicates the unique contributions of each type of simulation and points to the added value reached when you combine face-to-face and cyber rounds in one hybrid simulation. This way, you can familiarize yourself with alternatives for consideration when you think of hybrid learning and begin to plan the simulation that suits you best.

Rationale

For some of us, traditional and innovative teaching modes with high-tech tools are already a natural way of teaching. For others it is still a new venture. This section explains why it is useful to integrate simulations into a teaching routine. Table 1.1 summarizes the basic goals that simulations are designed to achieve, based on the extensive literature review described in chapter 3. You can use this table as a checklist for the goals you may want to achieve in any simulation you plan.

When you use simulations as part of hybrid learning you are bound to create a progressive and reinforcing learning experience that will enable students to (1) grasp the subject matter in a multidimensional way; (2) gain a better understanding of the complexities of world politics; (3) enjoy classes and course work; (4) develop and practice skills, like critical thinking, empathy, leadership, and teamwork; and (5) improve grades. All this is achieved when passive learning is replaced with active participation, solitary learning is transformed into a new experience with a creative search process to acquire knowledge, traditional resources are expanded, and the curriculum is redesigned to incorporate simulations into the course plan and learning process.

From the start, this book is designed to meet the challenge of education in the 21st century by pointing to the wealth of information at the fingertips of current digital natives. The virtual environment extends the physical campus location and drastically changes the meaning of time and space. If the academic calendar demarcates the learning slot on campus and its duration, the virtual milieu redefines it. You and your students can meet as often as needed on cyber forums. Each student can extend the learning process to interactions with peers. Many of the sources are always available, and the use of texts, photos, and video clips allows students to move in time to other periods that are central to the topics they study. Online resources let students see and hear how leaders act and even step into their shoes and feel what it is like to cope with the dilemmas of world politics. Such dynamics can also be achieved by screening movies in class, but the full intensity of a personal experience is profoundly enhanced when students actively engage in a simulation.

Access to web platforms also modifies the spatial boundaries, from the physical confines of the campus to the entire global village. A student can be at home and relocate, with the click of a mouse, to other conflict regions, like the Middle East, Central America, or South East Asia. Such a shift enables a challenging process of solitary learning beyond the confines of given state boundaries.

Even more so, the web forums and social networks make it possible to run simulations with participants from across the globe to create a genuine intercultural process among peers in faraway countries. This greatly helps students grasp the complexities of world politics

TABLE 1.1. Simulation Goals

Check if relevant for your simulation	Literature
Combine systematic, flexible and varied methods of study at individual and team levels	DeGarmo (2006); Goon (2011); Kelle (2008); Korosteleva (2010); Parmentier (2013); Raymond (2010); Rothman (2012); Taylor, Backlund, and Niklasson (2012)
Apply paradigms and theories, explore complexity, understand situations that have no analytical solution	Asal (2005); Asal and Blake (2006); Asal and Schulzke (2012); Boyer et al. (2009); Brynen (2010); Chasek (2005); Corbeil and Laveault (2011); Crossley-Frolick (2010); Dexter and Guittet (2014); Earnest (2008); Enterline and Jepsen (2009); Fowler and Pusch (2010); Goon (2011); Kelle (2008); Korosteleva (2010); Loggins (2009); Mintz (2004); Mintz, Redd, and Vedlitz (2006); Raymond and Sorensen (2008); Rothman (2012); Rousseau and Van der Veen (2005); Sasley (2010); Schnurr, Santo, and Craig (2013); Siegel and Young (2009); Stoll (2011); Stover (2007); Strand and Rapkin (2011); Weir and Baranowski (2011); Wolfe (2010); Zaino and Mulligan (2009)
Make the study more tangible so theories of international relations, political studies, social sciences, history and media come to life	Ben-Yehuda, Naveh, and Levin-Banchik (2013b); Blair et al. (2010); Boyer et al. (2009); Brynen (2010); Cioffi-Revilla and Rouleau (2010); Crossley-Frolick (2010); DeGarmo (2006); Dexter and Guittet (2014); Enterline and Jepsen (2009); Geller and Alam (2010); Goon (2011); Kanner (2007); Kelle (2008); Mintz (2004); Parmentier (2013); Raymond (2010); Sasley (2010); Schnurr, Santo, and Craig (2013); Simpson and Kaussler (2009); Smolinski and Kesting (2012); Stoll (2011); Taylor (2013); Wolfe (2010); Yilmaz, Oren, and Ghasem-Aghaee (2006); Zaino and Mulligan (2009)
Serve as a laboratory for practical training and research on decision-making, negotiations, journalism and other topics	Asal (2005); Asal and Blake (2006); Asal and Schulzke (2012); Ben-Yehuda, Naveh, and Levin-Banchik (2013b); Blair et al. (2010); Boyer et al. (2009); Brynen (2010); Butcher (2012); Crossley-Frolick (2010); DeGarmo (2006); Enterline and Jepsen (2009); Kanner (2007); Lay and Smarick (2006); Loggins (2009); Mintz (2004); Mintz, Redd, and Vedlitz (2006); Schnurr, Santo, and Craig (2013); Smolinski and Kesting (2012); Wolfe (2010)
Complement and enhance traditional study by increasing motivation and encouraging an attentive and active learning process	Asal (2005); Blum and Scherer (2007); Butcher (2012); Fowler (2009); Kelle (2008); Korosteleva (2010); Loggins (2009); Obendorf and Randerson (2012); Simpson and Kaussler (2009); Smolinski and Kesting (2012); Taylor (2013); Weir and Baranowski (2011)
Develop critical thinking and analytical skills	DeGarmo (2006); Kanner (2007); Loggins (2009); McMahon and Miller (2012); Obendorf and Randerson (2012); Raymond and Sorensen (2008); Taylor (2013); Weir and Baranowski (2011); Yilmaz, Ören, and Ghasem-Aghaee (2006); Zaino and Mulligan (2009)
Expose diversity of cultural, ethical and religious issues, value judgments, prejudice and subjective points of view	Asal and Schulzke (2012); Brynen (2010); DeGarmo (2006); Dexter and Guittet (2014); Fowler (2009); Parmentier (2013); Stover (2007); Weir and Baranowski (2011). See also *Statecraft* under websites in references
Facilitate sympathy and empathy, identification, and attitude modifications	Dexter and Guittet (2014); Sasley (2010); Williams and Williams (2011, 2010)
Expose underlying processes and causal mechanisms	Rousseau and Van der Veen (2005)
Teach to manage information and retain it longer	Asal (2005); Taylor (2013)
Allow informal learning between educators and students	Darling and Foster (2012); Taylor Backlund, and Niklasson (2012); Zaino and Mulligan (2009)
Increase the number of students reached, including "resistant populations"	Asal (2005); Chasek (2005); DeGarmo (2006); Glazier (2011); Goon (2011); Lay and Smarick (2006)
Elevate civic culture and rhetoric skills	Corbeil and Laveault (2011); Goon (2011); Lay and Smarick (2006); Sasley (2010); Taylor (2013)
Add creativity and improvisation to make learning emotional, intensive and enjoyable	Brynen (2010); Crossley-Frolick (2010); Kelle (2008); Parmentier (2013); Weir and Baranowski (2011)
Enrich postsimulation learning by linking simulation developments to real events	Enterline and Jepsen (2009); Goon (2011)
Encourage peer-based collaborative teamwork	Asal (2005); Corbeil and Laveault (2011); Darling and Foster (2012); DeGarmo (2006); Lay and Smarick (2006); Loggins (2009); McMahon and Miller (2012); Obendorf and Randerson (2012)

with different cultures, worldviews, and attitudes. These complexities are no longer a theoretical matter but rather a practical constraint each participant has to deal with while preparing class assignments, getting ready for the simulation, and for interactions with others.

The physical meeting place for each group may occur on a single campus and in a given course with traditional lectures. But a bulk of the interactions and learning process can take place on the web. Even in class, some deliberations can focus on the activities that had taken place on the web and discuss their meaning. Previous experiences in one's life, dogmatic positions, stereotypes, and in-group values are then put to a test and critical thinking may take place. Consequently, the global village or conflict zone may enter your lectures and the thoughts of your students to create a genuine experience of confrontation, coping, and management.

Cooperation with colleagues in other states may require some coordination efforts, but once you try out such encounters you will discover the extraordinary profits of partnership and maybe even find it hard to go back to the old ways of teaching.

Passive Learning Replaced

Figure 1.2 illustrates the transformed learning structure and multiple interaction processes that characterize simulations in hybrid learning. Simulations with cyber aids bring about a restructuring of the learning configuration from a traditional top-down one, illustrated by the bold arrows alone, to a more complex one, shown by the addition of multiple light arrows.

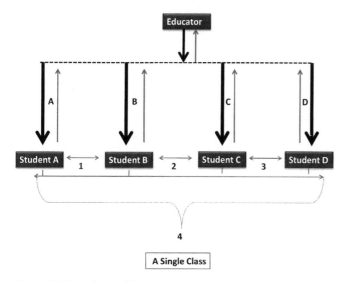

Fig. 1.2. Transformed learning structure

In a traditional setting, the *vertical interactions* include the transfer of knowledge from you, the educator, to your students. You are the most active, and your students are generally the more passive followers. These interactions involve lectures, assignments, exams, and discussions in class. Obviously, some students are more involved and assertive than others, but you remain the main driving force in the learning process. Most efforts are geared to ensure that students retain information, which is tested in the final exams. Within this setting you may have little time for the development of skills such as critical thinking or creativity.

The *horizontal interactions* among students in a traditional course take place mainly in class, sometimes in the process of preparing assignments together, while others remain out of sight, when students use the materials of a peer to save time and hand in an assignment without going through the independent search and study cycle.

In simulations as part of hybrid learning the volume of interactions is dramatically increased and fundamentally restructured: the vertical ones, A to D in figure 1.2, are eased, and the horizontal ones, illustrated in numbers 1 to 4, are considerably strengthened. So the light arrows indicating activities from student to educator contribute more to the learning process than the bold arrows that had taken the lead in the traditional setting.

Solitary Learning Transformed

The syllabus is traditionally the learning contract between the student and the educator. It presents the topic and goals of the course, the reading requirements, and the assignments needed for its completion. The main task for students is to read texts listed in the syllabus, sometimes coupled with the preparation of a short presentation for class or other assignments. To advance a more focused study and an integrative outlook, educators usually provide their students with a few guiding questions on the text and key concepts that are at the center of the inquiry.

In simulations with hybrid learning, the syllabus becomes a central tool in which you advertise the exciting simulation project, explain its distinctive assignments, and detail the progressive schedule you plan to inspire students from start. Beyond the syllabus much of the learning process develops by the active involvement of each participant, by dynamic interactions between students and educators and among peer students. This means that the reading requirements are the minimal starting point in the learning journey, which is shaped by the educator and each student in conjunction with others. So too are the written and participatory assignments as the learning process provides opportunities for creativity and growth.

A closer look at the solitary learning process reveals that the vertical student-to-educator roles shift, and the students find themselves contributing to the learning process, sometimes even more than the educator. Beyond the basic texts, students locate and assess much of the material that is essential for progress. Moreover, a multitude of horizontal interactions and creative initiatives take place by motivated students and among them and their peers. The amount of learning interactions increases considerably and the weight of vertical and horizontal interactions changes, in favor of the latter. This gives more room for a progressive dialogue and the gradual development of critical thinking. Simulations give your students a sense of the partnership in the development of the subject matter. The success of the simulation and consequently of the course becomes a shared goal for you and your class. When the relationships between you and your students become more flexible, inhibitions to opening up are slowly removed and the fear of making mistakes decreases. With simulations, students can feel much more comfortable to participate, ask questions, express their views, try out theoretical frameworks they have learned, and practice policy formation and activity in world politics.

To be sure, these changes in learning patterns and the more extensive use of online features are not accomplished without your guidance and support, but digital natives are usually comfortable with the virtual environment. They have the skills to surf the web and find what they are looking for and even more. This leaves a place for unexpected findings and serendipity. Active learning makes students enjoy their study and motivates many of them to engage more fully in the topic under observation. Once assignments are posted on the joint forum or social network, a sense of contribution and accomplishment leads to even higher interest, competition with peers, and extended commitment. Changes in solitary learning may also shape the lesson in class as you discuss short clips, select movie scenes, or review the contents of interactions within and among teams placed on the social network. This way your lecture becomes part of the activities the students had engaged in and a friendly session of feedback and encouragement.

The horizontal student-to-student roles, indicated by arrows 1, 2, and 3 in figure 1.2, are also drastically altered to form a larger part of solitary study, which becomes active and interactive. Students can coach one another, discovering that all of them gain via such co-operation. Working groups can be set up on social networks to tackle different aspects of a hard-to-resolve issue. By communicating in these forums, participants can gain pride on their ability to master topics, confront and solve problems, deal with complexities, and apply analytical thinking.

All these interactions may also take part on a university administered platform, with more or less similar results. But we find the social network quite promising because students navigate there as part of their daily habits. By meeting in a Facebook group created for active study, the boundaries of social and study time fade and most students are drawn into a more intensive encounter with the topic they are learning.

Traditional Resources Expanded

Simulations as part of hybrid learning can easily be incorporated into courses of political science, international relations, history, media, and area studies. Beyond the basic reading requirements for all course topics, the virtual platform offers a wealth of resources that considerably enrich the learning process. Among these are academic and nonacademic search engines, websites, and many applications, such as YouTube, Skype, and Dropbox, to store data, gain knowledge, share information, express opinions, and communicate with others.

To begin a search process to acquire knowledge, you should provide students with lead themes: (1) the *topic*, for example, the Arab-Israel conflict; (2) the *participants*, states like Egypt, Israel and Syria, nonstate actors such as the Hamas, or media organs such as *Aljazeera*; (3) the *decision-makers*, for instance, President Bashar Assad; and (4) the core *documents* that shape a given situation, for example, UN Resolution 181 of 1947 or the 1974 Israel-Syria separation of forces agreement.

After a brief introduction about how to use academic and other search engines, in class, the library, or on a virtual platform of your choice, the students can start their own inquiry. Once progress is made they are required to report on their findings to you and their classmates. Different students are bound to come up with a variety of sources, discuss their contribution, and evaluate their quality. One way to make this search more efficient is to request that all students post a link to the resources they have found, with a short comment on how it adds to the learning process. By the use of a virtual platform, a lively debate encourages students to express their positions and highlights the fact that more than one point of view may emerge from certain texts. Here the first steps toward the development of crit-

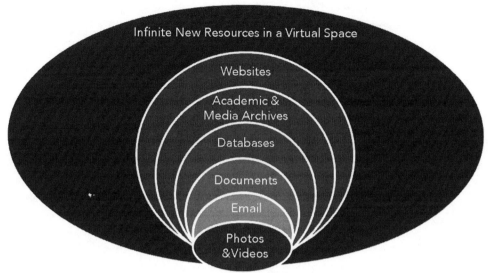

Fig. 1.3. Hybrid learning resources

ical thinking begin, and the transformation of a group of students into a learning community starts.

Figure 1.3 presents the hybrid learning resources in the form of concentric circles. The inner circles represent specific resources, while the outer ones contain multiple subsets with a variety of sources within each of them. Students can become familiar with the topic of the simulation by finding photos and video clips that let them see, hear, and feel the reality they are probing and add an authentic hue to the study. With photos and clips from YouTube some serious topics can be viewed with humor and through a lighter perspective, drawing hesitant students to the material under investigation. Visuals like caricatures, maps, and figures with data can add to the fun of building a joint knowledge-bank and enhance the learning experience as a whole.

Next, by resorting to the e-mail and documents circles, students can share and exchange information with one another, thereby increasing the horizontal interactions in hybrid learning. The documents may involve genuine agreements reached in the past among states, international organizations, or nonstate entities that are relevant to the topic under investigation and assignments written by students in preparation for the simulation.

By using resources in the three inner circles some students may come up with clips and photos of the decision-makers and events, thereby helping others become more familiar with the characters and atmosphere of the region and time. The addition of documents provides a wealth of information on the process under investigation. From a methodological standpoint, you can highlight the contributions of distinct resources to the buildup of a whole

picture and discuss the issue of validity and data manipulation in different sources derived from cyberspace.

Moving on to databases, the students compare the qualitative data they have gathered thus far with academic and professional information to expand and enrich their knowledge on the topic of inquiry. This integration can begin with (1) overview summaries and reports like the *CIA World Factbook*;[6] (2) qualitative and quantitative archives generated by states, alliances, international organizations, or media organs under investigation; and (3) academic databases like COW, ICB, MAR, MID, and PRIO.[7]

Next in the concentric circles are the archives of academic publications and newspapers that encapsulate resources of clearer reputation. You can point out to your students that archives like JSTOR, ProQuest, the International Relations Oxford Bibliographies, the International Studies Encyclopedia, and websites of individual academic journals contain research that has passed peer reviews for quality. Journals are also ranked, reflecting levels of academic excellence. But students should be aware that media archives, such as those constructed by Lexis-Nexis, Newseum, the *BBC*, the *New York Times*, or any local paper, reflect the unique profile each media organ seeks to promote and a built-in bias that each news archive represents.

Intercultural outlooks and cleavages within and among states help students understand disagreements among actors and the severity of the conflicts that will be handled later during the simulation. To cope with coverage discrepancies and interpretation differences, students may (1) post links to various sites with contents on media coverage; (2) highlight the contradictions in actor perceptions; and (3) discuss the meaning such practices unravel. Together, the objective and subjective data provide students with an idea about the main topic you teach and its multiple perspectives.

Almost at the last outer band are other websites of unknown and sometimes even problematic reputation that can also be used for study. Here your role of guiding and coaching is central to assure that students will avoid the pitfalls of disinformation. You can point out some core websites as essential resources and explain their qualities, warn against others, and bring to the attention of the class several websites that students have found and discuss their value. This can be done as part of your lectures in class or on any virtual forum you choose.

The web offers a dynamic environment for creative inputs in the future. So the last band refers to resources that are still unavailable at present but are sure to emerge after the publication of this book. As they appear, you can add them to your resource list, to enrich the inputs for theoretical or empirical investigation by students. Each of these resources serves as a specific piece needed for advancing the complex research puzzle you have assigned your students.

At the start, some students may be more active, have more motivation, or feel more at home on the web than others. So let your students know that the process of resource accumulation is an integral part of their grade. You may request each one of them to add a given number of resources to the joint knowledge-bank with a brief summary of the source, some questions on its contents, and an assessment of its reputation. With detailed instructions and some coaching you can transform your class into a learning community even at this early stage of solitary learning for the simulation.

The search process to acquire knowledge is a learning experience in itself. The wealth of resources illustrated in figure 1.3 make the buildup of knowledge a creative process that involves active thinking, far beyond passive reading of preassigned texts. Students quickly enrich one another, share the burden of finding and evaluating relevant sources, and gain more information jointly than they would have alone.

You can encourage students to engage in the inquiry endeavor by discussing interesting sources in class. Another way to go about is to couple a strong student with weaker ones to share tasks. When you follow individual and group activities on Facebook you can frequently add *"likes"* that show you are aware of the learning progress. From time to time you can upload comments on the posts

of your students to direct their study, pinpoint omissions, highlight quality contributions, and sharpen issues worth more thought.

Curriculum Redesigned

How does hybrid learning with simulations blend into the traditional academic curriculum to elevate the acquisition of knowledge? In your lecture-plan for a course that incorporates simulations you need to allocate some time to explain what they are and how you will use them as a new tool of study. You will also introduce the topic you plan for the simulation, such as the Palestinian quest for statehood, and the assignments required in preparation for the simulation. The first lectures may follow a regular sequence, but as part of the transformed solitary learning process discussed above, it is useful to devote some time to guide and follow collective learning interactions.

The course outline and the ways you structure your topics are the foundation of the learning process. As we show in the second part of the book on implementation, the classroom may remain an essential component, a place where lectures take place and horizontal or vertical interactions unfold between you as the educator and your students as part of active learning. But the experience you will be creating with simulations will be totally different from most ordinary courses. Simulations on social networks are usually an ongoing process that occurs parallel to your lectures. They can be used as a preparatory process for shorter face-to-face events on campus or via video conferences that enhance the human dimensions in negotiations and agreements. Your lectures, the solitary preparation carried out by the students, engagements on social networks, face-to-face meetings, and debriefing discussions all accumulate to form a new way of teaching designed to develop an open-minded approach to theory and findings.

Figure 1.4 summarizes the use of simulations as part of hybrid learning that begins with your lectures and proceeds via solitary learning throughout the course for each student individually. Once the simulation starts, all students discuss topics, share information, build foreign policy plans within teams, and engage in the practice of world politics. After it ends, an extensive debriefing process takes place to understand what has happened and why.

The preparation of research projects illustrated in figure 1.4 may be the main product of advanced graduate courses and reflect the full spectrum of knowledge gained by students. But individual research may also take place

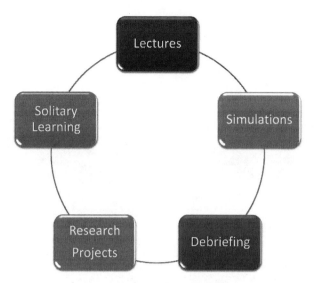

Fig. 1.4. Simulations in a hybrid learning cycle

on a much smaller scale for any level of study, even in undergraduate courses. For example, simulation participants may compare their encounters with real cases to highlight similarities and differences. Though "a game is only a game," as your students write their papers they will realize that the simulation is a source of insights gained by stepping into the shoes of decision-makers to practice policy formation and engage in world politics activities. Above all, your students will recognize the meaning of a complex international system, where no single actor can impose its will on others.

The information posted on social networks, like the Facebook groups, serves as a vast database for research on theoretical or empirical topics that you have raised in your course. The gradual buildup, from solitary learning and lectures, via simulation interactions to debriefing and research, covers a progressive learning cycle that suits the demands of college graduates of the current era. It is designed to help them develop from the academic point of view, prepare for the requirements of the professional world, or send them off to a successful academic career in the future.

Simulations as part of hybrid learning facilitate an in-depth learning process. Simulations enable you, the educator, to bring together many concerns that were part of world politics in the past, or are the major dilemmas of current events. They demonstrate the complexities of (1) multiactor decision-making; (2) threats and escalation management; (3) linkage among issues, actors, and activities; (4) media involvement and its impact on politics; and (5) character, motivation, creativity, and emotions that shape political outcomes. These and other topics

practiced in simulations are addressed in the second part of the book on implementation.

Simulations offer an innovative approach to the study of world politics nowadays. They build on traditional and novel resources and combine multiple learning platforms. The integration of different simulation types and topics into the curriculum provides your students with a personal experience and enriched perspectives. The use of friendly, free, easily accessible, and well-known cyber tools, the specifics of simulation you run, and the relative weight of the simulation experience in the overall learning cycle are all up to you. Whatever your choice, simulations are likely to gain a competitive advantage over traditional study modes of world politics.

Conceptual Framework: A Toolbox and Building Blocks

The conceptual framework, summarized in table 1.2, identifies the main components of a simulation and characterizes its core attributes. Why does one need a conceptual framework? What is it good for? Each simulation has a story of its own that can be described in detail. What does the framework add?

We believe that if simulations are to expand considerably beyond experimental exercises by some faculty and comprehensive use by a few others, there must be a systematic way to address simulations and to encapsulate their essence in a few useful terms that are common to all simulations. We define four such components below and explain their contributions to goal achievement.

Once scholars compare and classify simulations in a scientific manner, it becomes possible to (1) identify the differences among simulations; (2) uncover the range of options on what to include in a simulation; and (3) pinpoint cost-benefit tradeoffs. A fruitful dialogue can then emerge among simulation users on the assessment of simulations as a teaching tool in academe and on the adoption of more rigorous practices in the future, as discussed in chapters 10 and 11.

You can envision the conceptual framework presented herein, together with the typology outlined in chapter 3, as a theoretical toolbox and linguistic building blocks. You can apply them to the analysis of any simulation and keep them handy as you proceed to the second part of the book on implementation. After you are familiar with this toolbox you can use it to describe and compare all simulations addressed in this book and others you encounter elsewhere

TABLE 1.2. Conceptual Framework of World Politics Simulations

Component		Attribute
Platforms	Infrastructure	Physical/Virtual
	Web platforms	Websites, e-mail, social networks, academic and media databases, other virtual applications and resources like YouTube
	Theatrical setting	Costumes and decor, language, rhetoric, intonations, body language
Spatial boundaries	Players	Human/Machine
	Academic level	Unilevel/Multilevel, ranging from undergraduate to professionals Single/Multiple fields of study: international relations, political science, history, media, area studies, conflict and security research, scientific study of international processes, methodology and active learning
	Assignments	Compulsory/Voluntary Actor portfolio, character biography, values, goals, policy plans opening initiatives and negotiation proposals, press releases, media products, intra/interteam interactions, concluding remarks, feedback form, debriefing insights and research projects
	Number of players	Planned and actual participants
	Geographic spread	Single/Multiple: regions, states, campuses, courses
	Geographic diversity	Locale: campus and off-campus, home, office and en route
	Number of teams	Planned and actual teams with planned and actual players per team
	Type of actors	Superpowers, great powers, regional states, international organizations, military alliances, nonstate actors and media organs
Temporal boundaries	Phases	A cycle from preparation, policy formation, world politics, feedback, debriefing, assessment, and research
	Duration	Single lesson, semester, year
	Tempo	Upfront speeches or dynamic communications
		Slow/Fast
	Timing and turning-points	Driven by initial and opening scenario, add-hoc events, political and media teams
	Acceleration	Breakpoints create non-linear process initiated by simulation administration or teams usually before the simulation ends
Interactions	Topics/Issues	Historical, current, nonfiction, or fictional on peace, conflict and war events in regional or global politics
		Single/Multi-topic in one or several working groups
	Type of contacts	Within teams: political/media teams formulate policy and initiatives Political teams: threats and promises between two or more teams Political and media teams: media management, public diplomacy and coping with media manipulation
	Level of contacts	One sided, bilateral and multilateral
	Synchronization	Asynchronous flexible login on virtual platform and upfront speeches on-campus Synchronous meetings in preset times with all participants active online or face-to-face on-campus
	Negotiation	Bilateral/Multilateral with or without observers, mediators and media
		Formal/Informal
		Closed/Open to the media
	Mediation	By superpower, regional power or international organization
	Coaching	By educator to individual participants By participants within and among teams
Study efficiency of teaching and learning	Cognitive	Achieve advanced and improved comprehension of theory, empirical realities, area studies, methodology, multiple actor types, media involvement and the complex domestic-international linkages
	Behavioral	Practice leadership and teamwork in fields, such as decision making, information processing, policy formation, strategic planning, negotiation, mediation, public diplomacy and media management. Gain training, feedback insights and adaption skills
	Affective	Experience and develop emotional skills: empathy, identification, fun, frustration, uncertainty, surprise, stress, patience, persistence, anger, happiness, failure and success

or run on your own. Then you can adapt the contents of this toolbox to your own preferences and concerns.

To start with, we regard simulations as political systems, set up intentionally to replicate fiction or nonfiction situations. They involve at least two participants as individuals or teams, representing states, nonstate actors, international organizations, or media organs that interact according to a given scenario within a preset time frame and specific rules for activity. From the simplest, short, and ad-hoc role-play in class to a complex project, with multiple rounds, over an extended time, on cyber platforms and in face-to-face meetings, simulations have basic components that are common to systems in all fields of science and to political systems in particular.[8]

As political systems, all simulations are characterized by four components: (1) *Platforms* typify the physical infrastructure and virtual environments of the simulation. They involve a wide range of settings, from a lecture hall or conference room for a face-to-face meeting to virtual "rooms" for a get-together on social networks in a cyber simulation. (2) *Boundaries* include spatial and temporal elements that shape the contents and process of a particular simulation and tap its main features. As static attributes, teams, players, time frame, and topic set the boundaries for the simulation and map the preconditions for its interaction flow. (3) *Interactions* tell the dynamic story of the simulation and embody the complex patterns of planned and unplanned developments that occur among political and media teams. These activities include initiatives, negotiations, mediation efforts, and political outcomes. Some involve up-front speeches and individual role-play in a classroom setting or "nonlive" encounters on virtual platforms at flexible login times. Others include "live" engagements on virtual platforms with dynamic exchanges during fixed login times for all players as the counterparts of dyadic to multiplayer negotiations in face-to-face encounters. (4) *Study efficiency* captures the core function of simulations as an innovative method of teaching. From the point of view of both faculty and students, it makes simulations a dedicated exercise designed to fit an academic setting, a teaching curriculum, and well-defined goals.

Simulations trigger creative initiatives, increased motivation, and a wider array of experiences beyond the traditional modes of classroom teaching. Personal and team activity create an interplay among cognitive, behavioral, and emotional stimuli encountered in the simulation and make the overall learning impact much greater than the sum of its separate effects. By actual participation and repeated practice, students are able to reach an under-

standing of abstract paradigms, theories, and concepts. Such results are frequently mentioned by simulation participants in the debriefing session and in written feedback after the simulation ends. Advanced knowledge comprehension is often accompanied by memories of intense simulation episodes that endure far beyond short-term information retention for a final course exam.

Figure 1.5 introduces the four simulation components and specifies the links among them in graphic terms. It separates study efficiency into learning and teaching: the former is advanced before, during, and after the simulation encounter, the latter is assessed after the simulation ends and all feedback, debriefing, and final assignments are graded.

This framework follows the general systems theory's distinction between static elements of structure and processes of interaction, to characterize simulations as systems that replicate historical and contemporary political realities or create fictional ones. Platforms and boundaries are the slowly changing structural elements. They affect interactions, which is the dynamic element.[9] Platforms, boundaries, and interactions apply to simulations of all genres and influence the efficiency of simulations as a tool of learning and teaching.

The framework is designed as a practical toolbox to characterize any simulation, so you can become familiar with the goals and choices of simulations. Most of the discussion below is based on examples from three simulations described in the appendix. These simulations illustrate the different genres addressed throughout the book: (1) *The Gulf nuclear face-to-face simulation* on Iran's nuclear program and the ways to restabilize the region after a simultaneous exchange of military strikes initiated by Israel and Iran. (2) *The Middle East cyber simulation* on two interrelated issues of the Iranian quest for nuclear

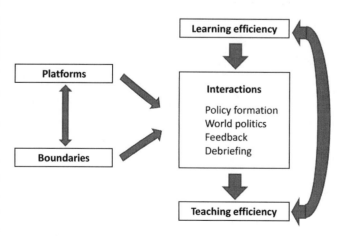

Fig. 1.5. Conceptual framework: components and links

status and the Palestinian quest for statehood. (3) *The Palestinian statehood hybrid simulation,* with cyber and face-to-face rounds spread out in time, designed to reach a compromise agreement between Israel and the Palestinians on the establishment of a Palestinian state.

In this chapter, we use the framework components and their detailed attributes to describe simulations and to indicate how the goals related to each component are advanced. In the second part of the book, on implementation, we link platforms and boundaries to interactions during preparations for the simulation, policy formation activities, and world politics interactions.

Platforms

This first framework component, *platforms,* characterizes the physical and virtual settings where the simulation unfolds. It defines the stage for the simulation and details the environments where encounters take place. Lecture halls or conference rooms host face-to-face meetings, and cyber "rooms" on social networks are their virtual counterparts, like those created for the Middle East and Palestinian statehood simulations. Decor and atmosphere on stage serve as the theatrical setting for the simulation, shape its interaction, and affect its outcomes.

How does the choice of platform promote simulation goals? Table 1.3 summarizes the core goals related to platform attributes and the most fitting type of simulation to reach them.[10]

Physical Infrastructure

Among world politics simulations, a face-to-face encounter is the most common genre. It is based on simple, natural, and ever-present elements of conventional education: a group of people at a physical location. While face-to-face simulations may diverge in topics, scenarios, and players, all of them require joint physical presence among participants who meet one another directly, see, speak, hear, and interact synchronously at close quarters. The Gulf nuclear face-to-face simulation, for example, took place at a round table in a formal and well-equipped conference room on campus. The room, which usually serves faculty, was very different from regular classrooms. It contained modern and high standard furniture, advanced screening facilities, sound equipment and Internet connections by cable for high-speed connection and via Wi-Fi, so students could use their personal computers. Most students also had smart phones so they could use cyber resources during the simulation.

Web Environment

With the emergence of the Internet and the development of Web 2.0 applications, the platforms available for running simulations were considerably expanded to the cyber milieu. On these vast, new, and rapidly changing spaces, players can meet and interact, although a full interpersonal exchange is hard to achieve in a virtual setting where computer screens separate people and change the nature of human experiences among them.

Despite the high-tech infrastructure, the only use of the web during the Gulf nuclear simulation was the screening of YouTube clips prepared by the media teams, in the midst of the simulation after the Israeli and Iranian teams decided to strike each other. It served as a visualization of the violent exchange and the development of an acute crisis scene. By contrast, the Middle East cyber simulation took place on a virtual platform only, since the physical location of players from across the globe made it impossible for them to gather in one place. A Facebook group created for educational purposes enabled International Studies Association (ISA) scholars from many countries to interact. Beyond meetings on the

TABLE 1.3. Platform-Related Goals and Simulation Types

Goals	Face-to-Face	Cyber
Create an authentic theatrical setting of decor and rhetoric	✓	✓
Allow quick and easy use of diverse information sources	✓	✓
Facilitate observation of students performance at real-time	✓	✓
Enable low cost setup, flexible design, and easy replication	✓	✓
Build on an accessible and familiar campus setting	✓	
Reduce dependence on technological knowledge, infrastructure, and glitches	✓	
Build on familiarity with Internet applications, offer a user-friendly interface, record and store meaningful communication		✓

social network, other important web applications were integrated into the simulation including websites, e-mail, YouTube, Skype, and Google Drive as a place for easy access to relevant documents and forms. The weight of these applications changed as the simulation progressed past its genesis stage. To begin with, an announcement of the Middle East simulation appeared on the ISA website and provided its members with basic information about a contemporary Arab-Israel conflict simulation they could join. The simulation had two rounds on Facebook and a face-to-face debriefing exchange during an innovative ISA panel at the 2012 annual meeting in San Diego. The preliminary notice allowed faculty to register in advance so they could act as political leaders or media professionals in a diplomatic negotiations simulation. The advertisement of the project and its schedule provided a link to the SIM2012 website to deliver an overview of the simulation plan and to guide prospective players till they joined academic Facebook groups that were open only to registered members. All further information and instructions were available in these groups, making the social network the core platform for all interactions.

Theatrical Setting

Any simulation you run is actually a dramatic script and your students are its actors. To be effective and fun, the story is enriched by a wealth of theatrical elements that build the setting for the simulation and help players leave their ordinary selves and step into the shoes of the characters they represent.

Like on stage, in an opera, musical, or theater performance, the decor, atmosphere, and rhetoric transform the players and the audience from here and now to a chosen topic and a background narrative. In other words, as your students put on a costume or change their profile picture on social networks, they act as if they were the character they had been assigned to play and have learned about in detail.

In the Gulf nuclear simulation, the use of a modern conference room with sophisticated technological devices helped create an atmosphere of a formal UN assembly that fit the simulation scenario of an emergency meeting on the nuclear situation in the Gulf. The UN logo was projected on the wall, and UN flags were positioned on the table along the nameplates of the speakers. The change from a typical classroom to such formal decor contributed to the students' sense that something new and important is going to happen.

Beyond room decor, the students added to the atmosphere by their choice of costumes: several students playing in Arab teams appeared in traditional keffiyeh or hijab, while some others came in formal suits to imitate the way diplomats show up to a negotiation session. But the simulation took place during a very hot summer day so the air-conditioned conference setting was not enough to prevent some students from wearing casual T-shirts and shorts. This diversity affected the general mood in the simulation since these classmates were not easily identified as committed decision-makers.

In a physical setting, rhetoric, intonations, and body language are also a central part of the theatrical setup and have a high potential to enhance the simulation's atmosphere. Regardless of the knowledge a student has, some individuals are better debaters than others. With such talents, they may contribute enormously to the simulation experience but at the same time challenge introverted students and intimidate shy ones.

To preserve the impact of atmosphere, decor, and interpersonal skills during negotiations, you need to ensure close supervision, sensitive coaching, and careful management of the teams in the simulation. Along with your guidance, peer student support and awareness by heads of team as group leaders may also help some participants loosen up and overcome their reservations. Others may stay rather aloof throughout the encounter. In a simulation with dozens of participants it is extremely difficult for faculty to notice each student. This is especially true during short and relatively intensive face-to-face simulations. By moving to virtual environments, such as the use of social networks for the contemporary Middle East simulation, even shy students can express themselves more freely behind the mask of an assigned profile photo, as no one sees their real selves.

So far we have used platform concepts to describe some core simulation features and the learning benefits they produce. As noted in figure 1.5 and described in the second part of the book on implementation, the choice of platform for the simulation affects its interaction process and overall study efficiency. Most platform-related goals, however, can be achieved by all simulation types so you can choose the platform you feel more comfortable to start with. To maximize platform utilities and goal realization you may opt for a hybrid simulation, with a mix of cyber and face-to-face rounds that suit your academic setting, as described in chapter 2.

Boundaries

This second framework component, *boundaries*, involves a myriad of spatial and temporal elements that define the

TABLE 1.4. Boundary-Related Goals and Simulation Types

Goals	Face-to-Face	Cyber
Integrate multilevel, cross-cultural and interdisciplinary expertise	✓	✓
Enable time management from routine to crisis	✓	✓
Fit most class sizes and multiple academic programs	✓	✓
Incorporate ad-hoc events	✓	✓
Provide immediate feedback and adaptation	✓	✓
Perform in any physically accessible place	✓	
Build on lecture slots and minimize the need for schedule adjustments	✓	
Transcend boundaries and allow worldwide simulations		✓
Perform anywhere within Internet reach		✓
Permit schedule flexibility and extend time for asynchronous contacts		✓
Enable anonymity and secure privacy		✓

structural contents of a simulation and shape its interactions. Boundaries, like the platform, are the static attributes of any simulation that act as fundamental preconditions for the interaction flow among actors. How does the choice of boundaries help promote simulation goals? Table 1.4 summarizes the core goals related to boundary attributes and the most fitting simulation type to reach them.[11]

Spatial Boundaries

The players who take part in the simulation, their number and academic level, the assignments they fulfill, their geographical spread and cultural diversity, as well as the number and composition of political and media teams, shape the interaction process and affect the overall study efficiency. The concerns and guidelines for choice of spatial boundaries are detailed in the second part of the book on implementation. Here we provide a brief overview of some core spatial attributes and their link to both learning and teaching efficiency.

A physical setting as the sole learning environment narrows the geographical spread of face-to-face simulations as all participants must be present at the same place and time. Such a setting suits single on-campus courses best because no extra efforts are required to get all participants together for the simulation, beyond the allocation of lecture time. A face-to-face meeting for students from different campuses may be a very challenging experience with complicated logistics. When the students live in different countries, face-to-face meetings become unrealistic or extremely expensive.

Social networks come in handy to overcome physical barriers of location and distances. Figure 1.6 shows how cyber simulations can extend the scope of interactions and enrich their intercultural reach across states or regions. This is true with respect to direct contacts among students who take part in the simulation, marked by the light arrows, among educators who plan and conduct the simulation jointly and between educator and students within each institution, marked by the small bold arrows.

The Middle East cyber simulation, summarized in the appendix, was unique as it brought together academic professionals from across the globe with a fully multiregional representation and high cultural diversity, though regretfully no Arab participants signed up for the simulation. The participants brought with them a wealth of outlooks that was further enhanced by their varied specialties in international relations, political science, history, media, area expertise, conflict and security studies, as well as specialties in the scientific study of international processes, methodology, and innovative learning.

Spatial boundaries also characterize the teams in the simulation and their composition, as detailed in table 1.2. The original plan for the political and media teams in the Middle East simulation included core adversaries and mediators in the Arab-Israel conflict: Egypt, the European Union, Iran, Israel, Lebanon, the Palestinians, Russia, Syria, the UN, the United States, and three media teams to correspond with the Israeli, Arab, and U.S. newspapers. But the original team composition had to be reduced in order to have a minimum of three members in each political or media team. So the simulation involved a superpower: the United States; regional states: Iran and Israel;

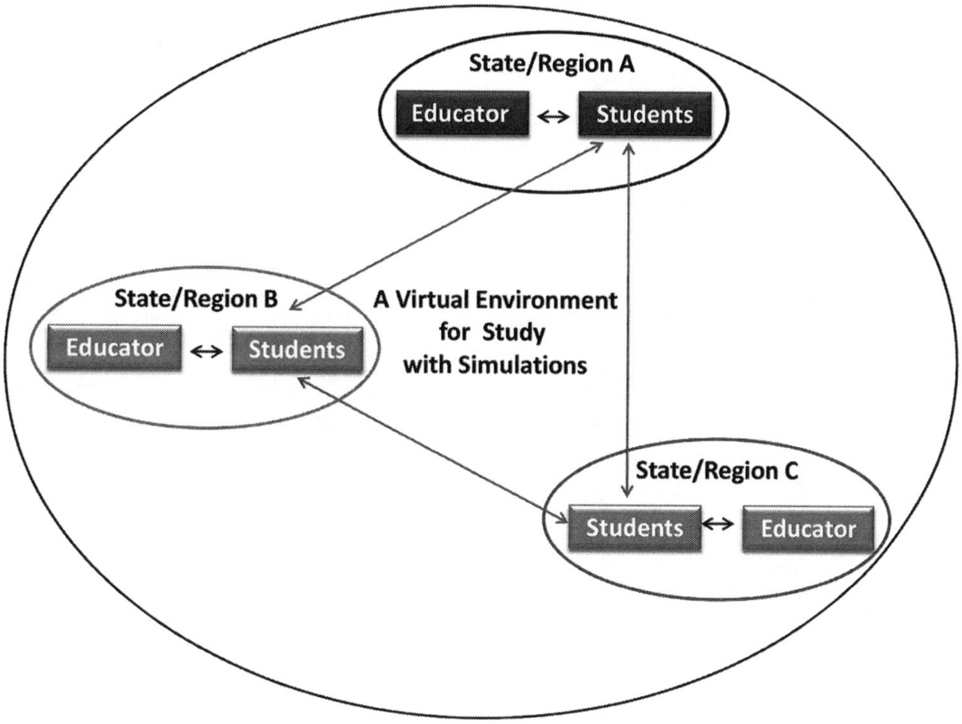

Fig. 1.6. Study of world politics in a global village

a nonstate actor: the Palestinians; and a media network: the *Global Crescent*. This choice of political and media actors made it possible for participants to confront the dilemmas related to the Palestinian quest for statehood and to work out an agreement between Israel and Iran to stabilize the Gulf region. More actors could have added detail and complexity, but the choice of fewer teams made it possible to have enough participants in each team to engage in a meaningful policy formation process and prepare initiatives for world politics negotiations.

Temporal Boundaries

The learning cycle phases, the number of simulation rounds, duration, tempo, timing, turning points, and the acceleration pace during the simulation shape the encounters among participants and affect study efficiency. In the second part of the book, on implementation, multiple aspects related to the temporal aspects are discussed, such as adjustments of the simulation plan to semester and yearly courses, to different academic settings, and to time constraints. Here we provide a brief overview of some core temporal attributes and their link to learning and teaching efficiency.

The Middle East cyber simulation, for example, consisted of four phases: (1) preparation, (2) policy formation, (3) world politics, and (4) debriefing. The short

preparation for the simulation was followed by longer policy formation deliberations among teammates. The two rounds of world politics with interactions among teams lasted two hours each with a reassessment break in each round and a longer one, of two weeks, between them. At the ISA conference a brief face-to-face role-play was followed by a postsimulation analysis of feedback submitted online, an exciting debriefing session, and plans for teaching collaborations and joint research.

The two phases of preparation and wrap-up analysis were brief and required limited efforts but their reward was profound. As a voluntary simulation among colleagues, the time investment during preparation was confined to a few deliberations within teams to get to know one another's academic background, to allocate roles and functions in the team, and to define policy goals and plans. Since each participant showed up on the Facebook group at different times from many different time zones across the globe, coordination was essential for the teams to make progress in policy formation and to ensure that all team preparations would be completed on time to meet the preset schedule of the two world politics rounds.

Most players in this simulation were familiar with current events of the Arab-Israel conflict so a short time was enough for them to formulate initiatives toward foes and allies and to promote their team goals by interacting in the world politics arena. Some participants initiated creative moves and others enriched their team's Facebook group with links to resources related to the simulation topic. This process enabled others to keep up with policy formation and strategic planning even as they invested limited time in the simulation. This pattern of creating the team's "public good" by separate contributions and learning from one another also takes place among students, but the relative share of the burden can be controlled and registered by educators so everybody is responsible for different but mostly balanced tasks and preparation assignments.

The short and relatively low-speed cyber exchanges within teams were a pilot run for the two scheduled rounds of world politics. They included flexible, nonsynchronized login sessions to the team's Facebook group. Simply put, each player joined the group at different times and posted a comment that was addressed later when others read it and reacted to it. So the intensity of interactions at this stage depended on each participant's time allocation, motivation, and actual availability in terms of time zones across the global village.

During the policy formation phase, the media carried out Skype video sessions to coordinate their coverage responsibilities and to build their media strategies for the simulation. These exchanges provided individuals who played media professionals with cyber encounters as surrogates for face-to-face meetings and facilitated some coaching needed for players who were assigned to the media team but were not familiar with media theories or actual reporting techniques.

All in all, this phase of relatively relaxed pace also served as a training period for individuals who were less familiar or comfortable with Facebook procedures and enabled each team to create its collective identity based on the personal traits of its participants, accounting for creativity, expression, leadership, negotiation skills, and decision-making proficiency. All these were necessary when adversaries, media, and mediators meet for intensive synchronous rounds of world politics.

While concepts related to spatial and temporal boundaries are useful to describe basic simulation attributes of all genres and some boundary-related goals can be achieved by all simulation types, other goals are specific to face-to-face or cyber simulations. So your choice of a particular simulation should depend on your preferences and on the goals you set. The mix of cyber and face-to-face rounds in a hybrid simulation can maximize goal attainment, as described in the second part of the book on implementation, but also requires consideration of its costs.

Interactions

This third framework component, *interactions*, contains the activities that take place during the simulation, tell its story, and embody the complex patterns of planned and unplanned developments that occur among political and media teams. Interactions provide a nuanced picture of political offers, negotiations, mediation efforts, and outcomes reached throughout the simulation. Even in face-to-face simulations that begin with up-front opening speeches, most meetings are synchronous and involve discussions within teams and negotiations among teams. In cyber simulations, interactions are classified into asynchronous and synchronous activities. The former "nonlive" encounters mean flexible login times on the social network, like short individual role-plays in class without immediate action-reaction processes. The "live" engagements are the dynamic simulation exchanges during fixed login times on the social network or the multiplayer negotiations in a face-to-face simulation. These interactions are usually very intense and create a microcosmos experience of world politics for the many participants who all at once take part, interact, and impact the process and its outcomes.

How does the choice of interactions help promote simulation goals? Table 1.5 summarizes the core goals advanced by interaction attributes and the best type of simulation to reach them.[12]

Interactions, as the dynamic aspect of the simulation, involve a struggle among actors over topics of contention. Contact levels, synchronization, and the number of teams and players characterize the complexity of the simulation as it unfolds. During the simulation, simple asynchronous within-team exchanges, at low pace, shift to intensive synchronous bilateral or multilateral world politics negotiations. Activities are driven by an effort to conclude an agreement or as an expression of coercive diplomacy geared to enhance soft power, gain time to maneuver, and promote one's goals.

Simulation interactions also involve coaching conducted by teammates or by you, the educator and administrator, to ensure the smooth progress of the simulation and to enhance individual as well as collective experiences. Most digital natives find it easy to join the simulation and even shy personalities add creative contributions and substance on the virtual platform. The gradual nature of the simulation works wonders for participants who are not confident enough from the start with how and what to do. Initial training on the social network during policy formation takes place at the team level, where the head of team and other members advise one another and show

TABLE 1.5. Interaction-Related Goals and Simulation Types

Goals	Face-to-Face	Cyber
Couple policy formation with world politics	✓	✓
Stimulate search for new solutions and leave room for innovation	✓	✓
Provide practice of international cooperation, real-life events, complex negotiations, models, and paradigms	✓	✓
Simplify complex situations	✓	✓
Replicate diverse activities, from secret to open or informal diplomacy	✓	✓
Draw players to respond to the theatrical setting and take part in the drama	✓	✓
Replicate human aspects of interpersonal activities	✓	
Use multiple human senses to interpret activity and political moves	✓	
Allow gradual and prolonged interaction with both asynchronous and synchronous contacts		✓

support by posting *"likes"* to the contribution of peers. At a relatively slow pace and within a small group, participants can comfortably assimilate into their roles. This makes all students better players during world politics interactions.

All in all, interactions during the simulations can occur face-to-face and on social networks, within and among teams. The most common interaction process involves political teams composed of states or international organizations. It can also be easily extended to include nonstate actors who may become central teams in some situations. Hamas, Hezbollah, the Palestinian Liberation Organization (PLO), and the Palestinian Authority are illustrations of such actors that we usually integrate in our simulations on the Arab-Israel conflict.

The inclusion of media teams is a novel contribution of all simulations addressed in this book. Surprisingly, most simulations of world politics described in our literature review rarely integrate a media feature into the simulation, let alone active media teams. The idea here is to project the complexities of world politics to participants in simulations by introducing media professionals who create products, add to the information density, and shape the news agenda of the simulation.

The need to integrate media and politics in domestic affairs has long been recognized and developed in the concepts and theories of media management, rally around the flag, embedded reporting in times of war, public diplomacy, and nation branding. The introduction of media organs into world politics simulations is also a logical step given the centrality of media reporting on crisis, conflict, and war and the recognition that specific patterns of press coverage by different newspapers and media channels exist.

Traditionally the media channels perform roles that fulfill social and political functions (McQuail 1994; Naveh 2002). They (1) decide what the news is, set the political and public agendas, and inform the political actors, leaders, and public opinion of relevant events and developments; (2) interpret the news and provide the context through the process of framing; (3) create an atmosphere and construct the mood for decision-makers to perform and the public to react; (4) participate in mobilizing support for the country/nation; and (5) generate patriotism in times of conflict and tension.

To understand the interaction between the media and politics it is necessary to add two aspects that influence the performance of the media in each political actor: (1) the political regime of states, ranging between authoritarian and democratic,[13] and (2) the economic setting, ranging from a state-controlled economy to a free market (Hallin and Mancini 2004; Limor 2003). Together, these two aspects set the base for a variety of media contexts from free uncensored press to limited and controlled media organs.

The technological platform should be taken into account as well, whether it is printed press, radio, television, or one of the new media channels.[14] The journalistic working process and the publications differ if the news is distributed on paper, wireless on the web, or on mobile devices.

Finally, political communication also deals with the relations between the decision-makers and the media. This involves a twofold relation: (1) how the leaders accept, interpret, and perceive the news, and (2) how the decision-makers and their professional aides use the media to promote their cause, a process that is defined as media management, or sometimes "spin."[15]

How does the addition of media teams help promote

TABLE 1.6. Media-Related Goals and Simulation Types

Goals	Face-to-Face	Cyber
Report multiple perspectives on the moves of decision-makers in the simulation	✓	✓
Enhance the awareness to the multicultural nature of politics in the global village	✓	✓
Increase the potential of the media to become meaningful actors	✓	✓
Replicate real-life use of digital and online technology by media teams	✓	✓
Drive participants to rely on actual news footage and images	✓	✓
Increase motivation of media players by reactions from other participants	✓	✓
Gain increased exposure to media products by the introduction of a media break during which all other interactions cease	✓	✓
Demonstrate the impact of interpersonal relations between political leaders and media professionals on the news agenda	✓	
Enable immediate and ongoing reactions to media products by all participants		✓

simulation goals? Table 1.6 summarizes the core goals advanced by the attributes of media participation and the best type of simulation to reach them.[16] The integration of media teams into simulations of world politics (1) adds new information; (2) widens the range of viewpoints and perspectives to be considered by all players; (3) generates creative simulation products; (4) creates opportunities to practice various skills, from media reporting and editing to critical thinking and empathy; and (5) produces a better understanding of the complex links between the media and politics.

Educators who run simulations and want the participants to comprehend the complexity and the authenticity of world politics have to introduce the intersection of both lenses: the political and the media. This adds a flow of information created by the media organs for all participants to consider. Such information and the interactions among political and media teams, described in the implementation chapters of the book, exemplify the notions of media management, media manipulation, and the power of the media in political processes. Beyond that, the option of including several media organs in the simulation exposes participants to diversity in style, perspectives, agenda setting, and framing of simulation activities. Inclusion of media teams adds not only a creative outlet for media players but a richer portrayal of the simulation world for all participants who can practice multiple skills like empathy, identification, and critical thinking by interacting with the media and following its products. More details on the necessity to develop skills and the means of doing so are found in the third part of this book, on simulation analysis.

In the Middle East simulation, one media organ was active: the *Global Crescent,* designed as an equivalent to *Aljazeera,* the major network in the Arab world. Like the real *Aljazeera,* the *Global Crescent* developed an "Arab-centric" viewpoint to world affairs, used a language that was fit for portraying their agenda, and chose to highlight certain events over others. It suffices to look at the *Aljazeera* website in English to get an idea of where the simulation media team got its inspiration. The *Global Crescent* provided all players with an alternative interpretation to most simulation developments and enriched the learning experience considerably. In simulations with multiple media organs, reporting gaps, differences in choice of terminology, headlines, and photos further enhance the multicultural diversity in the global village, making the world politics exposure more genuine.

You can attain goals by all simulation types, but the best way to maximize the impact of interactions on study efficiency is to use hybrid simulations. With a mix of face-to-face and cyber rounds the participants continue their learning process gradually, over a prolonged time, in different ways. This is achieved by use of knowledge they have acquired during solitary preparation, practice of policy makers' or media professionals' roles, and the integration of objective and subjective perspectives on simulation matters. As a result, participants are bound to feel and understand what theories mean in complex interactions.

As noted in figure 1.5, simulation interactions are linked to platform and boundary choices. They are a product of your academic setting as detailed in chapter 4 on the preparations for a simulation. Interactions are also affected by quality fulfillment of assignments during solitary learning, as detailed in table 4.3. Beyond policy formation, detailed in chapter 5, and world politics, detailed in chapter 6, participation also involves an analysis of the simulation process and its outcomes as detailed in the third part of this book. Once the simulation ends players step out of their roles and costumes to examine the interactions they created as observers from outside. This new type of participation includes feedback, detailed in chapter 8, and debriefing, detailed in chapter 9. Together these activities bring to bear all the knowledge gained and the skills acquired during the learning experience to form a multidimensional understanding of the simulation topic as a whole.

Study Efficiency

This fourth framework component, *study efficiency*, combines both teaching and learning efficiency to capture the core function of simulations as an innovative method of study. The main contribution of all simulations is to produce a comprehensive experience for individuals and teams, which is based on meaningful engagement and diverse study accomplishments. These include many cognitive, behavioral, and affective aspects of knowledge accumulation. Unlike most university courses that focus primarily on cognitive learning and enhanced comprehension, simulations add practice, increase skill attainment, and touch upon emotions, which together produce a deep understanding of complex topics.

Face-to-face simulations are a creative teaching tool. Compared to traditional lectures, they increase teaching and learning efficiency, but also its cost. They require students to work harder and sometimes even inspire them to do so. This in turn provides them with improved knowledge, practice in decision-making, and a unique experience. Simulations also demand more efforts from educators and often result in a great feeling of accomplishment. The Middle East cyber simulation started out as an exciting experience designed to motivate individual engagement, trigger curiosity, and mobilize creativity. Like all simulations, it generated a shared mechanism for joint learning, for each participant alone and together with others as a study community. It also involved many important learning aspects often missing in traditional teaching, such as expressions of creativity, excitement, and drama, a wide array of insights, intense escalations, frustration, coping skills, and the joy of success.

Given the attainment of many educational goals by all simulation types, indicated in tables 1.3 to 1.6, why use social networks? What are the distinctive contributions of meeting in cyber "rooms," like Facebook groups, to the learning process? To be sure, simulations are an exceptional way to make theory and practice meet, enhance the immediate learning experience, and raise the levels of knowledge acquisition for students of all levels and topics. By using Facebook you can apply role-playing even when your students are not within reach of one another, like the case of ISA scholars who took part in the Middle East simulation. The use of social networks as the major application for cyber encounters provides extensive benefits that can be easily replicated in simulations among students across regions, cultures, and continents of the global village. It is free of financial cost and enables learning blended with lots of fun on a virtual platform where participants show up frequently on a daily basis. Even the best educators may be trapped in a race to teach course topics in class and to complete reading assignments, so they forget that when fun and motivation are forsaken, the pursuit of excellence is often lost. Interactions on social networks are entertaining and provide instant feedback modes such as the number of *"like"* icons received from others on Facebook, or the short reactions from various participants creating a chain of comments to one's post. The option of adding web links, YouTube clips, and photos widens the variety of possible reactions, making feedback and revision a natural endeavor. Facebook messages also allow for bilateral communication when the subject is not to be shared by all participants, so secret initiatives can be tried out.

The integration of social networks into the learning process also blurs the demarcation line between study time and the custom of socializing on the web as a common routine. As a result of daily habits, learning hours increase and activities intensify. This overlap of study, fun, and habit is further supported by the fast speed of social network interactions and the ability to log in, keep up quickly with an ongoing dialogue, and add to it repeatedly during the day. Posting on Facebook and cooperating with others becomes an effective way to follow the complex realities of political science, international relations, history, area studies, and other fields related to the simulation.

The progressive buildup makes individual accomplishments possible and allows for diversity of character, creativity, and motivation. This makes the participants into a learning community, which generates collective benefits and a love of learning.

Last but not least, all posts can be identified by who uploaded them and tracked as far as date and time are concerned. After the simulation is over, all participants can revisit the entire log of interactions, within and among teams, to gain an overarching picture of what had occurred earlier and might have been overlooked under time pressure.

Together the different social networks features and communication options can be utilized to cover a full-range study cycle from preparation through playing the game of world politics and concluded with debriefing and research. Once a Facebook group is created and the students join it, the "wall" becomes a readily available environment for an academic study group on the web. The "wall" expands as the group of students learns and the simulation proceeds, with new posts that add to a growing substance, enriched with photos and links to other platforms. This accumulation of exchanges is a rich source of information and a vast self-created database for research projects by students and faculty alike. Research can span a wide array of theoretical and empirical topics. In the absence of a real lab in social studies and humanities, simulations on social networks are a handy substitute to test behavior, control select variables, and stage repetitive experiments. The data derived from these encounters can also be used in comparison to developments in the real world to assess the value of simulations as a teaching and research tool in academe, as detailed in chapter 10.

The particular choices you make regarding the four simulation components of platforms, boundaries, interactions, and study efficiency will shape the simulation you run. As a toolbox for planning simulations, a choice of particular framework components will have an impact on the attainment of goals you have set forth. To revisit the framework and grasp its utility you can always apply it to (1) a simulation you have ran in the past, (2) one of the simulations described in this book or in its appendix, or (3) a simulation that others ran throughout the generations, reviewed in chapter 3.

Summary

This chapter is designed to get you started with a new, creative, and promising academic tool for teaching world politics in a digital information age. To do so the chapter aims to familiarize you with (1) the use of simulations in hybrid learning and its basic goals; (2) the toolbox, a conceptual framework of four simulation components: platforms, boundaries, interactions, and study efficiency, which appear in table 1.2, and the links among them; and (3) alternatives for a simulation that best fits the attainment of goals related to each framework component, so you can start planning a simulation that suits your needs.

The conceptual framework is designed as a theoretical and linguistic toolbox you can keep handy as you proceed to chapter 3, where you will get familiar with a new typology of simulations. Together the framework and typology are the building blocks for all simulations described in this book and others you may encounter elsewhere or run on your own. They are also the foundation for the simulation project as a whole, from planning and preparation, via implementation, to analysis and implications, as the book structure suggests.

You may have already used table 1.2 to focus on topics of specific interest in the text or tested it to characterize simulations you have ran. It is also useful as a summary and checklist for following chapter 3, about the world of simulations in academe since 1945. The concepts of platforms, boundaries, interactions, and study efficiency systematically help the comparison of world politics simulations across genres. They also highlight opportunities that simulations introduce and the challenges they pose. With experiences of your own, you can add detail, remarks, and modifications to this table and make it reflect your particular setting and special concerns.

CHAPTER 2

Academic Setting and Simulation Choice

The purpose of this chapter is to consider the particulars of your academic setting and what they mean in terms of simulation choice. By *academic setting* we refer to the course you plan to teach by use of simulations. The main features of your course dictate the opportunities for and constraints on the simulation you choose to run. Courses differ in subject, on-campus or online teaching style, duration, class type, and extent of cooperation with other colleagues. In discussing these aspects, we outline a sketch for a wide range of courses so you can adjust the scheme to fit your particular academic setting.

Once you adopt simulations as a form of hybrid learning the novel learning experience for you and your students never ends.[1] Even as you run simulations for years, you are likely to encounter new insights, cope with challenges, and introduce creative adaptations. The learning experience starts when you enter the class on your very first meeting or encounter your students online and share with them the fresh and exciting way you will use to teach your course. Many of our students who participated in simulations kept in touch with us long after the course ended, and at graduation events some of them acknowledged that the simulation was one of their strongest college experiences.

As you consider what type of simulation to use and what its topic will be, ask yourself the following questions: (1) What is the main orientation of the course? Is it a theory course, a methodology course, a course dedicated to a specific subject, or some combination of these? The orientation of the course and its goals guide the choice of simulation topic and the appropriate setup, described in chapter 4. (2) Does the course run for one semester or for a full academic year? The duration of the course affects

the schedule for the simulation. (3) How large is the class? Class size shapes the number of teams you may have and the roles of the participants in each team. (4) Do you plan to cooperate with colleagues from other universities? If so, you can broaden the spatial and cultural boundaries of your simulation and considerably enhance the learning experience, but you will also need to make allowances for differences in academic schedules, time zones, and the preferences of each of the participating educators. (5) What is the academic level of your students? Graduate students who have more advanced knowledge and research skills and freshmen who have less knowledge of the subject and no training in research methods obviously require very different levels of preparation before the simulation begins. The students' abilities also shape the sophistication of the debriefing discussion, the range of feedback issues, and the quality of research products generated before and after the simulation.

This chapter looks at the academic setting and shows how the main course attributes are related to particular simulation options. Unless specified otherwise, the same guidelines apply to on-campus and fully online classes.

Course Subject

What you teach will affect the particulars of the simulation you will run. Academic courses cover an unlimited wealth of different subject matters that can be divided into four broad categories: theory, empirical theme, area studies, and methodology. While most courses have a major focus, some of them combine more than one of these divisions into the study program. Chapter 3 describes the evolution of simulations since 1945 and shows that simulations were used in academe to test theories, teach specific case studies, clarify the characteristics of a geographic region, or serve as a research lab and training tool for policy applications. Each educator then and nowadays applied simulations to help students develop critical thinking, understand the subject matter, and gain experience, practice, and knowledge.

Theory-driven simulations are designed to clarify the main concepts of the theory taught, pinpoint its assumptions, test its assertions, and evaluate its utility. As abstract constructs, theories are hard to master, let alone to apply and to criticize. By planning a simulation that relates to one or more theories, you can help your students "touch" the abstract themes, transform them into operational matters, practice them, and discover their strengths and weaknesses.

The realist theory is a natural starting point for our examination of the Arab-Israel conflict by students who live in the region and who are engulfed in the confrontation on a daily basis. The use of simulations makes it possible to try out alternative approaches like the liberal and constructivist theories. While players cope with the basic assertions of realism regarding the centrality of state actors and superpower impact in particular, they come to grips with the role of nonstate actors like Hamas or Hezbollah and media organs like *Aljazeera*. The clash between theories and the interactions in the simulation appears sometimes as frustration of participants in the U.S. or Russian teams who quickly learn that despite the power gap in their favor, the regional powers do not easily comply with the requests of the superpower. Similarly, participants who need to cope with terror organizations or to gain favorable media exposure learn about the illusive nature of soft power and its use in world politics. Early on, the meaning of theoretical terms like mixed-motive interests, deterrence, and mediation effectiveness put realist positions, liberal outlooks, and constructivist claims to the test of practical application in ongoing simulation interactions.

An international system, one of the most difficult concepts to teach in world politics, becomes a reality when your students engage in a simulation. The full and complex meaning of dynamic political systems can come to light through interactions with one another in a given regional or global simulation setting. Such interactions reveal the difference between a decision and its implementation made by one actor and its outcomes that depend on the powerful pressures exerted by multiple actors. This is even more so when you incorporate political and media teams alongside one another to test the effectiveness of new diplomacy and to validate media theories on the impact of agenda setting, framing, and priming on political practices within and among actors in world politics.[2]

So, if your course is theory driven, the choice of teams and their interactions should reflect the theoretical frameworks, concepts, and assumptions you teach. Similarly, the simulation scenario and the assignments students have to prepare should encompass the basics of the theories you include in your course. You may request students to follow specific hypotheses during the simulation, with the relevant variables and implications made explicit before the exercise begins, or to leave the hypotheses out till after the simulation ends and then to revisit the interaction flow by looking at different hypotheses.

To advance theoretical comprehension, you may (1) direct the flow of interactions according to a single predefined set of theoretical hypotheses that will be tested after the simulation, so that all participants focus on the same theoretical considerations; (2) play several rounds, with a different theory leading each round in order to evaluate the utility of each theory; (3) assign different theories to different teams in a single simulation so as to assess their validity; or (4) run a flexible format for the simulation with each participant free to play any theory-driven role, to be evaluated by all players after the simulation ends. This can be done in the debriefing after the simulation is over and in research projects. Such free choice and flexibility in the application of theories maximizes the impact of individuals and confronts all players with core world politics features like complexity, uncertainty, and interdependence.

In one of our runs on the Iranian nuclear program, we wanted Israeli students to come to grips with the liberal approach. While most students in class expressed strong personal inclinations toward a realist outlook, the Israeli team held negotiations with Iran under the auspices of a strong European Union team. In line with theoretical stipulations, they practiced a mixed-motive posture driven by the dominance of economic concerns, which led to the signing of a compromise agreement between Israel and Iran. This result from a 2009 simulation was very different from the one in 2012, described in the appendix, with military strikes exchanged between Israel and Iran and negotiations under UN auspices to settle the "day after" situation.

True, you, like us and many of the students, may think that such outcomes are unlikely given the predominance of realist concerns and clash of civilizations atmosphere in the Middle East that place the leaders of Iran and Israel on a collision course. But the simulation served its purpose from a theoretical perspective, by letting the players feel how a change of paradigm may bring about a fundamental policy shift.

Simulations are also a very effective tool to disclose and test the ethical dilemmas posed by a theory and to understand the normative meaning of theories, stated in either explicit or implicit terms. So, for example, you may want to demonstrate that the realist and the analytical decision-making theories are essentially value-free, that is, they do not imply a good or just policy from an ethical angle, or a moral outlook regarding right and wrong in terms of long-term policy evaluations. By playing an extremely fanatic actor, like Germany under Adolf Hitler or Mahmoud Ahmadinejad's Iran, students can learn to confront the hidden theoretical assumptions of bad and good policies and clarify the difference between the normative and substantive foundations of different theories.

So too is the use of terror events in simulations, which brings along not only the urge to strike hard against "evil" but the need to confront its heavy costs. The commitment to protect civilians is often forsaken due to the limited range of policy choices and effective means to combat terrorism. The paradoxes of democratic resolve come alive when students understand that impulsive acts and harsh retaliations play right into the hands of the terrorists and grant them media exposure.[3]

Simulations driven by an empirical theme cover an unlimited span of historical and current cases. The central goal in such exercises is to familiarize your students with a timeline, the contextual background, core events, and turning points, to gain in-depth knowledge about the actual happenings. By the use of cases that test diplomatic resolve, such as Nazi Germany, the 9/11 terror attacks, or the Iranian nuclear program under Ahmadinejad compared to Hassan Rouhani's regime, you can steer your students to acquire a broader command of information and to grasp the many facets that build up the empirical narrative with its different sides and complex activities.

In empirical-driven simulations, the role of data is essential, and the need to replicate a case is at the core of the interaction process. While a simulation will never fully resemble the reality you chose to focus on, a protracted simulation with several rounds can serve as a surrogate to deepen your students' knowledge. With adequate time and actual practice they can master the details and particulars of the case and greatly improve their study.

Simulations can effectively serve the dual goal of illuminating theory and empirical cases as long as you plan the simulation carefully to represent the historical setting in the configuration of teams and at the same time insert theoretically driven challenges in the scenario that sets the simulation in motion. In this way substance and technical aspects often interact, and with a proper setup you can advance a better understanding of theory without forsaking the buildup of empirical knowledge.

Simulations in area studies enable students to travel across time and space to a distant and often unfamiliar region, which comes alive via knowledge accumulation and practice. In many respects the planning of area study simulations is similar to that of empirical cases. But the time frame in area study simulations may cover longer periods to illuminate slow changes that occur in a region. To capture such developments it is advisable to divide the simulation into separate rounds taking place at different, not necessarily continuous, time frames, with the same political teams in all rounds. Students of the Middle East, for example, can play four rounds: (1) World War II and the German impact on the region; (2) UN resolution 181 to partition Palestine in 1947; (3) the transformation from war to diplomacy and peace agreements among Israel, Egypt, Jordan, since the late 1970s; and (4) turmoil in the Middle East driven by the Arab Spring uprisings since 2010. In such a simulation, the fundamental attributes of the area change a lot from one round to another and yet some basic features remain rather constant, like the involvement of powers from outside the region, the existence of cultural and religious differences, and the diversity in regime types. You can create a setting that will illuminate the unique characteristics of each period and successfully meet the goals of effective study by consecutive simulation rounds.

Methodology-oriented simulations seem to be a natural tool for application in methodology courses but unfortunately this is rarely the case, as shown in chapter 3. With the exception of classes that focus on simulations as a study tool, most research design programs use traditional on-campus or distance learning modes of solitary study, lectures, discussions, and assignments.

Being well aware of how important, yet hard, it is to teach research design in general and statistics or qualitative techniques in particular, it is not surprising to find that students dread these classes and often characterize them as the least attractive experiences they have had during their studies. We find that simulations are a very effective tool to advance methodological growth in an enjoyable manner with some innovative practices discussed in chapters 7 and 11 of the book.

In one of your introductory lectures you need to point out to your students that four interrelated goals are advanced by use of simulations: (1) demonstrate why a lab is crucially necessary in social sciences, humanities, and area studies, how it can be created, and what its contributions may be; (2) create a joint database of all deliberations, additional resources, and material from all simulation rounds, with extra ease through the use of social networks, a platform that automatically records and backs up all information. When the qualitative and quantitative products of the simulation are applied in research, all participants feel involved with the research source and are familiar with its substance, intrinsic value, and shortcomings. The use of sources one knows well and can evaluate from within is an important topic to discuss in class, compared with other types of resources used in research and the problems of assessing their validity. (3) Operationalize and test diverse research frameworks and models with the simulation-derived data. All students can be requested to use simulation-generated material, instead of their real sources, to cope with methodological concerns, conceptual definitions, and theoretical claims related to their own projects. As a surrogate source, simulation-generated data forces the students to completely disassociate theory and empirical work and then to unite them with important implications for their own research projects. For example, a simulation topic on the Arab-Israel conflict may be quite different from an empirical topic like the European Union or the behavior of a political party in the domestic politics of a Latin American state. But simulations may portray many insights on how concepts such as fanatic regimes, effective negotiation strategy, and inflexible policy may explain the occurrence of violence and its escalation. Insights and valuable practice on how to cope with hard-to-define and complex-to-measure substances related to political and social data are a good starting point for one's own research project. The added value of the simulation-derived data is that it is produced collectively so everybody is familiar with its contents, structure, advantages, and shortcomings. (4) Add innovative elements to a difficult and at times even a dull course. This is a very important contribution if you really want to keep your students focused on the subjects you teach and for your course to be a success.

If you are willing to try out simulations in methodology classes, be aware that the full meaning of the simulation as a methodological and research tool will only be brought to bear close to the end of the course once the students apply what they have learned from the simulation and the debriefing in their individual research.

Let us follow three different students in the course. The first is a journalism major who is probing the ways the media covers violent events in the Middle East, comparing Western and non-Western sources. The second is an area specialist who studies South American cultures and regimes and is looking into the impact of opposition groups on policy formation and relationships in the region. The third is a major in international relations who reexamines Samuel Huntington's clash of civilizations thesis in the Middle East after the outbreak of the Arab Spring. To illustrate how simulations can be used in research design courses, let's consider a cyber simulation on Nazi Germany as a rogue state that triggered major instability, a Holocaust of the Jewish people, and a disastrous war that changed the world entirely after World War II. During the simulation, a wealth of information was gathered on Facebook containing all the intrateam discussions on policy formation, the world politics interactions among teams, and the products created by the media teams. All this material was within reach of each participant with a click of a mouse. Once the simulation ends, all three students are instructed to draw on the posts of the political and media teams to further their specific research projects by presenting a theoretical model, some findings from a pilot study, and their methodological implications.

Since all three students have taken part in the simulation on Germany, they are familiar with the crises and the turning points in the interaction process. They have read the media products that have been created during the simulation. They have felt how hard it is to promote goals and to secure the assistance of allies. So, as they apply their different topics, based on the use of simulation-derived data, they can share their applications with the entire class. The examples from the German milieu they had practiced are used in class discussions to illustrate many theoretical aspects, and later all students can draw inferences from the proceedings in class to their individual projects and gain a comparative outlook. Next the class may consider a choice of variables and values presented in the models, offered by each of the three students, relevant to the media begets violence thesis, the impact of opposition groups on policy formation, and state relations in a clash-of-civilizations region. Finally, the variables and models are applied to empirical data derived from the simulation events as a pilot test by use of qualitative and quantitative methods.[4]

For this methodological exercise, the choice of a social

network is the best-fit simulation platform as it automatically records all posts and stores them for easy access by all simulation participants. A face-to-face simulation round can be used for a qualitative analysis, but the lack of stored data on many interactions in the process reduces its utility as a tool for practicing research design chores.

On-Campus and Online Teaching

Traditional on-campus classes are still the most common course types in academe but online ones are rapidly becoming popular. Simulations can fit both course types with some adjustments.

If you teach a course with lectures in class, you can enhance it with face-to-face or cyber simulations. You can first try a short role-play in class with a few participants sitting up front and others watching and commenting after the role-play is over. Or you can also engage students in teams, pitting one against the other or challenging them to reach an agreement. These two pilot runs may be the starter for more extended experimentation with simulations, as will be explained in chapters 5 and 6 of the book.

If you are teaching an online course, the option of running a simulation on social networks may be a fresh way to add cohesion to a group of students who have little opportunity to meet and to interact. You can use the regular web platform of your course for a discussion forum, but when you run a simulation on social networks you reap the fruits of blurring the line between study and nonstudy time. We provide more detail on simulation types in chapters 3 and 4.

Course Duration

The length of your course dictates the range of topics you can include, affects the reasonable workload you can request from your students, and shapes the type of simulations you can run. A face-to-face event is a great way to end a semester-long course or a yearlong one. But a one-time event hardly triggers the wealth of teaching advantages derived from a full learning cycle with simulations. So we recommend at least a single round on social networks, even in a semester setting, along with a face-to-face meeting.

In a yearlong course your options are more diverse since you can spread the schedule of the simulation rounds to fit the topics you teach. You have the choice of running one or two rounds on social networks each semester and climaxing the learning experience with a face-to-face conference at the end of the year. This setting maximizes the benefits of teaching with hybrid simulations and adds a lot of innovation and fun to your course.

The use of simulation rounds in a semester or yearlong plan may follow several patterns: (1) consecutive rounds on the same topic and empirical developments, with added detail, complexity, and knowledge accumulation from one round to the other; (2) rounds include a paradigm change from the first to the next, to show how different theories affect behavior and outcomes; (3) rounds cover different historical time frames and events among the same actors to illuminate the role of slow-changing variables and important turning points; or (4) rounds involve different actors and regions that are requested to cope with similar ethical problems like terror or civil war to investigate the uniform patterns and discover unique culture-embedded trends.

Options 1 and 2 fit all simulation genres in both semester and yearlong plans because they are relatively less demanding in time and necessary preparations. Options 3 and 4 require more study time and longer practice during the simulation, so the choice of a cyber or hybrid genre in a yearly course setting is advised. In chapter 4 various options for simulation schedules are discussed, based on a semester or yearly course plan.

Class Type

Each course has its specific class setting that includes the size of the class, namely the number of registered students; the nature of interactions among them in a lecture or seminar; and the academic level of students, undergraduate or graduate. Simulations can fit any and every class, but the specific class attributes affect the choice of best-fit simulation. For instance, too many participants at once create an overload of interactions, hide free riders who do not really contribute to the interaction process, and increase the risk that you might lose control. So if you are conducting a mass-participant undergraduate course, online or on campus, you need to split your class into several groups, three for example, each divided into a similar number of teams that will take part in different rounds on social networks or in class. This way, a third of the class takes part in the first round and the other two-thirds follow their activity closely. The use of social networks facilitates this type of class size best and allows all course participants to stay in touch with the simulation developments. In the second round another third of the class interacts and the last third of the class interacts in the third round. You may choose to have each round continue the previous one, or post a new scenario for each round.

A big class with many students can also enable a larger number of political and media teams, since it is effective to have at least three students on each team. Another way to have many players without increasing the number of teams is to divide the team into a ruling elite, opposition groups, and public opinion representatives, especially in teams that play democratic states. These participants are not decision-makers but they are meant to represent the bulk of the citizens in the real world. While the decision-makers shape policy, the opposition members argue for or against it, offering alternative policies and using the media. Public opinion representatives follow the developments, debate them, discuss their moral ramifications, interact with the press, and try to affect leaders and opposition alike. Opposition members and public opinion representatives extend the range of political participation alternatives and considerably enrich the understanding of democratic processes and their impact on world politics. At the same time, many interactions take place within teams and the overload of interteam world politics interactions is reduced to top decision-makers.

Cyber simulations on social networks are the best-fit type for the inclusion of opposition members and public opinion representatives because such platforms allow all participants to follow the unfolding interaction process simultaneously. In a face-to-face round, which is usually shorter, it is harder to incorporate and follow the activities of such players.

Seminar classes and small graduate courses are an ideal setting for the use of simulations as they build upon intensive solitary learning assignments alongside creative inquiries, the development of critical thinking, and individual research projects. If you teach more than one course, you can have undergraduates and graduates join the same simulation, with specific assignments and roles for each class in the same simulation. For example, graduate students may serve as strategic advisers to a team of undergraduates or as a national security council that offers political plans, follows the interaction process, and comes up with initiatives as the simulation progresses. Advanced graduate students can also team up with undergraduate students to improve their practices and elevate their achievements.

Such merging of students from different courses and academic levels necessitates careful planning and close follow-up to create a challenging and enriching learning experience for all participants. Blending in participants from different courses in face-to-face simulations is often difficult because each group of students has its own schedule on campus and finding a joint time slot for the simulation may seem almost impossible. The easy solution is to run social network rounds, with most intrateam work done during flexible time, whenever students are available to join their team on the social network. The world politics session may also take place online but it requires synchronous interactions at a fixed time, preferably in the evening when all players can partake in the exercise. Chapters 5 and 6 address the details on how to implement such interactions.

Academic Cooperation

When you bring together participants from different courses into one simulation, you notice how a broader expertise, in terms of qualifications and knowledge, enriches the exercise and its overall learning efficiency. You may also decide to cooperate with other colleagues and run simulations together. By doing so, you can share the workload of the joint project and reap the fruits of partnership for the benefit of all participants.

Cooperation can vary from a project that covers several academic institutions within one state to multiregional and even transglobal cooperation. As we describe in the implementation chapters, most of our simulations are multicampus within Israel, composed of political studies, international relations, and media majors at Bar-Ilan University and the School of Communication at Sapir College. Our partnerships have led to many simulations with students from different campuses who are excited to meet one another on Facebook and in face-to-face simulations. Beyond Israel, a broader intercultural experience took place in simulations we conducted with two universities in the United States, Carnegie Mellon University in Pittsburgh and Arizona State University in Phoenix. In these exercises, the teams switched roles to play actors different from their real location, so the Israeli students played the U.S. leadership and the students in the United States played Israel. Arab roles were spread among U.S. and Israeli students.

Some of the simulation rounds took place during the 2012 Operation Pillar of Defense, a violent escalation between Israel and Hamas in the Gaza Strip. The outbreak of violence and the uncertainties of wartime added considerably to the simulation experience on current events in a conflict region. Real events mingled with the simulation scenario, and stepping into the shoes of the other, located far across the globe, exposed all participants to new and very different viewpoints than one's own.

These examples of cooperation show how substance and technical aspects intersect to create a novel hybrid learning plan that maximizes the utilities of cyber simulations on social networks. In face-to-face simulations, the confines of the physical sphere dictate the geographic spread of simulation participants. With Facebook or other social media and the incorporation of multiple digital sources and tools, the abilities to transcend physical and political boundaries increase. What emerges is a genuine world politics encounter, designed to unravel the complexities of domestic and foreign politics all over the global village.

Summary

This chapter on the academic setting and simulation choice handles the attributes of the course you teach as basic contingencies, opportunities, and constraints that are likely to affect the choice of a face-to-face, cyber, or hybrid simulation and its particulars. It is designed to make you aware that your options for a well-planned and effective simulation build upon the academic setting into which you will integrate simulations. So as you think of possibilities for simulations you should consider the subject of the course, its on-campus or online teaching style, its duration, the type of class, and the academic cooperation you plan with other educators. The impact of all these contingences together is brought to bear in the plan you design for the simulation and the operational procedures you and your students will follow in preparation for the simulation, both addressed in chapter 4 on simulation setup.

Before we leave the first part of the book on theory and move on to the second part, on implementation, we look at the world of simulations to show how the simulations run nowadays build on a rich and progressive tradition of experimentation. We view the refinement of previous experiences and gradual accumulation of innovative knowledge as an adaptation process to new technologies combined with a reaction to emerging needs and problems. Together, technology and adaptation lead to new and exciting solutions, some of which we suggest in this book. Chapter 3 supplements the toolbox offered in chapter 1 with a typology of simulation genres you will find handy when you proceed to part II of the book, which covers implementation.

CHAPTER 3

The World of Simulations

The use of simulations in world politics has been an ongoing topic of inquiry. The present chapter adds to this growing body of knowledge by looking at the role of technology in shaping the available range of simulations for teaching and research. It offers a new typology of simulation genres that goes beyond the traditional human/machine classification and applies it in a review of publications on simulations in political science and international relations.

The purpose of this chapter is to investigate the relative weight of different genres in the simulation landscape since World War II. The chapter takes a close look at the spread of simulations in the digital information age since the introduction of Web 2.0 in general and social networks in particular, like Facebook in 2004.

Unlike the rest of the book, which is essentially a practical guide for educators, this chapter integrates important segments of scholarship on simulation on which we build. To fit the focus of our book on world politics simulations in the global information age, we had to streamline the wealth of scholarship on the topic of simulations and concentrate mainly on publications in the 21st century. And still we acknowledge the outstanding value of work achieved by the pioneers who ventured the less-traveled paths of innovative learning as soon as new technologies emerged. Without their work and many earlier developments in the field of experimental learning by use of simulations, we would not have reached the experience we offer and share throughout the book.

The literature review offers a rich foundation of essential concepts from leading paradigms and theories combined with a variety of case studies across periods and regions. These studies also provide many helpful guidelines

for educators who want to design simulations of their own. Together, the framework presented in chapter 1 and the new typology suggested herein is meant to serve as a toolbox for simulation users. Experienced ones and newcomers are invited to build upon the framework, typology, and examples from previous publications to extend the range of choice for their simulation designs.

The chapter begins with an introduction of the simulation experience in world politics through the generations with an emphasis on how technological innovations rippled into new simulation modes. An unequal use of simulations of different genres triggers a discussion on the costs related to face-to-face and cyber simulations. The chapter points to the common costs of all simulations and to those linked to particular genres. It ends with six guidelines on how to reduce the costs of all simulations and to pick the best-fit one as an active learning tool.

The Simulation Family: A Typology

At the second decade of the 21st century, this book highlights players and environment as the two criteria to accommodate for the latest digital information age innovations in core simulation features. The first criterion builds on the traditional *human/machine* distinction while the second one focuses on *physical/virtual* diversity. Table 3.1 summarizes the eight possible simulation genres based on this twofold classification, which covers human or machine players, in a physical or virtual setting. Table 3.2, discussed later in the chapter, provides examples of simulations that appeared in publications since 2004, classified into genres.

TABLE 3.1. Simulation Typology

Players	Environment		
	Physical	Virtual	Physical and Virtual
Human	Face-to-Face	Cyber	Hybrid: Face-to-Face and Cyber
Machine	Software	Cyber Software to Software	
Human and Machine	Human and Software	Cyber, Human, and Software	Complex

With respect to the players, by humans we refer to all levels of participants, from students at different educational centers to professionals and practitioners who train for a certain purpose or test a specific topic. By machine we mean a real construct, a robot whose interactions are structured by a preinstalled formula, or software that generates behavioral outcomes.

Related to the platform for the simulation, by the physical environment we capture the concrete location of the simulation: a classroom or simulation lab on campus or at a professional establishment for training, a military base, or a government compound. By a virtual environment we mean all abstract, nontangible milieus where interactions occur, like the well-known International Communication and Negotiation Simulations (ICONS), as professional software created to run the simulation, university-administered remote learning systems, social networks in general, or Facebook in particular.

Cyber tools, like YouTube clips or photos that enhance the theatrical atmosphere, may be used in both physical and virtual environments, but this does not make a face-to-face simulation into a hybrid one. By a *hybrid simulation* we mean a set of several world politics rounds, each one of them taking place on a different platform, as discussed in chapter 6.[1] Most of this chapter, beyond the genealogy section, focuses on three major genres with human players: face-to-face, cyber, and hybrid simulations of the typology.

The common simulations of the past were face-to-face, as in role-play exercises of a selected historical case study in class, or the software modeling of arms races and complex game theory situations. The virtual environment emerged later, once technological innovations enabled the development of connections among humans or machines from a distance by way of phone, cable, or broadband. It drastically changed the range of human interactions from the immediate proximity to the endless cross-globe sphere. Unlike the face-to-face deliberations that take place in physical setting like an auditorium, the interactions of a cyber simulation occur on the web. The Internet also introduced vast changes in the connections among machines. The software-to-software connections via cyber channels allow for contacts and behavior manipulations among clever robots, directed from afar. In a growing number of cases, preprogrammed machine interactions in an industrial plant or drones and other nonhuman equipment on a battlefield carry out a variety of chores. These advanced and complex machines also allow for software modifications and activity correction from a remote location, based on feedback and revision. While the integration of groundbreaking human-machine simulations as a teaching tool still awaits future developments, traditional face-to-face and software genres are still popular. Web 2.0 and social networks offer a novel technology-based option for an exciting encounter among human players on a cyber platform like the Middle East simulation or the Palestinian statehood hybrid simulation summarized in the appendix.

There are many different types of simulations, each of which comes with its own advantages and shortcomings. One can think in terms of an extended family of simulations, whose members share core traits and diverge in others. The family distinctions include (1) mainly face-to-face simulations with little integration of cyber applications; (2) mainly cyber simulations with strong reliance on the Internet along with very few face-to-face encounters; and (3) a balanced weight of physical and virtual platforms in separate rounds, for encounters of hybrid simulations where a variety of interactions contribute more or less equally to the overall learning experience, as in the Palestinian statehood example. Among the family groups, the first plays it safe and mostly disregards the new, technologically driven options for enhancing world politics simulations. The second eagerly replaces the traditional in-class encounters with the new virtual surrounding and features, but in doing so risks giving up the wealth of successful simulation precedents and the rich body of knowledge they triggered. Only the third, by balancing physical and virtual features on social networks, preserves the benefits of the well-tested face-to-face modes and at the same time considerably incorporates the virtues of the most recent cyber innovations. The choice of a particular simulation type depends upon your simulation goals and academic setting, as described in chapters 1 and 2.

The Simulation Genealogy: A Temporal Mapping

The genealogy of simulations in international relations described below highlights the most common simulations addressed in the literature. Beyond a long and mostly undocumented genesis period, we point to four generations and demonstrate how new technologies led to major changes in simulation features.

When looking at simulation genres and the types within them, as they appear through the temporal mapping of simulations, we find that the emergence of a new generation does not mean that successful simulations of a previous one cease to exist. The face-to-face genre, for example, has maintained its lead throughout the generations and is likely to keep doing so within contemporary simulations. This is especially true in current simulations that aim at maximizing the learning experience by bringing together players from afar without forsaking the human element. In this respect, consider for instance, how a computer lab and high-quality video conferences on broadband, like Skype, can facilitate interactions among participants from distant locations and at the same time promote excitement in class during such meetings with peers on virtual environments.

The four generations follow a temporal sequence though the duration of each generation varies. How did simulation literature and actual conduct reach the current state of art? When did the different genres develop? Do the leading genres change over time? Does technology affect this progression, and how fast does this happen? We show that a shift from one generation to another is driven by technological innovations and their introduction into simulations. It is difficult to define exactly when the *first generation* of simulations started, but it was sometime in the 1950s when face-to-face simulations were integrated as a mode of teaching in academe. The *second generation* of simulations emerged a decade later, with the introduction of mainframe computers in the 1960s and the increased use of human-software simulations for teaching and research. *Third generation* simulations evolved in 1991 with the development of the Internet and the World Wide Web, which transformed computer connections among universities to virtual platforms as a mainstream public domain. At this point, the human and machine on

a virtual platform appeared on the simulation scene. The *fourth generation* of current simulations began in 2004 when Facebook was introduced and Web 2.0 offered rapid, dynamic, and interactive connections on multiple virtual platforms. From this point, social networks proliferated to become a daily habit for people all over the globe, broadening the options for communication between educators and students of world politics and the range of simulations to choose from.

To understand recent developments it is necessary to look back briefly at the earlier stages of simulations. Young animals play to learn the social skills of life (Morell 2013). So do children in many of their real and imaginary activities (Gopnik 2012). For years humans have used simulations and participated in role-playing for leisure, teaching, training, and experimentation (Shubik 1968). Not less important was, and is, the use of simulations for operational military purposes, including rehearsals, dry runs, and field maneuvers for planning offensives (Shubik 1972). In the midst of the 20th century simulations were introduced to academia for teaching and practice in various fields, such as economics, political science, and international relations, allowing players to "feel" the actual environment as presented in the simulation (Robinson 1963).[2]

First generation. The early application of simulations was mainly role-play encounters held in small environments, most of them in classes on campus (Schelling 1961). So the ordinary simulations of this early period took place between human players and belong to the face-to-face genre (Goldhamer and Speier 1959). When these political simulations were applied in the 1950s, computers already existed but were not yet integrated for calculation purposes during simulations between human players. But a potential for change and a promising new mode for evaluation of theories appeared with new machine simulations for testing models based on formulas with multiple elements (Helmer and Rescher 1959). Some of these early exercises dealt with arms races or complex game theory situations like the prisoners dilemma (Luce and Raiffa 1957).

Richard Brody, one of the first simulation developers, provides a good starting point for exploring the emerging field of innovative teaching and research with his definition of simulations as representations of systems designed to replicate sociopolitical processes. In other words, he regarded simulations as theory-based models that are supposed to provide information about unit and variable changes over time (Brody 1963, 671).[3] In his overview on simulations of his day, Brody emphasized that the great advantage of this technique in theory building and testing is summed up in the idea of "control." Because the researcher is to a large extent the "master" of his system, he can work with many variables that interest him and explore their consequent impact on particular subsystems or on the model as a whole.[4] This way, scholars can evaluate outcomes associated with a variety of alternative policies in relation to a preset or desired outcome, or, in other words, test future states of the system under study. As such, simulations serve as a much-needed lab for the social sciences in general and for political studies, international relations, and area studies in particular.

Further technological developments in computer science as well as the emergence of new communication options led to the adoption of computers as efficient tools for complex calculations and triggered changes in teaching and learning.[5] The first generation of simulations also witnessed the engagement of human beings and computers on the same study/playground known as "man-machine" games, setting the stage for the more sophisticated ones of the next generation.[6] So scholars who were used to running simulations wondered how to incorporate these innovations into their curriculum.

Second generation. The start of a new generation occurred sometime in the late 1950s and early 1960s as Harold Guetzkow and his associates introduced the Inter Nation Simulation (INS). INS was a giant leap forward in human-machine simulations, with scholars and students who played the roles of a variety of decision-makers in a long list of fictional countries and different international scenarios. Guetzkow and his associates used calculators and early generations of mainframe computers as an interface to run programmed assumptions and restrictions upon the behavior of actors in the simulation. The complexity of the routines involved in the model allocations required machine help and made the computer a useful tool for figuring out the consequences of human decisions (Guetzkow and Jensen 1966). For example, researchers used special formulas developed for the simulations to calculate the use of force and the results of interactions in world politics (Guetzkow 1959, 1962; Guetzkow et al. 1963). The INS project opened the door for a variety of simulations on historical topics (Hermann 1965; Hermann and Hermann 1962, 1967) and current events (Brody 1963; Hermann, Hermann, and Cantor 1974) dealing with a variety of political and international relations processes. The proliferation of INS-type simulations also led to further developments in the human and

software genre that eventually matured into the ICONS project.

The use of mainframe computers tempted scholars of that era to develop simulations that dwelt mainly on machines with hardly any human intervention, leading to the rise of a software genre where the human player was absent and the entire run took place on a preprogrammed machine. A famous computer simulation called Crisiscom was developed by De Sola Pool and Kessler (1965). It focused on national decision-makers processing information during a crisis. By simulating a variety of possible crises they illuminated the process of deterrence and explored how far psychological mechanisms can explain the behavior of political decision-makers. At the same time, Singer and Hinomoto (1965) used a simplified computer simulation to analyze possible future events and to study the costs of various inspection methods of nuclear weapons by use of a semidynamic model. Another stage in developing the INS simulations was Guetzkow's Simulated International Processes (SIP) project designed to increase the coherence, solve problems of validity, and accelerate research activities in the field of simulations. This project also focused on clarifying the differences between the processes and behaviors in the simulation and the occurrences in the real world (Guetzkow and Jensen 1966).

Other software genre simulations run on machines were developed during the late 1960s and early 1970s. Howard (1961) at General Motors had an all-computer simulation of a colonial socioeconomic development system. His colleague Kaehler (1961) had been preparing for the study of problems of international conflict with an analog computer. Abt (1961), at Raytheon Company, developed Technological, Economic, Military, Political Evaluation Routine (TEMPER), intended to be used to analyze the Cold War and limited wars in some 20 conflict regions.

By 1969 the total literature on simulation exceeded 2,000 items including business and war simulations (Tansey and Unwin 1969). During the 1970s many scholars followed the footsteps of Guetzkow and the other academics and developed offshoots of the earlier simulations or introduced their own simulation variations. One of them was Coplin (1970) with a simulation illustrating the dynamics of the factors affecting the stability of the international system. Other examples were the Princeton Inter-nation Game (PING), which studies global war, limited war, and peace (Terhune and Firestone 1970), and the Computer-Aided System for Handling Information on Local Conflicts (CASCON), developed by MIT scholars Bloomfield and Beattie (1971) who tackled some problems for which policy analysts or planners needed solutions. Bremer (1977) developed the Simulated International Processor (SIPER), a full-machine simulation, and Pollins (1985) continued in a similar direction, using formulas in a simulation model of the international trade system.

More and more simulations were applied to academic as well as to training purposes, accompanied by a variety of articles and manuals that enabled the dissemination of simulations all over the academic, military and business world. Gilboa (1979) developed a simulation used to introduce and train military officers in the realities of the Arab-Israel conflict.

Thus far, all simulations belonged to three genres: traditional face-to-face between human players in a physical location, formula or software simulations where machines completely replaced human players, and human-software simulations that integrated the advantages of human contacts with the benefits of machine calculations.

The first personal computer (PC) was introduced by IBM in 1981 (Kleinrock 2008, 14), and a year later the next major development in international relations simulations occurred with the emergence of the ICONS project. Early ICONS, also known as distributed simulations, planned as a coordinating and facilitating system for a series of online multiweek simulations, was developed in 1982 by Jonathan Wilkenfeld and Richard Brecht at the University of Maryland. Their simulations were scheduled for specific times each semester and involved students from schools around the world taking part in negotiations on pressing global issues. The academic institutions paid a fee for participation and enjoyed the benefit of an advanced computer program as a platform for the simulation, together with detailed manuals and guidance on how to run the events on each campus. As part of the education program, ICONS combined computerized simulation experiences on an interuniversity network as well as face-to-face on-campus discussions in the teams played by each campus.[7] So while all academic partners shared the same manuals and created joint products, each participating institution contributed to the progressive development of the ICONS project as a whole.

ICONS developers regard the project as human driven and machine supported so the project fits the classification of a human-software genre. It began as a computer-assisted simulation run in different physical centers, by use of a single professional software that shaped and integrated the interactions between all players. ICONS has grown through the years and included thousands of participants throughout the world. By the early 1990s,

advanced ICONS began to use the Internet as its communication platform (Kaufman 1998). Once all campuses were connected to the Maryland system via the Internet, the project was transformed into a complex genre of human-software on physical and virtual platforms. These simulations signaled the potential for Web 1.0 cyber communications that were about to begin shortly thereafter.[8] The entire archiving system for message flows and the possibility of distant interactions were based on a computer platform that was used to connect students from one campus with others, to teach, practice, and conduct analytical research. As such, ICONS symbolizes an ongoing trend in simulation genealogy where the technological innovations led to a new simulation generation and novel genres but the successful simulations of previous generations and genres still maintain their hold.

While ICONS gained popularity, further advances, with increased complexity, were made in the field of computerized models to simulate a variety of issues. For example, the Ward and Mintz (1987) model focused on military spending in Israel from 1960 to 1983, trying to simulate future trends. It included 12 variables, such as domestic expenditures, military aid, and foreign defense purchases, that were used to evaluate possible trends in Israeli military spending until the end of the 1980s. Based on mathematical calculations of several counterfactual experiments, with pessimistic, optimistic, and no-change scenarios, all models predicted that Israeli military spending would grow rapidly at least until the end of the decade examined. Experiments of this sort relied on the availability and integration of more advanced computers and software than had been available in the first generation.

The traditional face-to-face genre with human players in a physical location kept its lead along the generations together with new human-software and cyber human-software genres. Yet it is surprising to find that beyond ICONS, the introduction of a virtual platform and especially social networks into political science simulations was slow and rather limited. Till the second decade of the 21st century, with a fully fledged digital information age, it has not yet captured a mainstream status or left its mark on contemporary simulations.

Third generation. After the emergence of ICONS, the time came for the application of new technologies and the emergence of a new generation of simulations. The Internet and Web 1.0 browsers were introduced in the early 1990s, Tim Berners-Lee made the first website available in 1991 (Kleinrock 2008, 14), novel technologies allowed for improved computers, and with the proliferation of

PCs came the early stages of online communications.[9] Cable connections, although few and slow, enabled interactions on the web, on and between campuses. The next stage saw the introduction of websites as a tool assisting the conduct of simulations in a regional context, like the Israeli Neighbors on the Web project (Naveh 2001), or the global one with Model UN or the advanced ICONS project.[10] At the end of the 20th century, simulations became a source for some commercial profit with the development of gaming on PCs and on the web, which paved the way for the development of simulations as a professional business.

One such example is PeaceMaker, simulation software for PCs, based on Middle East realities. The game dictates that the "winner" situation is a two-state solution. The trick is for students to figure out how to balance Israel and Palestinian public opinion needs to get there from both the Palestinian president and Israeli prime minister starting point.[11] The simulation is inspired by real events in the Israeli-Palestinian conflict and preprogrammed to contain diverse options of conflict evolution and resolution. In the game, human participants play the roles of the Israeli prime minister or the Palestinian president on their PCs, immersed in programmed event variations to learn from their experience about the conflict.

Another example is Statecraft, a fully automated, multitopic online simulation that, as its developers suggest, is inspired by strategy concerns that allow students to experience the challenges, opportunities, and complexities of international relations. Statecraft brings participants to a world where they use trade, war, spying, and diplomacy during several weeks. Unlike PeaceMaker, which focuses on the Arab-Israel conflict, Statecraft covers many fictional narratives related to theoretical aspects, like the security dilemma, world peace, equality, cooperation among nations, the rule of law, and anarchy.[12]

Despite extensive use of computers, professional software, Internet sources, and elaborate websites, the web has not become a core platform in these years and its potential was left as a promise for future generations.

Fourth generation. After the turn of the millennium when the Internet environment was transformed into a social networks milieu, new platforms enabled cyber simulations among participants near and far.[13] The online communication systems and computer technology went through fast developments with the shift to Web 2.0, which signaled the democratization of knowledge production and novel online media platforms: podcasting, blogging, YouTube, Twitter, and Facebook. These technologies and platforms made it easier for all users to create and share information on the World Wide Web.[14]

This dynamic high-tech environment offered improved channels of communication and online interactions based on broadband Wi-Fi and 3G Internet with multiple users in many distant locations. The options of on-campus and home use of high-speed communication and access to information sources across the globe influenced the development of all academic studies and simulations as well. The availability of social network systems, handheld tablets, and smart phones opened the road to expanded modes of interaction. Most radical was the change in the storage locale, which in turn enabled a dramatic transformation in daily interactions between people. The shift from a race for increased PC-based memory to huge storage capabilities on remote servers led to a widespread habit of people who interact on the infinite web for more and more aspects of their personal, professional, and social life. The use of the Cloud, a concept that reflected a metaphor of a remote location, actually meant commercial servers at distant and unknown sites that provide free and paid storage and host a multitude of websites, accessed quickly from any hardware device. This infinite range of connections and storage options changed the ways in which we regard computer hardware in general and PCs in particular. All devices became simple docking stations that let humans connect to the enormous web as a core platform for their interactions. Rather than being sophisticated calculators, computers shrunk in size and overlapped with phones and cameras to become interaction gateways. These technological innovations and changes in lifestyle had to leave an impact on the popularity of cyber and hybrid genres and signaled a wide range of innovative applications in what we call fourth-generation simulations.

The literature review summarized in table 3.2 applies the typology, discussed earlier, to map fourth generation simulation genres at a time when human communications spread to the virtual environment and flourished on Facebook as the leading platform.[15] To systematically characterize genres in this generation and to determine their weight, a set of 77 articles and two PC/web games were reviewed. The articles were retrieved from the online databases of ProQuest, JSTOR, and Google Scholar, screened by nine keywords and their intersections: simulation, web, Facebook, social networking systems, computer, PC, virtual, Internet, machine, and games.[16] All sources had to answer four criteria: (1) they represented specific simulations of world politics; (2) they were designed for and applied in higher education institutions; (3) they contained details regarding the simulation experience; and (4) they were published in English between 2004 and 2013.

The temporal spread of these reports was uneven but indicated a growth in the documented use of simulations in the literature with hundreds of students and scores of educators who developed and ran the simulations. The number of participants in the simulations ranged from 15 to 100, while the groups or teams varied from 3 to 16. Latin America was the most common region used in the fourth-generation simulations followed by the Middle East and other regions such as Africa, Europe, the Balkans, Asia, the Caucasus, North America, and some multiregion cases. The United States appeared in almost half of the simulations, followed in descending order by Israel, Afghanistan, China, Russia, and Iraq.

Among the leading concepts and main theories applied during this generation, war and violence were still at the center and a crisis or conflict was a common way to drive simulation participants into action. Soft power issues, environment, and ecology appeared, but did not become mainstream yet.[17]

In terms of empirical coverage, more than 40 percent of the simulations dealt with historical or current case studies and only few of them were based on a fictional narrative. Less than 20 percent of the simulations were designed to test theories of foreign policy or international relations with no empirical details on a real, imaginary, or science fiction case. It seems that tangible events are more popular than abstract theories, which may have been harder to run and more difficult to test.

As far as the typology is concerned, the share of simulations among genres varied greatly. Most simulations in this fourth-generation contained interactions between human participants. About 65 percent of the simulations are classified as traditional face-to-face or newly introduced hybrid genres that coupled high-tech facilities with human interactions in physical and virtual environments. More than 30 percent of the simulations belonged to the traditional face-to-face genre, which has maintained its lead since the early 1950s. About 20 percent of the reports surveyed were of the software genre with no human participation and only a few simulations belonged to the human and software genre.

These findings indicate that the use of computers is mostly integrated into simulations played by humans who use them to reach website resources, test theories by applying computerized formulas, or use the high-tech infrastructure to communicate by e-mail or by professional software generated for university teaching. Most often, the human experience is epitomized as the essence of simulations as a learning tool. The small share of software-only simulations could be explained by the difficulty of developing a real-life situation that conveys a human experience between players in such experiments. Moreover, most students in the social sciences and humanities may not be familiar enough with advanced mathematical-statistical tools to benefit from software games that translate complex situations into formulas and models run on computers.

Surprisingly, the use of the media as part of a simulated environment and, even more, the recognition of media organs as powerful actors appeared in only few of the recent simulations in this literature review. For example, Shellman and Turan (2006, 101–6) required participants in media teams to report the news of the day, hold press conferences, and uncover information about actors' relations. They provided instructions for reporters on how to write stories and broadcast them on the Internet. They even suggested eavesdropping as a good information source for their reporters.

The use of the media as a reporting agent was also described by Zaino and Mulligan (2009) in a department-wide crisis simulation with a *CNN*-type channel that monitored the developments in the simulation. The students used smart-classroom capabilities for that purpose, such as PCs and LCD projectors and the university Blackboard computer system.

In another simulation, Siegel and Young (2009) introduced news channels in a simulation on terrorism with a meaningful role devoted to the media. Reasonably, when playing a simulation on terror it was impossible to ignore the media and its influence on the unfolding events. Students had to choose *CNN, ABC, Fox News*, the *BBC*, or *Aljazeera* as the organ they were reporting for. Divided into two media teams, the simulation reporters used cameras, computers, and other means to present material in a creative way that, as the authors' state, would help increase student motivation and interest in assignments and summary reports. Siegel and Young (2009, 767) also introduced the "citizen's media" by allowing members of the public to become bloggers, to create their own reports, to prepare written material for the other groups, to talk with them at any time, and to report on the crisis simultaneously. This way, a full process of political communication was established for the media teams, and the political actors also played a role as media sources by sending written messages from spokespeople and team leaders to each other. Siegel and Young presented these information tracks as secret back-channels. The lesson drawn from the simulation on terror and media was that both government and terrorist groups utilized selective media strategies to achieve their goals.

Brynen (2010) also used the media by dedicating two e-mail lists (listservs) to broadcasting the simulation news.[18] In a project simulating war-to-peace transitions and peace building in a fictional country called Brynania, separate e-mails were used for routine items and for official news reports generated by the simulation administration or the simulation regional newspaper and flash alerts. To these Brynen added a simulated online *New York Times*, which was published at the start of each day, summarizing the previous day's events and any overnight developments. No details were provided as to how these news organs operated, that is, if they were run by specific media teams and how they collected and edited news items during the simulation. It was also hard to assess if and how the media influenced the simulation, its outcomes, and the learning process as a whole.

Simpson and Kaussler (2009) suggested traditional role-playing with a digital age touch for the study of strategic-military interactions and diplomatic and conflict resolution skills. They used online tools for communication, such as Blackboard or Web-CT, and Facebook, as a social utility forum. To prepare for the simulation, Simpson and Kaussler offered the integration of films as an important tool to enhance the readiness of players for their roles. During the simulations, country teams interacted on two levels: domestic politics and foreign policy, in seven crisis scenarios: the Cuban missile crisis, interventions in Africa, Yugoslavian civil wars, terrorism, failed states, 9 /11, and Middle East politics. News teams such as *BBC*, *Aljazeera,* and *Fox News* updated all teams with "news flashes" and press release statements from the teams. News teams were also able to interview country teams and establish contact with terrorists. Especially dedicated news teams recorded their interviews with terrorists and hostages and broadcasted them on YouTube. Despite this active media participation, the role of media in world politics and communications was not highlighted as a major theoretical issue and its contributions to simulations as a teaching tool was not discussed.

While more than 30 percent of the simulations in the fourth generation encompass a virtual environment, perhaps the most fascinating finding in this review is that social networks are still a rare learning environment.[19] By the last year of this literature review, few simulations integrated Facebook as a core platform for interaction. Smolinski and Kesting (2012) introduced chat on Facebook as an internal channel of communication among students from remote sites, together with other tools like Skype and MSN. Darling and Foster (2012) created a Facebook group with the class name, inviting regional experts as well as the students to join the group and discussion forum. Facebook also served as an additional online tool in response to student interest in coordinating group projects and study groups. However, the authors emphasized that the students did not embrace the Facebook group as much as they had hoped because it was an optional platform that blurred the lines between informal and formal learning. By contrast, Simpson and Kaussler (2009) claimed that Facebook, as a social utility forum, proved to be the most popular and effective online tool for communication among students.

Beyond the 2013 cutoff date for our review, recent publications add findings on the use of simulations for the study of war and peace. Alhabash and Wise (2014) used the PeaceMaker game and report that players changed their evaluations of adversaries, moderated implicit bias, and changed stereotype perceptions. With a similar idea of training and education, Nannini, Appleget, and Hernandez (2013) ran the Game for Peace simulation during United Nations' Peacekeeping Operations courses for practitioners to achieve progressive education in peace operations. Schulzke (2013) relied on video games by letting players step into the role of a terrorist and describes the value of such simulations to familiarize participants with narratives from the perspective of the terrorists.[20] Harding and Whitlock (2013) also emphasized practice as they focused on an educational intervention involving the training of regional conflict early warning analysts by application of a networked, case study/simulation hybrid tool called COUNTRY X. Their results show that no run has resulted in an outcome of mass killing and a single attempt to reach a "final solution" was prevented by other players. But these applications and other publications do not highlight the web as an environment for interactions or the use of social networks as a core platform for cyber simulations.[21]

Since 2004, the year Facebook was introduced to the world, other articles on simulations have not reported extensive use of social networks even though teachers and students had already become more and more familiar with this social network as a common means of social communication (Yang et al. 2011). Studies on Facebook have progressed considerably, with hundreds of peer-reviewed articles published between 2005 and 2012 (Caers et al. 2013; Wilson, Gosling, and Graham 2012). Yet even among educators who use Facebook in their social life, few tend to use it as an educational tool in their teaching (Prescott 2014). Despite widespread Web 2.0

TABLE 3.2. Typology Applied

A. Human Players		
Physical Environment	Virtual Environment	Physical and Virtual Environment
Face-to-Face ($N = 30, 38\%$)[a]	**Cyber** ($N = 2, 2\%$)	**Hybrid: Face-to-Face and Cyber**[b] ($N = 18, 22\%$)
Role-Playing and Board Games (8 items, 10%) Mason and Patterson (2013) – the Afghan PRT board game; Ansoms and Geenen (2012) – Monopoly revised board game; Glazier (2011) – Uganda conflict; Korosteleva (2010) – European integration; Fowler and Pusch (2010) – 53 culture-specific packages from the Arab Gulf to West Africa; Williams and Williams (2007) – Ocean Wind board game; Boyer, Trumbore, and Fricke (2006) – on International Political Economy; Shaw (2004) – Zodora and Colombia, foreign policy decision making and peacekeeping Case Studies (12 items, 15%) Bartels, McCown, and Wilkie (2013) – water conflict and Russian foreign policy; Taylor (2013) – UN; Rothman (2012) – Iranian nuclear, Chinese and U.S. economics, environment; Whaling and Myanmar human rights; Butcher (2012) – U.S.-Iran, Middle Eastern conflict; Asal and Schulzke (2012), Williams and Williams (2011, 2010) and Sasley (2010) – on ethical dilemmas in contemporary Iraq; Crossley-Frolick (2010) – UN model on AIDS conference; Siegel and Young (2009) – on terror in Lebanon against Americans; Chin, Dukes, and Gamson (2009) – Global Justice Game on the World Trade Organization; Switky (2004) – European Union voting rules Fictional (3 items, 4%) Ebner and Winkler (2009) – Pasta Wars negotiations; Enterline and Jepsen (2009) – on territorial dispute; Chasek (2005) – fictitious serious terrorist attack in Singapore Theory (7 items, 9%) Powers and Kirkpatrick (2013) – Take-a-Chance, prisoner's dilemma variation; Schofield (2013) – nuclear dilemmas; Dexter and Guittet (2014) – on terror; Goon (2011) – on peacekeeping and peace-building; Kelle (2008) – arms control simulation; Asal (2005) – prisoner's dilemma; Corbeil and Laveault (2011) – negotiations	Case Studies (1 item, 1%) Parmentier (2013) – OAS and Latin America, historical and contemporary Practice (1 item, 1%) Taylor, Backlund, and Niklasson (2012) – on coaching	Case Studies (13 items, 16%) Landwehr et al. (2013) – Cosmopolis applied to Sudan, avatar style with human interaction; Darling and Foster (2012) – OAS; Schnurr, Santo, and Craig (2013) – Convention on Biological Diversity; McMahon and Miller (2012) – Camp David 2000; Obendorf and Randerson (2012); Zaino and Mulligan (2009) – Middle East; Loggins (2009) – U.S. foreign policy decision-making; Stover (2007) – Cuban missile crisis; Simpson and Kaussler (2009) – multiple cases, with Middle East emphasis; On Model UN: Raymond (2010) and Raymond and Sorensen (2008) applied to the Middle East; Fowler (2009) – on peace processes in Guatemala, Hebron, and Armenia/Azerbaijan/Nagorno Karabakh; Shellman and Turan (2006) – transnational insurgency in Iraq, face-to-face and online role-play Fictional (4 items, 5%) Brynen (2010) – with active media organs; Kanner (2007) – War and Peace; Kuperman (2000) – human vs. computer in simulated fishing dispute; Bos, Shami, and Naab (2006) – ethical dilemmas in international business, face-to-face and online role-play Theory (1 item, 1%) Smolinski and Kesting (2012) – on negotiations

Physical Environment	Virtual Environment	Physical and Virtual Environment
Software (*N* = 12; 15%) Case Studies (6 items, 8%) Morey (2011) – Second Greco-Turkish rivalry, 1866–1925, Testing the Conflict and Rivalry Model (CAR); Weir and Baranowski (2011) – Civilizations competing against one another in the Cold War, Middle East, Iran-Iraq War, Rebuilding of Iraq, India/Pakistan, and Korean War; Strand and Rapkin (2011) – UN; Wolfe (2010) – Taiwan Straits Crisis 1996; Geller and Alam (2010) – current Afghanistan; Blair et al. (2010) – U.S.-Russia Theory (6 items, 8%) Stoll (2011) – civil wars; Cioffi-Revilla and Rouleau (2010) – the RebeLand model; Yilmaz (2007) – computational multisimulation; Yilmaz, Ören, and Ghasem-Aghaee (2006) – multimodels and multisimulation; Rousseau and Van der Veen (2005) – identity, threat, and international cooperation; Stoll (2005) – realist theory and civil war computer game	**Cyber Software to Software** (*N* = 1, 1%) Case Studies (1 item, 1%) Earnest (2008) – U.S.-NATO	

Physical Environment	Virtual Environment	Physical and Virtual Environment
Human and Software (*N* = 4, 5%) Computer Games (2 items, 2%) *PeaceMaker* (2007) – the Israel-Palestinian conflict; Gonzalez, Saner, and Eisenberg (2013) – *PeaceMaker* Computerized Board Games (2 items, 2%) Mintz, Redd, and Vedlitz (2006) – counterterror policy; Mintz (2004) – poliheuristic decision-making theory	**Cyber, Human, and Software** (*N* = 12, 15%) Computer Games (7 items, 9%) Harding and Whitlock (2013) – COUNTRY X educational simulation; Lisk, Kaplancalo, and Riggio (2012) – Infiniteams and Eve Online multiplayer video game; Bachen, Hernandez-Ramos, and Raphael (2012) – Real Lives computer game; Earnest (2009) – counterinsurgency online role-playing games; Power (2007) – America's Army digital war games; Schut (2007) – Civilization, Total War, Sid Meier's Pirates and Battlefield historical games; *Statecraft* (since 2002) ICONS Applications (5 items, 6%) Boyer et al. (2009) – negotiations and gender; Blum and Scherer (2007) – European Security; Asal and Blake (2006) – the International Whaling Commission (IWC); DeGarmo (2006) – refugees and internally displaced persons, conflict resolution and peacekeeping, terrorism and public health; Lay and Smarick (2006) – U.S. Senate lawmaking	**Complex[c]** (*N* = 0, 0%) None

[a] The percentages in this table are rounded.
[b] Examples of hybrid simulations include face-to-face and cyber platforms in a single simulation.
[c] Advanced ICONS uses Internet connection between campuses and can be classified as a complex genre, but no articles in our review reported such simulations.

environments and major technological developments, this review makes it clear that a major impact of social networks is not yet noticeable in fourth-generation simulations. Perhaps the introduction of Facebook into academe must first overcome the murky status social networks had gained as platforms for social gossip and buzz, which is deemed inappropriate for inclusion in higher education and academic research. But, over the years, Facebook has changed considerably and has by now gained mainstream status in many respectable fields such as economics, business, media, and politics.[22] This transformation is captured by the widely spread "Find Us on Facebook," a slogan added to most respectable websites. Moreover, political leaders are already shifting their attention to Facebook interactions as a means of contact with voters and activists all over the world. So perhaps it is already time that the study of world politics will also adjust to these changes.

We contend that the remarkable gap between social networks used in daily life and their relative absence in simulations needs to be addressed. It can be expedited by dialogue between scholars, shared knowledge, and joint development of practical applications for the use of social networks, like Facebook, in academic simulations. To overcome this lacuna, part II of the book, on implementation, applies the conceptual framework and typology as building blocks for planning and running a wide variety of simulations, with suggestions on how social networks can enhance the simulation experience.

In Search of Successful Simulations

The findings on the unequal spread of simulations across the different genres can also be attributed to the costs associated with running simulations. Table 3.3 summarizes the costs of two leading categories of the typology, face-to-face and cyber, by looking specifically at issues and problems related to the core framework components of platforms, boundaries, and interactions, which were presented in chapter 1.

Costs

Table 3.3 shows that some simulation costs are built-in to the method, irrespective of genre, such as (1) dependence on logistics and budget, (2) considerable time investment, (3) schedule constraints, (4) coordination difficulties, and (5) class size limitations.

All simulations embody difficulties related to interactions. They (1) depend on personalities and group dynamics for cohesive team activity, so not all voices are heard; (2) limit complex bargaining and realistic outcomes, and make it hard to define clear-cut winners; (3) involve rigidity in assumptions, decision rules, political plans, and activities; (4) tend to be manipulated by players in order to win; and (5) make coaching essential to prevent deadlocks at the cost of interrupting the simulation flow.

With such costs, it seems natural that faculty may be hesitant to use simulations as a teaching tool. While simulations may advance a large array of goals, as discussed in chapter 1, the price of applying them seems rather high.[23] But if this is the case, why do some educators and researchers across the generations continue to use simulations as a teaching mode? Apparently, a lot has to do with the unique contributions that simulations make to learning efficiency along cognitive, affective, and behavioral dimensions, as explained in chapter 1. More has to do with the specific costs that are attributed to the different genres and the ability to reduce them with experience, proper awareness of academic setting constrains, and careful planning to avoid common pitfalls. We provide practical tips on these subjects in the implementation chapters of the book.

The summaries of different simulations in the appendix indicate that simulations have distinctive features that make them fit certain purposes. So, for example, the Middle East cyber simulation is the most appropriate scheme to capture and illuminate the complexities of world politics in the multicultural global village. The hybrid Palestinian statehood example is a preferable simulation design for most academic courses as it brings together the advantages of physical and virtual encounters over a protracted learning period. Role-playing alone, like the one in the Gulf nuclear face-to-face simulation, is a relatively easy exercise to implement. But it lacks an important aspect of politics: the prolonged nature of interactions. So we suggest that when you plan a simulation on campus, you may consider coupling it with interactions on social networks to capture the continuous landscape of most confrontations, the inputs of the media, and the complexities of multiactor negotiations, live and open or secret, in back-channel settings. All in all, we believe that hybrid simulations, despite their costs, are the best choice to illustrate how complex and dynamic processes unfold in the real world of politics.

TABLE 3.3. Simulation Costs

Platform	Face-to-Face	Cyber
Depend on logistics and budget	✓	✓
Necessitate physical attendance	✓	
Make it difficult to keep records and monitor the simulation	✓	
Reduce human touch and personal relationships and lack body language, eye contact, and rhetoric skills		✓
Require technology skills and depend on smooth running of technology		✓
Some projects charge for participation		✓
Lack physical presence, so commitment to the simulation is lower		✓
Boundaries	**Face-to-Face**	**Cyber**
Require high time-investment	✓	✓
Require schedule modifications and coordination	✓	✓
Require adjustments to class size	✓	✓
Make intercampus cooperation expensive	✓	
Confined to a single locale and time slot	✓	
Limited time for breakthroughs, feedback, and debriefing	✓	
Leave room for participants to hide in plain sight	✓	
Extend spatial breath at the expense of depth		✓
Increase time pressure due to multiple and overlapping stimuli		✓
Political interactions	**Face-to-Face**	**Cyber**
Depend on personalities and group dynamics for cohesive team activity, so not all voices are heard	✓	✓
Limit complex bargaining, realistic outcomes, and make it hard to define clear-cut winners	✓	✓
Involve rigidity in assumptions, decision rules, preprogrammed moves, or formulas	✓	✓
Tend to be manipulated by players in order to win	✓	✓
Make coaching essential to prevent deadlocks at the cost of interrupting the simulation flow	✓	✓
Disagreements may deteriorate into hostility and violence among participants	✓	
Make back-channel and secret communications difficult	✓	
Lack visual contacts: hard to express one's feeling, "poker face" and related skills remain undetected		✓
Simultaneous interactions increase disorder		✓
Media participation	**Face-to-Face**	**Cyber**
Require a stage and time slot to publicize media products for consumption by political teams	✓	✓
Come at the expense of allocating participants to political teams, so require a large group of students	✓	✓
Lack transcripts on interactions, so coverage is dependent on reporting skills	✓	
Depend on technology and require professional skills to produce media products		✓

Guidelines for Choice

The face-to-face, cyber, and hybrid genres come with built-in costs, so we offer six guidelines that add to successful simulation management, reduce costs as much as possible, and serve as remedies to familiar pitfalls. Together, these guidelines can enhance the use of simulations as an integral part of teaching in academe. Unless mentioned otherwise, the same guidelines apply to simulations in on-campus and fully online courses.

1. Plan the simulation scheme for the long run. When you read this book, you should think of the short and long run at the same time. In the short run, you may be excited to use simulations as a teaching mode, but as you become aware of its costs you might change your decision. The adoption of a long-range outlook is likely to offer a more positive cost-benefit calculation. Despite immediate costs in the short run, after you have completed the first simulation you can reduce the costs of future runs. Most setup preparations discussed in chapter 4, such as creating a website, opening groups on social networks, drafting assignment sheets, and constructing feedback forms, are a first-time investment for many simulations you run in the future. In the Gulf nuclear, Middle East, and Palestinian statehood simulations, for example, we used the same feedback form with only minor adjustments to cover the particulars of each simulation. The format, platform, and many feedback questions remain unchanged, like those on overall satisfaction with the simulation, extent of learning, involvement in policy formation, or evaluation of the media role. Such universal issues serve as a readily available foundation for all our subsequent simulations. So the balance between short- and long-run considerations should make simulations a rational decision for teaching in the 21st century.

2. Clarify your immediate goals to make a choice regarding the best-fit simulation genre for any particular simulation you plan. Chapter 1 highlights the many goals that are effectively advanced by the use of simulations, and chapter 10 describes how to assess the contribution of each simulation you run after it ends. To reduce costs, you need to clarify the most important goals you want to advance in a particular simulation and to choose the most appropriate genre to reach them. In the Middle East simulation, for example, our primary goals was to introduce ISA members with the idea of simulations on social networks as a useful teaching tool by bringing together campuses across the global village. The use of a cyber platform was

therefore the best choice to reach this goal, especially given the worldwide spread of our target audience. In the Gulf nuclear simulation, by contrast, our immediate goal was to familiarize students with the complexity of current developments in the Middle East region, focusing on the Iranian nuclear program and the dilemmas it involves. Any type of simulation could be useful to reach this goal, but a whole-day on-campus encounter was the most suitable one to highlight the emotion-laden aspects that affect decision-making in a tense protracted conflict. So the face-to-face genre was the proper choice for this empirically driven simulation.

As you change your goals, you will need to reevaluate the utility of face-to-face or cyber simulations and only pay the costs of what you really want to gain. Hybrid learning means that the web is a handy environment in class, during solitary learning, the simulation rounds, debriefing, and research after all simulation interactions end. Consequently, to meet your teaching goals you might run a face-to-face simulation and enrich it with many web-based tools and processes at low cost, as detailed in chapter 4 on setup preparations. Or, for a new run, you might replicate the tools you had already created for a cyber simulation in the past with minimal adjustments and low update and maintenance costs, as addressed in the three implementation chapters of this book.

3. Adjust the simulation scheme to your academic setting. Though you may be personally inclined to use one particular genre over another one, the costs of face-to-face and cyber simulations, summarized in table 3.3, show there is really no universally better one compared to all others. As chapter 2 explains, the academic setting is a major constraint that affects the best-fit simulation. So careful consideration of academic concerns related to the topics you teach, the size of your class, and the duration of your course will help you decide on a simulation genre, setup, and practical preparations that will reduce costs without forsaking the goals you want to promote. In the Middle East simulation, for example, our preferable option was hybrid genre with one world politics round on social networks and another as a face-to-face encounter. Yet the geographic spread of the participants across the globe made the face-to-face round unrealistic and dictated a cyber genre. Although we met many of participants in person during the innovative workshop at the annual ISA convention in San Diego, we decided to devote the limited time for personal exchanges to debriefing. This choice enabled us to complete a full simulation cycle and accomplish our immediate goal of demonstrating the

efficiency of simulations as a teaching mode, even as we had to give up on the hybrid genre.

4. Cooperate with other educators to share the load and increase the payoffs of the simulation project. Most costs remain the same whether you cooperate or not. To be sure, if you run a face-to-face simulation and students from other campuses join, the project requires transportation arrangements and the costs increase. But the costs of a cyber simulation stay the same, even if students from outside the state or region join. So, in principle, try to find colleagues who will cooperate with you in the simulation, to share the load of setup preparations and to promote goal attainment by making a multicultural experience possible. With a few educators who take part in the project from the start, each one lowers the costs by distributing responsibilities and preparation tasks. The Arab-Israel conflict simulation in 2014, for example, involved close cooperation between two Israeli campuses and one campus in the United States. Each educator taught a different course for a different audience: a methodology-oriented course for graduate students in international relations, a theory-based seminar for undergraduates in communications, and an empirically driven course for undergraduates in history. And yet all three were part of the joint simulation project, with the same guidelines for teams, rules, scenarios, schedules, and feedback forms. Decisions on each of the shared procedures and tasks were made jointly by all colleagues, with unique contributions made by each one of them. For instance, after the first version of the scenario was written by one of educators, it was revised and enhanced with fresh ideas by another. Each version of the scenario was evaluated by our methodology colleague to check that the narrative fits the characteristics of a good scenario, as explained in chapters 5 and 6, and to assess its applicability to the theoretical hypotheses that guided the course. The history expert added a few historical nuances to the story, and the media specialist transformed the text into a creative newspaper format, with pictures, maps, and dramatic headlines, quite similar to the ones in figure 5.4 and 6.2. The gains accomplished from such cooperation in the simulation are exponential because expertise and experience diversity increases the challenge and creates awards that are not only greater but different in kind.

The fact that not all players are alike adds to the success of the simulation. This has to do with the geographic location and cultural backgrounds of the players, their academic level, and the topics they study. Cross-discipline simulations that involve undergraduate and graduate participants tend to enrich the simulation process and its outcomes. A larger number of teams in the simulation and many different roles within the team are likely to illustrate the complexities of politics in the real world. All these are easier to reach when you cooperate with others, reducing costs and making a profound difference in shaping the overall learning experience, as outlined in chapter 2.

5. Remember the importance of time elements and human attributes. The success of a simulation requires some plasticity to accommodate the unknown and the unplanned impact of time elements and human attributes. In the simulation schedule it is wise to leave some flexibility to cope with unexpected events and gradual adjustments by all players. This is especially true at the beginning of the intrateam policy formation debates and during intensive and rapid world politics interactions. Careful planning of duration, tempo, timing, and pace of acceleration in the simulation makes the difference between a dull or dramatic experience. The appropriate temporal calculations depend on many aspects, such as the topic, the number of participants, their skill and motivation, the number of teams, and the importance of the simulation in the course as a whole. If the duration is too long, even motivated fans lose interest or get carried away by competing assignments in other courses. If a simulation slows down, you may add inputs of terror, violence, or diplomatic events to enliven the encounter. Such inputs test the political resolve of different teams and teach skills related to coping with drawbacks and failure. But overwhelming exposure to frustration and disappointment may leave its impact on the overall learning experience.

In terms of duration, just keep in mind that a simulation that is too short may not meet its planned objectives and might trigger frustration, resentment, and detachment even by good students. In the Gulf nuclear simulation, for example, the time devoted for a breaking news session was insufficient for broadcasting of all products prepared by three media teams. So we urged editors to limit the number of publications to only one or two video clips and save other products for possible use after the simulation. Unfortunately, this request frustrated some of the participants in the media teams, especially those whose products were left aside. But we decided to leave the simulation schedule intact to ensure that the diplomatic negotiation process remains the main focus of the simulation.

Timing is also related to the gradual disclosure of scenario elements and to designing its complexity. You should be aware of the time constraints created by adding events into an ongoing simulation process, approving initiatives offered by participants, and allowing for media manipulations that may considerably increase uncertainties. The same is true with respect to the introduction of stress-generating events, meaningful changes in the scenario and leaps in time, such as a shift to "five years later" during a second round, with a detailed outline of all changes assumed to have taken place during this time frame. Acceleration is an effective way to practice crisis management and coping, but escalation driven by you as the simulation administrator by use of ad-hoc events is often matched by team behavior and might lead to the loss of control over events and to possible failure of the simulation project. However, if the duration is long enough, the simulation may include a shift in guiding paradigm that offers creative insights during the debriefing process and interesting research after the simulation ends. For example, a regional crisis with the superpowers as mediators may start out by following the assumptions of a liberal approach and shift after the first round to a confrontation based on realist considerations with adjustments in mediation goals, style, intensity, and effectiveness. By use of paradigms you can get students to handle and practice the most abstract components of the teaching curriculum. The same is true with regard to different modes of decision-making and within team debates. Participants may be instructed to do their best to follow a rational process during the first round and during the second round shift to apply an organizational or personality-driven one.

The human element is about the students as individual participants and as a group. Keep in mind that personality, previous experiences, peer pressures, motivation, study load, and academic expertise are among the core aspects that may affect the successful flow of the simulation and the overall learning experience.

From the start, you should assume that the appeal of simulations, face-to-face in class or on social networks, is not shared equally by all individuals. The idea of a cyber or hybrid simulation on social networks builds upon the familiarity and habits of digital natives who form the bulk of our current student body. This trend is most likely to increase in the future even if a new web-application replaces Facebook as the leading social network. But what about late adaptors or those who are simulation/ web avert? Coaching by faculty or, better yet, by peer students in conjunction with joint chores where a web fan accompanies a newcomer often serves as a quick cure and overcomes individual reluctance. Assurances regarding the privacy settings of educational groups set up on Facebook can further reduce fears connected with interactions on the web. Finally, the simulation experience is usually so powerful and enriching for the majority of students that an exceptional solution should be improvised for the few who end up refusing to take part in the project. In the simulation on the Arab-Israel conflict, in 2014, a new role of a correspondent on gossip was introduced and assigned to a less active student. This role dramatically increased this student's motivation, curiosity, and involvement in the simulation and added a creative, amusing, and theatrical contribution to the interactions between the political and media teams.

Full engagement in the simulation is an individual choice. Some become enthusiasts from the start and contribute way beyond their role and formal obligations. Others take more time to feel comfortable with the proceedings. Once the students feel that they actually play an active part in shaping the simulation project, their motivation to participate and fulfill simulation-related assignments increases considerably. A close and sensitive follow-up by educators can detect immersion dynamics and help overcome most difficulties with flexibility, patience, and coaching.

6. Reappraise the simulation scheme, goal achievement, and costs based on your experience. Simulations are about study, experimentation, practice, and adjustments. This is true for all participants and for you as the administrator of the simulation. In the third part of the book, on analysis, we look at the simulation project as a whole and evaluate its contributions for students and faculty. Chapter 8 offers tools for feedback, primarily a student activity that helps you tap the achievements of the simulation through the eyes of its participants. Chapter 9 explains how interactive debriefing between you and your students blends into the learning experience, and chapter 10 focuses on the assessment process, including the grading task. It also calls for a fresh look at the goals you set and at the outcomes you have reached so as to repeat the use of effective tools in the future and learn from mistakes. The data and insights you gain from each simulation and its debriefing process allow you to look back at the simulations you have run in a critical manner so as to maximize cost-benefit choices for current and planned projects. All simulations provide lessons to be learned, and often a simulation that you regard as a failure can be a source of valuable inputs for change, better goal fulfillment, and lower costs in the future. The Palestinian statehood simulation, for example, was an opportunity to learn by trial and error as we were

coping with unexpected difficulties that emerged during our experimental use of Facebook as a platform to bridge across distant campuses. During setup preparations, we asked each student to create new Facebook account for academic purposes and to add "sim" at the end of user-name. This way we reduced privacy concerns to the minimum and at the same time all participants could easily identify other students from different campuses. This practice worked well during the slow asynchronous process of policy formation but caused serious problems during synchronous world politics interactions. When all 60 participants with "sim" in their names acted simultaneously on the joint Facebook group, the social network automatically blocked many of them, thinking they were bots. So, we immediately guided participants that were blocked to use their personal Facebook accounts, a spontaneous solution that worked excellently and became our routine practice in all simulations on social networks. For sure, we were aware that the first round of world politics could have been a disaster if students could not function due to technical matters, but we learned that it is never late to adapt and improve.

Overall, by knowing your constraints, making the right choices, and sharing the burden of running the simulation with other partners, you can minimize the common costs of all simulations, such as dependence on logistics and budget, high time-investment, schedule shortcomings, coordination difficulties, and class size limitations. You can handle other costs related to interactions by adjusting your immediate simulation scheme to reduce problems of personality and group dynamics, oversimplification in bargaining, unrealistic outcomes, rigidity in assumptions, rules, plans, and activities, or the negative effects of coaching, which interrupt the simulation flow. These concerns and many others are discussed in chapter 2, on academic setting, and chapter 4, on simulation setup. They are further developed, with an emphasis on planning and implementation, in chapter 5, on the policy formation process within teams, and in chapter 6, on world politics interactions among teams.

PART II

Implementation

CHAPTER 4

Simulation Setup

This chapter focuses on the plan for simulation setup and the procedures you and your students will carry out as you get ready for the interactive event. By *simulation setup,* we mean all the preparations and study that take place before the simulation begins. The chapter is divided into three sections: the first addresses the plan for the simulation, the second explains the procedures that translate the plan into a well-defined operational tool, and the third contains instructions for simulation participants. Table 4.3 and 4.4 summarize core simulation-related assignments and basic guidelines for students. These tables can serve as useful checklists to help you make sure you have (1) taken into account the relevant considerations related to your academic setting; (2) made your decisions regarding the choices that are available to you, as addressed in chapter 2; and (3) completed all the necessary preparations for each simulation round and for hybrid learning in your course as a whole, as explained in this chapter. You may also use the detailed table of contents of this book to focus on specific topics of interest within the chapter and change the sequence of your reading as you proceed with the text.

Many setup procedures are common to a face-to-face, cyber, and hybrid genres. For example, beyond short and simple role-play exercises, each character in the simulation is part of a team, so you always need to divide your students into teams, with a role for each student within the team. Thus, we indicate a genre only when the measure to be taken is characteristic of a particular kind of simulation, like opening Facebook groups for each team when you plan to run a cyber simulation.

The chapter, like chapters 5 and 6 on implementation and chapters 8 and 9 on simulation analysis, provides a detailed account from a dual perspective: yours and that of your students. Since learning with simulations is a dyadic matter, it requires coordinated and synchronized progress in the learning stages by you as the educator who takes the lead and by your students who follow and at times have an important impact on the interaction process. We end each of these chapters with a section on instructions for participants. You can adapt this section to your specific choices and use it as an overview for students.

We enrich the chapter with examples from the **Gulf nuclear** face-to-face simulation, the **Middle East** cyber simulation, and the **Palestinian statehood** hybrid simulation summarized in the appendix. These examples are meant to make the analysis provided herein more vivid and to share with you options, consequences, pitfalls, and advice from our own experience. The three simulations also serve as templates you may choose to use in your runs. Teaching with simulations is efficient: once you have mastered the tools needed for the project and laid the infrastructure necessary for its setup, you can repeat the exercise from year to year. The addition of new story lines and a fresh scenario is an easy modification as all other setup procedures repeat themselves, on a preset skeleton, from one round to another and from one simulation to the next.

In a way, this chapter may seem to be the most complex of all implementation chapters, since it lays the groundwork for all the following stages of the simulation. If your first reaction is that you are overwhelmed with information regarding the plan and necessary preparations, so that you lose the big picture, we suggest that you proceed directly to chapters 5 and 6 or to the appendix, with short summaries of different simulations, to get a better idea of what the simulation is actually like. Then you can return here to read more about the chore of structuring the simulation of your choice, one that serves your teaching goals and fits your course setting.

Setup Plan

In preparation for the simulation you will need to make your first five decisions regarding the *type of simulation* you will run, the *topics it will cover*, the *teams* of the simulation, its *schedule*, and the *assignments* your students will have to prepare for the simulation, before, during, and after the interaction process.

Simulation Type

Part I of the book on theory addresses three core simulation genres: face-to-face, cyber, and hybrid. Basically, you have a choice between the first two or you can use both, so in effect you run a hybrid simulation with cyber and face-to-face rounds. The choice of simulation type affects further decisions you will make, so it should be regarded as a strategic move that is based on your academic setting, the goals you want to advance, and your personal inclinations. Earlier in chapter 2, we have also seen that the academic setting imposes constraints and offers opportunities for the choice of simulation genre. If, for example, your course is conducted online and involves students from different countries, you have to run a cyber simulation. Similarly, social networks as a platform for the simulation is a suitable option if your class is very large and the on-campus logistics make it difficult to work out a suitable time and place for a face-to-face gathering.

The decision on the type of simulation is also based on the goals you want to achieve, as detailed in the framework section of chapter 1. Given some flexibility in your academic setting, we highly recommend a hybrid simulation, which maximizes the utilities of both genres and overcomes many of their shortcomings.

By individual inclinations, we mean your personal preferences for cyber over face-to-face encounters or vice versa. As a starter, we suggest that you try out one type, then proceed with the other, and later move on to conduct hybrid simulations. If you are more comfortable with the idea of human interactions in a physical setting and a condensed time slot, disregard the sections that detail setup measures concerning cyber rounds. Similarly, if you like the notion of interacting over a prolonged but less in-

tensive period on social networks, you can skip the setup sections that outline how to proceed with a face-to-face simulation. The choice of a hybrid simulation means that you follow the guidelines for both simulations, although you will not be running both face-to-face and cyber rounds at once. The move from one round to another, as you change the platform from physical to virtual or vice versa, is what makes the simulation hybrid. So essentially you can focus on each genre separately to get ready for each round you conduct.

Once you have decided on the type of simulation, you are ready to proceed with the other four setup decisions on topics, teams, schedule, and assignments outlined below, which are needed in all simulation genres.

Topics

Your course may be theory-driven, empirically focused, area-study-based, or methodology-oriented, as detailed in chapter 2. Courses of all four types may benefit considerably from the application of simulations to increase learning efficiency. However, each of them leads to a somewhat different simulation topic and a specific emphasis in setup preparations to suit the course you teach.

For a simulation topic, you need a good story. You choose a historical, current events, or fiction narrative for the simulation and detail it in the simulation scenario. In chapters 5 and 6 we describe how to write a good scenario and suggest different formats to dress it up so as to add to the simulation atmosphere. You can format the scenario as an official invitation by a government or international organization, a proposal for negotiation, a newspaper with few relevant events to start the interaction process, or a YouTube video clip with a breaking news broadcast. No matter which format you pick, you need to make sure the story you build suits the subject of your course, as mentioned earlier with respect to academic setting concerns. In other words, the simulation should capture the core subjects and major issues you cover in your course— theory, empirical case, area study, or methodology—while its topic encapsulates the narrower focus of specific details necessary to begin a process of policy formation within teams and world politics among them.

When you run a simulation in a theory-driven course you want to improve the understanding of the theories covered in the curriculum. So your choice should include a case that embeds the core issues, concepts, and dilemmas included in and raised by the theories you teach. For instance, you can play the Arab-Israel conflict to test the dynamics of the realist paradigm, the difficulties of coping with terror, the dangers of crisis escalation, or the complexities of conducting negotiations when the adversaries belong to different cultures, religions, and civilizations. However, if you want to highlight the liberal paradigm or the impact of constructivism on policy formation you may be better off setting your simulation in a European context that is more relevant to these theoretical outlooks.

You may still choose the Arab-Israel conflict as a challenging anomaly for a liberal or constructivist simulation, keeping in mind that the combination of theory and empirical setting you have chosen may lead to simulation developments that do not resemble the actual events in the region. Such simulations may have a huge impact on your students as they demonstrate that behaviors are deeply embedded in theoretical and normative assumptions that shape goals and policy alternatives.

When you integrate a simulation into an empirically based course or part of an area studies program, your decision on the topic is usually preset by the case or region you teach. Still, you have a wide array of alternatives to choose from. For example, you may be an area specialist teaching Central American politics so you probably would not choose to play the Arab-Israel conflict, but you could narrow or expand your focus by (1) the states represented in the simulation, (2) the periods you cover in the scenario, or (3) by the emphasis on cooperation, conflict, or transformation from one to the other. So the simulation may cover the protracted Nicaraguan Contras' struggle, the relations between the United States and Cuba during the 1962 missile crisis, or the activity of the UN and regional organizations and their contributions to stability in the region.

When you blend simulations into a methodology-oriented course, your range of topics for the simulation is infinite. You should make it clear to your students that the main goal of the exercise is not to replicate a real event but rather to observe how the lab setting you have created is an effective tool for testing theory or evaluating the impact of variables from different fields and distinct models. Here, the emphasis shifts from a project designed to match an empirical setting to the observation of a tool and an assessment of its utility. In doing so your students will become more aware of the importance of creating a lab in social science and humanities, even if unsophisticated, to advance critical thinking and theory reformulation by hypotheses testing with multiple controls over several rounds and consecutive runs. You may change the leading theory each round you play, keeping the teams, roles, region, and topics constant to demonstrate how theoretical

outlooks and guiding principles affect policy formation, cooperation, and conflict. But as a lab, the simulation will contain part of the big picture, not all of it, as it is never intended to be an exact and full replica of reality. The use of an anomaly, a rare or a nontypical case is also useful in methodology courses, to illustrate the links between assumptions, data, and research outcomes. So the choice of an empirical topic and the selection of theories shape the process of the simulation and the results of the research based on its written products.

Once you have decided on the type of simulation and its topic you are ready to consider what teams to include, the third setup decision you make before you run the simulation.

Political and Media Teams

The minimum number of political teams in a simulation is two, with at least three participants in each team so as to have intrateam and interteam activity. You can include two states, a state and a nonstate actor, a state and an international organization, or two nonstate actors. Media teams may be added to enrich the simulation, as we explain in chapters 5 and 6, but they operate alongside political teams. To conduct interactions of world politics, each team has to prepare its policy plan and opening initiatives. When two political teams meet, the dynamics of world politics in the simulation begin. This minimal number of two teams does not imply this is the optimal number, which is dependent on the number of students in your course.

You should have at least three participants in each team so they can interact and plan their foreign policy, in the case of a political team, or their coverage strategy, in media teams. Two players could suffice, but when one of them becomes inactive, for whatever reason, the other player remains alone. The whole idea of simulations is to learn by taking part in a process. One person alone does not produce a process of policy formation. Moreover, when the number of players is too small, the workload and responsibilities are heavy, placing a strain on them that you may prefer to avoid.

As noted earlier, your academic setting becomes an important determinant: a small class means fewer teams and a narrower representation of domestic attributes, like regime characteristics, political parties, opposition groups, and public opinion within each team. Surely, you can create teams with different sizes, since a democracy or an international organization require more players and an autocratic regime or nonstate actor can function with fewer participants. For nonstate actors, you may choose to have a separate team for each group, such as Hamas and the Palestinian authority, or blend them into a one team, such as the Palestinians, to reveal the hardships of policy formation that authoritarian actors may confront and the costs of splintering or secession.

When you have a large enough class you may include some players as public opinion representatives or create a team that represents an international organization like the European Union or the UN that operates in a conflict region such as the Middle East or mediates to resolve a destabilizing issue like the Iranian nuclear program. To incorporate the diverse points of view, structure, and politics in the organization you need several students who play different states within the organization, such as France, Germany, Spain, or Greece in the European Union, or Russia, the United States, and other state members of the Security Council in the UN.

The question of how many teams to create depends on your choice because too many teams might trigger control problems and make it hard to run the simulation effectively. From a practical point of view, if you are operating all by yourself, plan on fewer teams, but if you have colleagues or assistants, you can add teams with less risk.

To capture the complexity and the authenticity of world politics, we suggest that you include media teams alongside political ones. This, we believe, is essential in simulations that cover 21st century events, but it also contributes considerably to all historical periods and diverse topics. Media teams generate a flow of information for all participants to consider. Such information and the interactions between political and media teams, described in chapters 5 and 6, exemplify the notions of media management, media manipulation, and the power of the media in political processes. You may add one or more media teams to reflect different media sources, styles, and biases.

Once you determine the number of teams and players within them, you can decide on the roles each player fulfills in the simulation. Given your class size, the choice regarding roles is linked to the range of domestic elements you want to illuminate in the simulation. If you want to have at least three top decision-makers on each team—a head of state, a foreign minister, and a defense minister—but you also want to assign players to represent interest groups, opposition parties, and ethnic minorities, you may have to compromise on the overall number of teams to add more participants to each team. Similarly, a media organ should have a chief editor and assistant editor as well as two to three reporters to cover interactions. A smaller team would reduce the team's ability to function

and limit its ability to produce quality media products, in real time, during the simulation.

In planning your teams and the roles within each team, you need to remember that teams that are too large may also hamper the simulation and reduce its effectiveness. One of the negative aspects of a large team is the existence of free riders who do not share the burdens of preparation and frustrate other team players who carry the load. From your perspective, such situations mean inadequate control over the players and their interactions and a problem of how to grade these students.

Depending on your academic setting, an ideal team size lets each player contribute to the simulation, preparing and learning from the process and its outcomes. When the team is too big, some students work and others hide in plain sight. Everybody in the team knows the burden is not shared by all members, but students rarely should or want to police their teammates. In these instances, you need to use considerable coaching to enhance the motivation of participants who bandwagon, to make them take an active role in the simulation, thereby lessening the frustrations of motivated others, and maintaining control over the interaction process.

The rule of thumb for effective and fun encounters is to let all students contribute, in order to prevent overload and to guide participants to share tasks and engage in activities that promote the entire team. Such practices increase the experience each student gains and the learning efficiency of the class as a whole. Guidelines and tips on how to implement such practices are included in chapter 5, on policy formation, and chapter 6, on world politics encounters.

After you have made your choices on the number, size, and composition of teams, your fourth setup decision relates to the simulation schedule and how it blends with your study plan for the entire course.

Schedule

The time plan for the simulation has to do with how and when the interactive project fits into your teaching scheme. The choice of time frame depends on your academic settings, on the type of simulation you choose, and on the complexity of the topic. To illustrate schedule options, tables 4.1 and 4.2 summarize the details of two examples for semester and yearlong plans that you can follow and modify according to your particular setting. A face-to-face or cyber simulation can be incorporated in both plans, or you can run a hybrid simulation of at least two rounds: one cyber and the other face-to-face, or vice versa.

TABLE 4.1. Simulation Schedule for a Semester Course

Two rounds, one cyber and one face-to-face, with a limited time break between rounds		
Week	**Main Activity**	**Simulation Choice**
1 to 3	Student preparation for the simulation, by solitary learning and in class meetings or distance learning instruction by the educator	Cyber and face-to-face
4 and 5	Intrateam activities for policy formation with flexible login time	Cyber
6	Round 1 of world politics for two hours at a fixed time	Cyber
7	Debriefing and intrateam reevaluation	Cyber and face-to-face
8	Round 2 of world politics as a daylong on-campus event	Face-to-face
9 and 10	Final simulation analysis: summary, feedback, debriefing, and assessment with personal, intrateam, and interteam perspectives	Cyber and face-to-face

A typical schedule for a single semester detailed in table 4.1 devotes at least two weeks for in-class preparation and solitary learning and another two weeks for intrateam consolidation and policy formation on the social network, at a flexible login time. Next comes the first round of world politics interactions, for a two-hour meeting on the social network at a fixed login time. After the first round ends, at least a week should be devoted for the teams to debrief, reevaluate their achievements, and adjust policy plans. This reassessment can be done on social networks, in class, or both.

The second round, a daylong on-campus face-to-face event, continues the first round. The simulation ends with a full debriefing and an evaluation of both rounds and the simulation as a whole on the platforms you decide. A detailed discussion of the postsimulation activities is found in the third part of the book on feedback, debriefing, and assessment.

Table 4.2 offers a plan for a yearlong course with a hybrid simulation of four rounds. It can follow developments in a single empirical case with three consecutive cyber rounds and a final face-to-face round. Alternatively, it can focus on one case in the first two rounds and shift to another case in time or region, but related in teams, topics, or theories in the other two.

The advantage of consecutive rounds on the same topic is in a gradual disclosure of information on policy changes, choices of actors, uncertainty, pressure, coalition buildup, negotiation management, and the promotion of desirable policy options. Often in a short simulation, some feeling is gained of what the politics are about, but due to a shortage of time the negotiated outcomes are not fully developed and some participants are left frustrated.

The benefit of shifting the interactions to a new scenario in the last two rounds is in advancing a comparative perspective that helps students understand the differences and similarities between cases, with some basic features common to both. For example, in the first semester the class can play the Arab-Israel conflict in 1947 with UN Resolution 181 as a major focal point. Then, in the second semester, the focus can shift to the Palestinian quest for statehood in 2012, with the major actors remaining the same and many of the issues raised in Resolution 181 still valid, but with new and important developments to consider. Though the schedule we present for a yearlong course suggests four rounds, you can easily adjust it to your preferences, with fewer rounds and a longer break between them. Too many rounds in a single course may impose an impossible workload on students and make the excitement related to the simulation project disappear. So plan your schedule carefully to maintain study efficiency and ensure the momentum.

All in all, a single semester course requires a tighter schedule than a yearlong course, with fewer rounds, a shorter duration for each round, and breaks between them. But the schedule is also dependent on the type of simulation you choose. Face-to-face simulations are mostly short events compared to cyber or hybrid encounters. This does not mean that in a single semester course you should only run a face-to-face simulation but rather that cyber or hybrid simulations give you more options for effective time management.

Assignments

The fifth and last setup decision you need to make concerns the assignments for your students to prepare before, during, and after the simulation. Most assignments described herein are an integral part of the simulation and are necessary for the simulation to proceed effectively. Others are suggested for undergraduate seminar courses or for graduate courses with an emphasis on individual research.

TABLE 4.2. Simulation Schedule for a Yearlong Course

Four rounds: three cyber and one face-to-face, with a major time break between the second and third rounds		
Week	**Main Activity**	**Simulation Choice**
First Semester		
1 to 3	Preparation for the simulation, by solitary learning and in class meetings or distance learning instruction by the educator	Cyber and face-to-face
4 and 5	Intrateam activities for policy formation with flexible login time	Cyber
6	Round 1 of world politics for two hours at a fixed time	Cyber
7	Debriefing and intrateam reevaluation	Cyber and face-to-face
8	Round 2 of world politics for two hours at a fixed time	Cyber
9 and 10	Debriefing and intrateam reevaluation	Cyber and face-to-face
Second Semester[a]		
1 to 3	Preparation for the simulation, by solitary learning and in class meetings or distance learning instruction by the educator	Cyber and face-to-face
4 and 5	Intrateam activities for policy formation with flexible login time	Cyber
6	Round 3 of world politics for two hours at a fixed time	Cyber
7	Debriefing and intrateam reevaluation	Cyber and face-to-face
8	Round 4 of world politics as a daylong on-campus event	Face-to-face
9 and 10	Final simulation analysis: summary, feedback, debriefing, and assessment with personal, intrateam, and interteam perspectives	Cyber and face-to-face

[a]In the second semester you may run a new simulation on a different but related topic, so rounds 3 and 4 are the first and second rounds of the new simulation.

Your experience with simulations will lead you to develop useful assignments of your own, to replace or supplement the ones suggested herein. The main reason for these assignments is to get the students ready for the simulation, as individuals and as teams. Assignments are intended to make sure the simulation experience advances the goals of your course, adds the most to the learning efficiency of your students, and extends their expertise in theory, empirical cases, area studies, or methodology.

Table 4.3 summarizes twelve assignments related to the simulation, divided into tasks for (1) all participants regardless of the actor they play; (2) political teams only, be they a state, nonstate, or international organization; and (3) media teams only. Each assignment is described in terms of its contents and explained further in chapters 5 and 6 as well as in the third part of the book with respect to postsimulation feedback and debriefing. Many assignments are offered as individual ones and are easy to grade, based on a detailed instruction sheet for each one of them. These assignments trigger solitary learning, which is later expanded and enriched by collective discussions in class, on cyber platforms, or both. Some assignments are collective from the start and raise concerns on how to grade individuals, like heads of teams or other committed participants, who have contributed considerably more than others to the final collective product. An advanced discussion on the assessment of students and of the simulation project as a whole is presented in chapter 10.

Assignments 1 and 2 include the preparation of an actor portfolio and character biography for a political or media team the student was assigned. These tasks apply to all students and include presimulation preparation and individual hand-ins based on solitary learning. Actor portfolio is suggested as a 10-page report on the actor, like an essay on Russia. Character biography is designed as a one-page summary, like a short review on Vladimir Putin. Both may include graphic as well as written items, starting with the icon that represents the actor or character, be it a flag, a logo of a media organ, a seal of a character role such as the president, defense minister, or foreign minister; and photos of leaders, chief editors, and reporters. Maps, official information, academic publications, and statistical data also contribute to the students' knowledge about the actor they play.

The purpose of the actor portfolio assignment is to stimulate solitary learning about the actor and to have the students integrate a wealth of relevant information and diverse aspects in a single report. We include two parts in

TABLE 4.3. Simulation Assignments

#	Task	Time Frame	Preparation and Grading
For participants of all teams			
1	Actor portfolio for states, nonstate actors, international organizations, and media organs	Before policy formation begins	Individual and collective by each team
2	Character biography for political decision-makers and media professionals	Before policy formation begins	Individual
3	Participation in intrateam policy formation	As the simulation progresses: before, during, and after the world politics rounds	Individual and collective by each team
4	Participation in interteam world politics process	During world politics rounds	Individual and collective by each team
5	Participation in all feedback activities and debriefing sessions from the individual and collective outlook	Mainly after the world politics rounds end. Most feedback is solitary, some is added during the interactive debriefing sessions	Individual and collective by each team
6	Final summary report, evaluation of team performance, simulation achievements, and other research topics	After the simulation ends. The report, evaluation, and research project are optional tasks	Individual and collective by each team
Only for participants of political teams			
7	Actor and character values and ideology	Before the simulation begins	Individual and collective by each team
8	Actor and character goals, policy plan, and alternative moves	Before the world politics rounds begin	Individual and collective by each team
9	Operational proposals, agreements, interviews with the media, and policy briefings for the media	Before and during the world politics rounds	Individual and collective by each team
Only for participants of media teams			
10	Network orientation and goals, media professionals' values	Before the world politics rounds begin	Individual and collective by each team
11	Reporting plans, product assignments, and division of labor	Before and during the world politics rounds	Collective by each team
12	Newspapers, video and audio broadcasts, photos and news flashes	Before and during the world politics rounds. For presentation, mainly during the media break	Individual and collective by each team

the report: first on the actor and second on the topic. You can modify the components of the report depending on the topics you want to include in your teaching.

In the first part, on the actor, the report contains a short description of the political actor including its core attributes: (1) regime type, ideology, and major concerns of domestic politics for states or media regime, editorial line and internal management structure for media organs; (2) capabilities and status, based on a variety of hard and soft power elements, like territory, population, military and economic resources, national cohesion, and leadership for the political actors, or rating, audience size, income, and geographic spread for media organs; (3) membership in international and regional organizations, economic bod-

ies, and military alliances for states, and participation in salient media events for media organs; (4) core allies, rivals, and competitors in the region and outside it for states and media organs; and (5) fundamental and long-standing values, interests, orientations, and policies.

The second part of the actor portfolio provides a short overview of the simulation topic from the actor's perspective. For example, the Arab-Israel conflict, nuclear proliferation in the Gulf, or the civil war in Syria can be explored from the outlook of a state, like Israel; a nonstate actor, like Hamas; an international organization, like the European Union; or a media organ, like *CNN*. The overview focuses on five aspects: (1) the main issues, as the actor defines them; (2) a basic timeline of core events, including the actor's previous involvement related to the topic of a simulation, for example its positions on and roles in peacekeeping attempts, violence, or negotiations. The report should cover a longer period than the one planned for the simulation to provide some historical background for the specific developments that are likely to appear in the scenario; (3) relevant documents and agreements; (4) the relationship between the main actors and the issues at stake, from the point of view of the actor. This characterizes the matrix of existing and prospective partners and their positions on issues as the actor perceives them; (5) important domestic and international constraints and opportunities the actor considers, such as unemployment, civil war, obligations to ethnic kin in neighboring states, or the activity of nonstate and intergovernmental actors.

The reference list for the report should include sources of diverse types: digital as well as traditional books and articles, newspapers, and journals, some of which will later be placed as links on the team's Facebook wall, if you choose to run a cyber simulation on social networks, so all team members can enrich one another based on their individual search for information.

In an Arab-Israel conflict simulation, for example, the students that played Israel had to learn about that country and to look for information regarding their actor in the period from 1947 to 1949, with the transformation from the British mandate in Palestine to a newly independent Israeli state.

For a student assigned to the role of the Israeli prime minister, the civil war events in Palestine and interstate war that followed serve as the immediate historical context. The official United Nations website provides a wealth of relevant resources on the proposals and political processes that occurred before and during the escalation to the 1948 war. The official Israeli Ministry of Foreign Affairs website adds documents from the Israeli perspective. YouTube clips, media sources, biographies, autobiographies, and academic studies supplement the basic overview to create a nuanced foundation of knowledge for the simulation.

In a current events simulation the *CIA World Factbook* and official state and media websites are a good starting point for basic data on each actor represented in the simulation. Other resources are detailed in chapter 1, on hybrid learning, and their value to learning efficiency is explained.

The character biography is a short one-page summary on the leader, decision-maker, or media professional the student is assigned for the simulation. The biographies of real characters, such as President Barack Obama, should be based on empirical facts, preferably with regard to the topic of the simulation. For media actors, the website of the newspaper or network can be enriched by searching for data on the core personalities relevant for the topic of the simulation or for past publications of the media organ and information about its orientation, strategies, and impact. In terms of character profile, students may step into the shoes of famous editors and well-known reporters or make up a fictional biography, based on relevant contextual facts and the creativity of the students.

For example, in the Middle East simulation a biography of an imaginary Hamid Mahmoud was composed by one of the media correspondents. It highlighted a dual Arab American background, upbringing, and education to explain his relocation from *Fox News* to the *Global Crescent*. It also hinted that the orientation the reporter had adopted is local Middle Eastern rather than Western or American.

When you choose a fiction narrative, you will need to instruct students carefully about how to prepare these two assignments. They may choose to use their imagination and creativity but (1) integrate details that relate to the main theories they have learned, and (2) draw upon relevant historical analogies to construct their assignments. Theories help participants define the values and policy of fictional characters while historical analogies help them add details and shape alternative polices to a fictional scenario. More details on how to proceed are discussed in chapters 5 and 6.

Once all participants have completed their individually prepared actor portfolio and character biography, handed them in or uploaded the digital file online, these reports are used to compile a collective actor portfolio to guide the team's policy formation and actual behavior. Crafting the collective document takes place during the policy formation stage detailed in chapter 5. Thus, the knowledge base created by each student supplements and enriches that of others, demonstrating the contribution of a learning community that develops among simulation participants.

Assignments 3 to 5 are related to the simulation itself and to the debriefing sessions after it ends. Players are graded according to their involvement in the simulation and the quality of their contributions to the interaction process. In a face-to-face simulation it is rather difficult to monitor individual contributions with limited records in writing or sound/video formats. So the assessment of a student's grade is mainly qualitative, based on the available observations from the simulation. However, when the encounters take place on social networks, grading has a strong quantitative basis, taking the number of posts each participant adds to the exercise into account. The intensity, continuity, and the quality of content are also considered. By quality posts we mean comments that indicate knowledge, critique, and creativity. Sometimes students just react to the moves of others, to show up on the Facebook wall. For the purpose of grading, you should differentiate between substantial contributions and superficial ones. You can also request that students summarize their posts and special contributions so your evaluation includes what the participants consider as their major inputs into the simulation. These measures, and others, are addressed in chapter 10 with an emphasis on how to produce a rigorous assessment of individual students and of the simulation project as a whole.

Assignments 7 to 9 are specific to students of political teams. They include the application of knowledge gained by creating the collective actor portfolio for the sake of defining the team's goals and policy plans as well as the preparation of proposals that will be presented to other teams when the world politics simulation starts. Goals and policy are first prepared on an individual basis by each player in the team and handed in. Then they are discussed among team members.

Assignment 9 also includes activities that take place during the world politics round, such as the drafting of agreements, the publication of policy briefings for the media, and the conduct of interviews with the media designed to explain the team's position and gain soft power. Forms and more explicit examples of these assignments appear in chapters 5 and 6 on implementation.

If you choose to run a cyber simulation, much of this activity usually takes place in the relevant collective environment of the social network, such as the Facebook group, as detailed in chapter 5. These collective deliberations are essential contributions that help transform individual students into representatives of a cohesive political body with defined responsibilities and a sense of priorities for application during the world politics round.

Assignments 10 to 12 are specific to students of the media teams. As with the political teams, here the students apply their individual research toward defining common goals and a collective orientation for the media organ they represent. They also plan their coverage of the simulation, decide on the media products they expect to create, and outline the division of labor between teammates. The editors and reporters have to define the orientation of the media organ and its symbolic language or jargon, like in the real world where the *New York Times* and *Aljazeera* may cover the same events differently. Their headlines and agenda setting in text and photos also reflect their divergent orientations.

From an operational standpoint, each media team has to decide how to divide the reporting and coverage responsibilities between the team participants, by region, state, or issue. Then teammates have to agree on a timetable with deadlines for team deliberations on matters such as choice of language, headlines, photos, and space allocation for each item and leave time for final editor decisions before the media product is publicized.

The preparation of most media products, such as newspapers, video clips, photos, and news flashes, is done before the world politics round begins. This reflects the work of the media in times of routine, when time pressure is relatively low. During world politics interactions, as during escalations and confrontation in the real world, severe time pressure builds up. In such situations the competition for information is highest so media coverage during real time is the hardest. We explain more on the work of the media during the world politics round in chapter 6.

An optional postsimulation task is detailed in assignment 6, prepared on an individual or team basis, if your schedule permits. It involves a written report on the simulation as a whole, on the teams' performance and achievements, or on any other research topic as detailed in chapters 7 and 11. In a face-to-face simulation the resources for these assignments are mainly qualitative as the backed-up material on detailed interactions may be limited. But, systematic interviews with team members to evaluate the different perspectives in the team may add a quantitative dimension to aspects that were not captured earlier during the simulation, in writing or sound/video recording. When you run a cyber simulation on social networks, the participants can easily revisit the posts they wrote and reacted to. By taking a fresh look at the interaction process, the posts, comments, links, and media products accumulated on social networks allow students to evaluate their performance and achievements in a qualitative and quantitative manner. This assignment is a good way to reappraise the relationship between planned goals, actual behavior, and final achievements. It also demonstrates the interdependence within and across actors and illustrates the constraints of operating in an international system and shaping its processes.

All written assignments may be handed in on paper or as a digital file that can be sent by e-mail or uploaded on the cyber platform used for hybrid learning during the simulation. We frequently use digital forms for some of the assignments, such as the registration, values, goals, and feedback forms. The use of digital forms is based on available web applications, such as Google Forms, where you can structure a document, place it on an accessible platform, and provide a link so all participants can submit information and answers to your questions. Completed forms are stored online for easy retrieval, and some web applications even generate summaries and quantitative reports that can be used for debriefing and research, as detailed in the third part of the book on analysis.

All forms, on paper or digital, may be structured as (1) closed, (2) open, or (3) combined. A closed form contains questions and a set of possible answers, and the students have to select their answer from a set of predefined choices. An open form consists of questions and an open space for answers that may reflect creativity, original thinking, and topics that are important from a subjective point of view. A form with a combined structure blends closed and open styles to allow for easy focus on particular information you specify in the closed questions and items that are important from a subjective point of view, but are sometimes sidestepped in a closed form. A more detailed overview of the different forms appears in chapters 5, 6, and 8.

If the participation in the simulation is compulsory it is a good idea to provide your students with a detailed rubric on how their different assignments and participation tasks will account for their overall evaluation. Be careful to balance the weight of participation and written assignments. The former, though hard to assess, requires many hours of interaction the students have to invest. To reflect the interactive contributions, you may request that each participant prepare a simulation logbook and use it to grade this aspect of the course. But make it clear to all players that participation does not mean mere presence. Substantive contributions based on solitary and collective active learning count more than just speaking loudly or adding posts. Placing links, photos, or short comments on the social media platform is a good quantitative starting point. Meaningful content, thoughtful insights, critical thinking, and interactions based on knowledge are the qualitative counterparts of the final grade.

So far we have explained the 12 core assignments summarized in table 4.3. Beyond these tasks, some supplementary assignments and research projects designed for advanced undergraduate and graduate seminars are addressed in part III of the book, especially in chapter 7. These tasks are connected to broad topics of research on theory and empirical studies via the application of simulation-generated data alone or in comparison with real case studies. Such assignments highlight the utility of simulations as a social science lab and may help improve the tools for testing theory in the future.

In the next sections we describe how all the decisions that you have made so far—on simulation type, topics, teams, schedule, and assignments—blend into a well-defined operational plan for the simulation. This happens when you perform a set of implementation procedures.

Setup Procedures

After you have defined your plan for the simulation it is time to move on to the more tangible aspects of the simulation setup, summarized by six verbs: create, introduce, distribute, build teams, assign dates, and follow-up. Once these procedures are completed, you will be ready to begin the simulation.

Create

As the simulation administrator you need to make sure you have a *place for the encounter*. By a place we mean two interrelated aspects: a site where all the information for the simulation is stored for easy access and a location where the interactions occur, on campus for a face-to-face meeting or on social networks for a cyber simulation.

Irrespective of the simulation genre you choose, we advise you to create a *website*, because in the current digital era it is the natural place for all the information and instructions for the simulation. You may choose to upload all the relevant contents and necessary material on the university network, so that only your students may log in, but we find it useful to build a website that is open to everybody so that the students can share their experience even with peers who are not enrolled in the course. Such open access to basic information regarding the simulation makes it possible for students to engage in the project with their friends, adds to their motivation, and may sometimes improve their devotion to the exercise.

If you have chosen to cooperate with other colleagues, from your department or from other campuses, a joint website is the best choice as it does not require login permission or passwords. But, unlike the information on the website, all activities on social networks are restricted to students who take part in the project from your course and that of others with whom you collaborate. These activities take place in closed groups to ensure that privacy is protected.

The basic components we recommend that you include in your website are portrayed in figure 4.1. Each com-

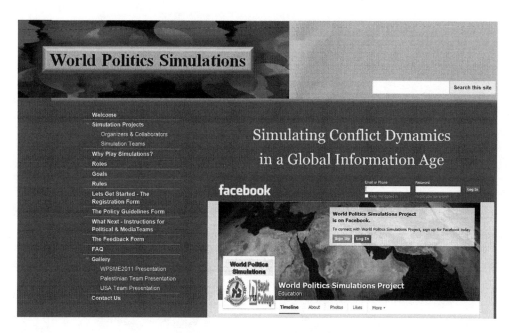

Fig. 4.1. Simulation website

ponent on the left-hand side is a link for easy access to a page or more with extended information for all simulation participants. Items (1) to (4) outline the core plan of your simulation, while items (5) to (9) present its operational aspects. Item (10) leaves room for your own additions to the website based on your preferences and experience.

(1) The *simulation schedule and plan,* which contains a detailed outline of the simulation time frame and describes the historical or fictional setting for the project. This information will give your students some idea of when and what they will encounter in the simulation. It serves as a starting point for all students to get acquainted with the topic they are going to role-play and the deadlines they have to meet. This page can also contain a link to a registration form that students are requested to fill, letting you know who they are, what they are interested in, and what they would like to do in the simulation. (2) The *goals* of the project, that is, an outline of what the simulation is geared to achieve. It explains how the simulation is integrated into the course and why it serves as a useful study tool. (3) The *organizers* specifies the staff behind the simulation, including your colleagues, graduate students, or teaching assistants who take part in the project with contact information so everybody can be reached when needed. (4) The *teams and social network links* detail the groups that will be represented in the simulation and their location on the social network for a cyber simulation. The links to the social network groups make it easy for all participants to find and join the teams they are assigned to, after filling a registration form.

(5) "*Let's get started*" focuses on the short-term measures and immediate step-by-step activities your students are going to implement so as to get ready to role-play the simulation. These instructions are discussed in the last section of this chapter and summarized in table 4.4. The reason to have a table like this, adjusted to your specific plan and posted on the website, is that all participants can check its contents and know what they need to do as the simulation preparations proceed, during policy formation activities and world politics rounds. (6) *Simulation rules* are a set of instructions that all participants must follow, as discussed in chapter 5. The rules are posted to make sure that all participants know what is allowed and what is forbidden in the simulation. (7) "*What next*" refers to the longer time span and describes a more complete picture of the simulation sequence so your students know where the simulation exercise is heading and how it will unfold. Here a full list of assignments and deadlines is published along with detailed *instruction sheets* that contain explanations on the contents, form, and weight of each assignment in the final grade. This item also refers to the feedback and debriefing activities addressed in chapters 8 and 9. (8) *FAQ* looks at the simulation from the students' perspective and addresses topics related to registration, schedule, time allocations for the simulation, team composition and roles, freedom of players to express creativity, and the need to strictly abide by simulation rules. FAQ is a component you can update as your students bring up matters that have remained unclear. This is a practical way to add guidelines, clarify assignments, address new

ideas, plan changes if needed, and make it easy for the class as a whole to follow what is going on and to enjoy the simulation. (9) *Forms, documents, and summary tables* includes links to uploaded files on the website or to files located elsewhere with forms and instruction sheets you prepare for your students to guide them with their assignments. The summary tables help your students follow the details related to the solitary and collective learning. Such summaries appear in the last section of chapters 4, 5, 6, 8, and 9 under the section instructions for participants.

(10) *Optional components* such as a photo gallery, calendar of events, presentations related to the simulation, or other material you consider necessary. These additions can highlight events from previous simulations to enrich your site and increase the curiosity of your students. They are likely to motivate students to play an active role in the simulation you are about to run.

The website holds all the relevant information, before, during, and after the simulation. So it is a permanent location where you and your students can always find information regarding the project you run. Once you build a basic website of your own you can add items, components, and content as you develop new simulations and fit the site to your academic setting and particular needs.

The permanent nature of the site makes it a simple starting point for your students who can easily get familiar with its structure. Furthermore, the website serves as your business card for the simulation project you are conducting and as a place to which your colleagues and students can go whenever they look for information related to the simulation.

You can create your website on many free web applications, like Google Sites. It will serve you for many simulations in the future, so the investment is well worth the effort. From one simulation you conduct to the next, you will need to update only a few sections of the site, enriching it based on previous experience and making it into an effective study aid for your students.

Given the popularity of Facebook pages, you may also consider creating a *Facebook page*, as illustrated in figure 4.2, and advertise it on your website asking students to "Join us on Facebook" with an icon and link to the page you have constructed. As your students access the page on the social network and click its *"like"* icon, they will receive updates you post thereafter to their own Facebook and stay in touch with contents you decide to post on the social network. This way you will be drawing them to the platform you use to run a cyber or hybrid simulation and build upon their daily habits as digital natives. By seeing the number of *"likes"* increase on the Facebook page of

your simulation, a feeling of an emerging learning community gradually develops.

Besides the website and Facebook page as permanent virtual sites, the place for the simulation also involves a designated location where all dynamic encounters occur. The location may be physical for a face-to-face round, like a conference hall, or virtual, that is groups set up on the social network as "rooms" for a cyber exercise. The physical location may be your regular classroom for a couple of sessions, or preferably a set of proximate classes so that each team can have its own "territory" and a bigger hall for an international conference where all teams meet to negotiate.

In a cyber simulation you need to create separate *groups on the social network* to host each team. To do so on Facebook, or any other social network, you need to sign up for an account of your own. From the start we recommend that you open an academic account on Facebook and use it for all the simulations you run. On this account you can manage all the groups you create and follow all activities taking place in them. Facebook automatically e-mails notifications on all activities to members in the social network group, including you as its administrator. If you want to avoid an overload in your mailbox, it is wise to use an academic rather than a personal account on the network.

On Facebook, you create three sets of groups: the first, for each of the political teams; the second, for each of the media teams; and the third, as a collective group for all simulation participants. In the first and second set of groups, the participants of political teams convene to plan their policy and the players of media teams discuss their reporting strategy and coverage products. The third set serves as a joint "room," a location where the participants of all teams meet for the world politics round. When you plan a hybrid simulation you need to make arrangements for both physical and virtual locations.

As an example of preparing a place for the simulation, consider the Middle East cyber simulation summarized in the appendix. It had a permanent virtual site and several virtual "rooms" on Facebook as locations where cyber interactions took place. To start with, the plan for the simulation was announced on the ISA website with some basic information about the project and a link to the SIM2012 website, as shown in figure 4.1. This simulation website was set up to guide prospective players till they were invited to join closed academic Facebook groups, as the location for all simulation encounters. Prospective participants filled a detailed registration form displayed in figure

Fig. 4.2. Simulation
Facebook page

4.3 and were allocated to teams. The registration form contained basic information such as (1) name, (2) e-mail, (3) areas of expertise and study, (4) previous experience with simulations, (5) familiarity with social networks, (6) requests for desirable team and role allocations, and (7) other specific remarks and requests.

The registration process and the data derived from it are an efficient way to keep in touch with your students, to record their initial information, and to learn about their requests and expectations. But you should make it clear that the simulation requirements will dictate the final allocation and you can't promise participants that their choice will be met.

Chapter 8 provides details on the forms we use during the simulation with examples and explanations regarding registration form questions and format. The registration form, like the website, becomes an essential tool when you cooperate with other colleagues and have students from separate courses, campuses, or countries take part in one simulation. In such instances a single university network for managing the simulation and its interactions is not suitable.

The last essential setup procedure relates to detailed instruction sheets with full information regarding contents, relevant forms, and due date, for all the assignments you select from table 4.3 and others you create on your own.

Beyond explanation in class, it is advisable to place these instruction sheets on the simulation website for everybody to download and know exactly when and what to do for each assignment.

Introduce

Once the simulation website, registration form, and instruction sheets are ready, it is time to introduce the simulation plan to your students, in class or via your communication platform in the case of an online course. An effective way to do so is to run a presentation that contains information about (1) the website, (2) the topic and goals of the simulation, (3) the teams and roles, (4) the schedule, (5) the assignments, and (6) due dates. You can enhance the presentation by adding recommended resources and reading material, maps and photos of leaders, flags or symbols and screenshots from the Facebook groups you use. You can also include photos from previous simulations you have conducted to create an exciting atmosphere and make the planned encounter more tangible for students who have never taken part in a simulation. Make sure to mention the FAQ page on the simulation website as a place where students can find answers to questions they may have and clarifications on issues addressed during your lectures.

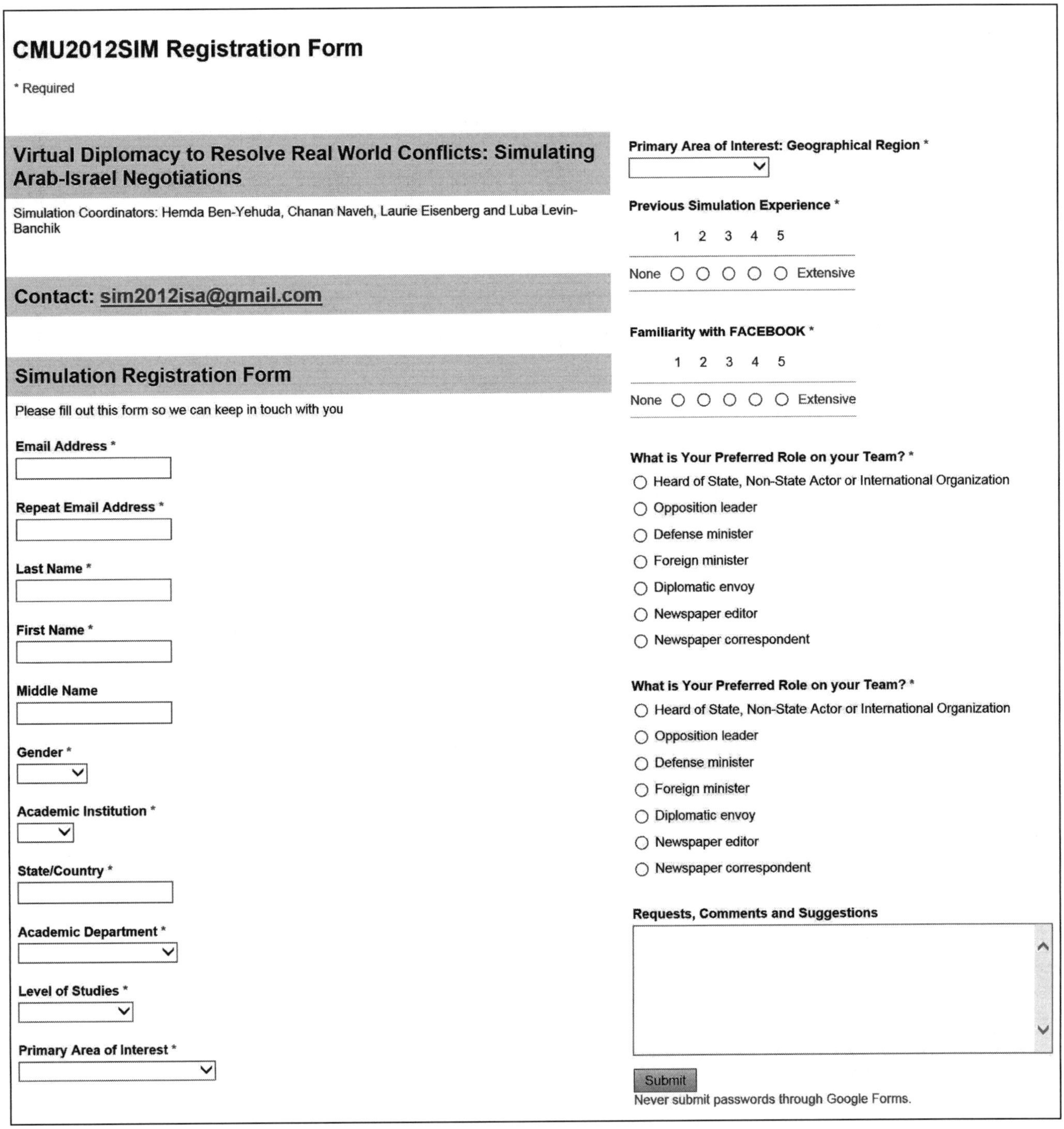

CMU2012SIM Registration Form

* Required

Virtual Diplomacy to Resolve Real World Conflicts: Simulating Arab-Israel Negotiations

Simulation Coordinators: Hemda Ben-Yehuda, Chanan Naveh, Laurie Eisenberg and Luba Levin-Banchik

Contact: sim2012isa@gmail.com

Simulation Registration Form

Please fill out this form so we can keep in touch with you

Email Address *

[   ]

Repeat Email Address *

[   ]

Last Name *

[   ]

First Name *

[   ]

Middle Name

[   ]

Gender *

[▾]

Academic Institution *

[▾]

State/Country *

[   ]

Academic Department *

[▾]

Level of Studies *

[▾]

Primary Area of Interest *

[▾]

Primary Area of Interest: Geographical Region *

[▾]

Previous Simulation Experience *

    1   2   3   4   5

None ○ ○ ○ ○ ○ Extensive

Familiarity with FACEBOOK *

    1   2   3   4   5

None ○ ○ ○ ○ ○ Extensive

What is Your Preferred Role on your Team? *

○ Heard of State, Non-State Actor or International Organization

○ Opposition leader

○ Defense minister

○ Foreign minister

○ Diplomatic envoy

○ Newspaper editor

○ Newspaper correspondent

What is Your Preferred Role on your Team? *

○ Heard of State, Non-State Actor or International Organization

○ Opposition leader

○ Defense minister

○ Foreign minister

○ Diplomatic envoy

○ Newspaper editor

○ Newspaper correspondent

Requests, Comments and Suggestions

[   ]

[Submit]

Never submit passwords through Google Forms.

Fig. 4.3. Online registration form

Distribute

After you have presented the simulation plan you are ready to distribute the registration forms and assignments, in class, via e-mail with links to where you have placed the necessary digital files, or through any communication mode you regularly use.

Build Teams

Once you have all the relevant information from your students on their preferences for the simulation, it is time to decide who will play what role. If you are conducting a cyber or hybrid exercise you are ready to invite them to enter their virtual "rooms," that is, to join the groups you have created on the social network of your choice. As students become part of these groups, all communications and procedures unfold within these groups, and they become a location where participants store all the information and material for the simulation for easy access by all players.

At this point you also need to assign roles within teams, unless you choose a very flexible administrative approach and let each team make these decisions on its own. From previous experience we have learned that some students like to take the lead and want to be heads of team or play an essential role. Others prefer to step into a less demanding position, either because of personality inclinations, motivation, or inability to invest extended time and effort. Your goal is to make sure that all teams will have a more or less equal share of dedicated students who want to play leading roles. It is useful to emphasize that the allocation of roles may change during the early preparation stage but not during the ongoing simulation, to ensure the best-fit personality composition within each team. If you know some of your students ahead of time, from previous courses, it is a good idea to allocate capable and motivated ones more evenly to each of your teams so as to increase the efficiency of all simulation interactions.

Assign Dates

As far as the schedule is concerned, you now have to set the dates for (1) publication of an initial and opening scenario, (2) the start and end of each simulation round, (3) the hand-in date of the individually prepared actor portfolio and character biography, (4) the start date for the policy formation process, (5) the hand-in date of individually prepared assignments on values, goals, and policy plans, (6) the date for conclusion of the collective actor portfolio, values, goals, and policy choices by each team, and the time world politics encounters commence, (7) the completion of feedback forms and debriefing remarks, during and after the simulation, and (8) the submission of final research papers or summary assignments.

Follow-Up

After all setup procedures are completed, you are ready to begin intrateam and interteam politics. This means you start to monitor and carefully follow (1) the registration data; (2) requests to join groups on the social network, if you choose to run a cyber simulation; and (3) initial interactions among participants in each team as they prepare for the simulation.

Since not all players are alike in terms of their backgrounds, academic level, and topics of study, you must assume that the appeal of simulations is not shared equally by all individuals. The idea of a cyber encounter on Facebook builds upon the familiarity and habits of the current student body. This trend is most likely to increase in the future even as a new web application may replace Facebook as the leading social network. But some students are late adaptors or web averts so you need to coach them or couple others with experienced peer students. A web fan who accompanies a newcomer usually serves as a quick cure for individual reluctance.

Another effective mode to achieve motivated participation and comprehensive learning is by coupling a simulation devotee with a hesitant peer to produce specific, well-defined, and short chores together, or to find areas of excellence where even a reluctant student will contribute to the team's conduct. For example, political inclinations, previous experiences, or hobbies may invoke greater familiarity with certain topics so a student may be assigned as a team adviser or a media professional to cover those topics and make a contribution that really matters to other participants. You must add assurances regarding the privacy settings of closed educational groups set up on Facebook to further reduce fears connected with interactions on the web.

The simulation experience is usually so powerful and enriching for many students that for the few who end up refusing to take part in the project, exceptional solutions should be improvised. A good example we encountered were students who for security reasons were prohibited by their employers from surfing the web or engaging in social networks. For those individuals we made within-team adjustments, nominating them to the role of team advisers or devil's advocates. They were supposed to keep an updated logbook of (1) major developments in the simulation, (2) meetings with teammates on campus, and (3) detailed reactions and proposals submitted to the heads of team in person or via phone messages or e-mail. In this way, personal constraints were overcome and the simulation experience enriched all players.

Beyond awareness of individual character, motivation, experiences, and constraints, anyone who has participated in simulations or conducted them knows that practice does not always make perfect, but it does result in a better simulation. With flexibility, patience, coaching, and sensitive follow-up you can detect immersion dynamics and help your students overcome most difficulties. Eventually, you and your students will enjoy the project and its promise as a study mode.

TABLE 4.4. Setup Instructions for Participants

Task	Details
Get familiar	Read and learn about the simulation plan, schedule, topic, teams, and assignments on the simulation website or other platforms used in your course
Study	Once the teams and roles are announced, conduct research on the political or media actor you represent and on the character you play in the simulation. For both assignments, see instructions and submission date on the simulation website or other platforms used in your course
	Prepare *actor portfolio* for states, nonstate, or media actors
	Prepare *character biography* for political decision-makers or media professionals
Follow instructions	See FAQ on website Fill out registration form Register for social network groups and introduce yourself briefly to your team Hand in assignments on time

So far, we have explained the various substantive and technical setup procedures. Simulations, however, require coordinated activities between educators and students, so we now summarize the setup instructions for students. Each setup procedure you have taken is paralleled with instructions for student activities. We use the term "instructions," conveying the traditional top-down interactions you require from your students, as reflected in the bold arrows of figure 1.2 in chapter 1. However, as the learning process unfolds, much of these instructions are transformed from vertical interactions alone to horizontal ones demarcated by the light arrows, that is, between the students as a learning community.

Instructions for Participants

The setup procedures needed in preparation for the simulation are summarized in table 4.4. They are captured by three verbs: get familiar, study, and follow instructions. Explanations in class or in any other form of communication are essential to supplement this table and to ensure that your students understand the requirements and cooperate in fulfilling them.

This summary table, together with other basic information regarding the simulation, should be presented on the simulation website so all participants can get familiar with the simulation plan, make the necessary accommodations to follow the simulation schedule, and take an active role in the simulation. Then they need to study an empirical case and an assigned character, real or fictional, so as to be able to step into the shoes of a team and role and play based on their knowledge of the simulation

story lines, relevant theories, and specific simulation instructions.

This section on instructions for participants summarizes the main points, described in this chapter, in a concise form. It is designed as a quick checklist you can present to your students, especially the summary table that you can hand out in class, upload on the simulation website, post on the social network platform, or send by e-mail. The brief explanations provided in this section assume that the reader is familiar with the details of the previous sections of this chapter.

Get Familiar

A rule of thumb for enjoying the simulation and learning from it is "the greater the investment, the broader the gains and the leap from low to mid and high levels is a step-level, not an incremental one." This means that at higher levels of involvement the awards are much greater and different in kind from those of lower levels. Thus, a full commitment to the project really makes a difference and pays off in shaping the individual and overall experience. When motivated participants step into the shoes of a character in the simulation, the overall impact of the learning process is immense at the cognitive, behavioral, and affective levels.

To get familiar with the simulation, participants need to read and learn about the simulation plan, schedule, topic, teams, and assignments on the simulation website. In this way, as the preparations progress, each student knows how to blend into the group as a whole and what contributions are expected from each player.

The simulation website is the best place to start with, a site where one finds the detailed plans, schedule, and assignments that are introduced and explained in class or in any other communication mode suitable for an online course. The availability of all information, in one permanent site that is easy to access, helps all students plan how to meet their formal participation obligations as well as the deadlines for their various assignments.

The simulation experience makes it possible for a variety of contributions so that people with different personality traits can express themselves and add to the individual and collective learning process. Some players take the lead, others follow. Shy ones can add important content to the team's wall on the social network and raise provoking comments that may trigger policy revisions and new initiatives. Such activities advance tolerance and critical thinking and are essential to prepare all participants to cope with the realities of the 21st century, within and outside academe.

It is important to emphasize to your students how solitary and collective learning are embedded in the simulation and blend together into an exciting and rewarding experience. You can also explain that, by following the guidelines for the simulation, each participant can advance their knowledge and grades, while understanding that the process also involves interdependence. Hence, the schedule and assignments are the fixed setup for the simulation and demarcate the mutual obligations and shared tasks for all players.

Study

The simulation experience is designed to maximize solitary and collective learning. Each participant is obliged to learn about the core topic played, the temporal setting of the empirical case, based on history, current events, or fiction and a specific team and role placement. This will later help each team to define its adversaries and allies in the simulation and to implement an in-depth and systematic process of policy formation, as described in chapter 5, and interteam activities of world politics detailed in chapter 6.

Follow Instructions

To ensure that each participant makes progress and the team functions effectively as a cohesive group, all students are requested to (1) fill out the registration form on time; (2) join Facebook groups if the simulation takes place on social networks or on Facebook as a supplementary platform for policy formation in a hybrid simulation; (3) prepare the individual and team assignments listed in table 4.3; (4) introduce oneself to the team on the social network and describe the role to be fulfilled in the simulation; and (5) progressively contribute to the buildup on the team's wall as the core learning environment. On it, information, critique, planning, and ideas are then exchanged, examined, and processed into operational goals and policy choices toward friends and foes in the upcoming simulation of world politics.

All preparations for the simulation are essential to reduce the uncertainties related to the innovative new project that is about to start and to ensure that all participants will be ready to cope with the tempo and complexities of world politics.

Summary

This chapter on simulation setup takes a close look at the plan you design for a face-to-face, cyber, or hybrid simulation and at the procedures you and your students implement. The chapter addresses the plan for the simulation, details the procedures that translate the plan into a well-defined operational tool, and outlines the instructions for simulation participants.

Simulation setup begins with the plan for the simulation along with five core decisions you need to make regarding the type of simulation you will run, the topics it will cover, the teams of the simulation, its schedule, and the assignments your students will have to prepare for the simulation, before, during, and after the interaction process. Setup continues with specific procedures in preparation for the simulation, encapsulated by six verbs: create, introduce, distribute, build, assign, and follow-up. Since the success of the simulation depends on you and your students alike, the chapter concludes with guidelines for students in the form of a summary table of instructions for simulation participants and a short outline based on the entire chapter but with an emphasis on the students' perspectives.

After the plan and procedures are set, the simulation actually begins and the dynamic process of activity within and among teams takes the lead in hybrid learning, as detailed in chapters 5 and 6.

CHAPTER 5

Policy Formation

Policy formation in simulations refers to the decision-making process and teamwork among participants within each political and media team. This is an essential phase that requires students to *discuss* and *decide* on their collective actor profile, values, goals, policy plan, and many other core elements that make up a coherent policy for the team. In doing so, students practice decision-making and learn to transform the knowledge gained through solitary learning during the setup preparations for the simulation into a collective strategy that will guide their team's behavior during world politics interactions with other teams.

This chapter addresses policy formation in simulations and shows how it can benefit from hybrid learning on social networks. First, it explains the rationale for including a policy formation process in your simulation. Second, the chapter focuses on the plan for policy formation that involves the formulation of a scenario, the clarification of simulation rules, and a detailed description of the activities that take place during the policy formation process. Third, the chapter deals with the core policy procedures in preparation for a collective actor portfolio and the definition of joint values, goals, and policy plans. Additional procedures include a close follow-up of intrateam debates and continuous coaching of your students. The chapter ends with a concise outline of instructions for simulation participants.

The policy deliberations may take place in a face-to-face meeting, on the social network, or, in accordance with hybrid learning, on both platforms. When you design intrateam discussions as face-to-face only, you will often need to schedule additional time and dates for meetings beyond routine class sessions. If you plan policy

formation on a cyber platform, a more careful follow-up of group dynamics is needed to ensure active participation and to avoid stalemate. The added value of hybrid learning lies in the integration of traditional teaching and digital tools. So the best way for a team to work out its policy is by combining face-to-face deliberations in class with discussions on social networks. The weight and sequence of the two platforms may vary from simulation to simulation and depends on your choice.

Rationale

Some world politics simulations skip policy formation altogether. This often happens due to temporal and logistical constraints. Scheduling time for intrateam discussions during the lecture may come at the cost of learning other topics you need to teach or at the expense of some world politics encounters. Beyond lecture slots, it is extremely difficult to coordinate meeting times among all students. You may count on the good will of your students to meet during their free time to formulate the team's policy and make sure they are ready for interactions among teams. Most likely such events will take place without your presence, so policy formation will lack your supervision and coaching. As a result, you may decide that solitary learning and written assignments provide each team with sufficient knowledge and adequate preparation for policy implementation at the start of the world politics round.

With hybrid learning and interactions on social networks there is a way to overcome the constraints of time and location. In the global information age, you can create discussion groups for each team on social networks, as described in the previous chapter, so your students can take an active part in policy formation 24/7, even when they are on the go. Such platforms provide unlimited options to choose from in order to share and discuss one's thoughts with teammates. All one needs is an Internet connection. You, as the educator, are able to follow and monitor policy formation at any time and place. Moreover, you can provide immediate feedback to the entire team or privately to each of the team members through messages or chat provided within the social network platform.

The virtual domain enables asynchronous and synchronous contacts, provides easy access to information, and facilitates protracted communications among participants. It overcomes many temporal and spatial constraints characteristic of the physical platform, supplements it, and adds to the learning process as a whole. So it makes sense that at least some of the policy formation process, if not the bulk of it, should take place on the social network.

To illustrate, in the Palestinian statehood hybrid simulation summarized in the appendix, each team first gathered in class for a relatively brief face-to-face meeting so as to get know each other and begin some initial discussions on policy plans. To make the identification of characters and actors easier, we used flags and symbols for each team, prepared tags for students with details on their name and role, assembled sitting places in circles to keep their discussion secret, and screened the initial scenario up front to mark the beginning of the policy formation activities. The face-to-face meeting was vital to trigger a sense of being a coherent team. But it was too short to finalize all policy formation requirements. Intrateam discussions continued online in closed Facebook groups for several weeks. Students logged in to their group at flexible times in order to read, comment, and initiate discussions with teammates. At the same time they continued to attend regular classes and some of them initiated ad-hoc face-to-face meetings during the breaks before or after class. The social network platform made it unnecessary to allocate more lecture time to implement an effective policy formation process.

Given the option of developing a full-fledged policy formation process on cyber platforms, this early part of the simulation may become more and more meaningful in the simulations of the future. When this happens, it can become a full round just like the world politics encounters.

The content of intrateam discussions described below remains the same in face-to-face and cyber meetings, but

their conduct differs in the following five ways. (1) Dialogue on social networks is mostly asynchronous, so each participant can communicate at any convenient time. This interaction mode gives participants time to think about their reactions. It also allows all voices to be heard because any group member can post a comment without being interrupted, as frequently happens in face-to-face debates. (2) The accessibility of online information facilitates sharing of knowledge among participants who can easily paste links to Internet sources, such as YouTube clips, pictures, maps, historical documents, and newspaper articles. (3) In a face-to-face meeting, enthusiastic debates may become loud and disrupt the discussions of other teams in the room. By contrast, on social networks each group is open exclusively to the members of a given team. Excited debates add to the exchange of ideas, and the risk of spying is minimized. (4) While in-class sessions of policy formation are usually brief, the process on social networks may be as long as you plan, thereby providing opportunities for protracted engagements, practice, and learning. Some students join the discussion immediately. Shy or slow adaptors may join hesitantly at first, but eventually add to the evolving process and gain considerably from the intrateam debates. (5) While your presence in all face-to-face meetings is impossible, especially in the ones initiated ad-hoc by students, on the social networks you receive an alert when a new comment is posted. This enables close follow-up of all comments in all groups, which are also saved and can be retrievable later for grading, debriefing, and research. All these attributes make policy formation on social networks a useful, innovative, convenient, and interesting way to conduct intrateam deliberations over extended time periods, either as the main platform or as a supplementary one.

Though hybrid learning makes policy formation easier to implement, domestic politics and decision-making may be of marginal importance in your learning curriculum. So why bother with policy formation? Consider the following example of a simulation on bargaining with terrorists in a multinational hostage-taking event. The scenario was designed to illuminate moral dilemmas and the difficulties democratic states face in responding to terror. The students were split into five groups, three of which represented states whose citizens were taken hostage, one team represented the terrorists, and there was one media team. Each group consisted of three to five players, as suggested in chapter 4. All participants saw a breaking news clip prepared by the educator on the hostage-taking event, which served as the initial scenario for the simulation and marked the beginning of policy formation activities. Students were asked to solve the crisis by negotiation. Each team tried to coordinate their positions with teammates, but since the educator "skipped" policy formation, they were tempted to do the same. In the absence of a coherent policy, students from the same team presented different demands and offered contradictory proposals, making it hard to interact and to make progress as a team. The simulation involved negotiations between individuals rather than among teams as consolidated actors.

The appearance of divergent positions confused most participants, and no one could trust anyone else. As the result, even occasional attempts to come up with an ad-hoc policy failed, most students were disappointed, and the learning experience was limited to insights about complexity and uncertainty in world politics. These aspects, however, were not the main topics initially planned as the central themes for the simulation. The choice of how to react, its price in terms of a moral dilemma, and the outcomes of behavior were shadowed by a myriad of uncoordinated activities. Effective policy formation could have added important knowledge on coping with terror, practice with the demands for the release of hostages, the price of compromise, and the centrality of the media in such encounters. So even when world politics interactions are your primary destination, policy formation is the main road that leads your students there.

Policy formation is sometimes your final destination in the simulation, with no follow-up of world politics encounters. An internal outlook fits courses on decision-making or on the link between domestic and foreign policy. In this case, you may split your class into several teams that represent different government institutions, regime types, ethnic or religious minorities, and other groups representing domestic constraints or decision-making styles.[1] While this chapter assumes that policy formation is followed by a world politics process, it is written as a stand-alone module so you can use it to design simulations that focus solely on policy formation within teams. In this case, the interteam engagements, detailed in chapter 6, are totally skipped, or the world politics process is replaced with domestic politics encounters. In simulations of local politics the process of policy formation within each team, discussed henceforth, prepares participants for negotiations among teams, all representing different entities within the same actor, that is, within a local environment of a state, an international organization, or nonstate actor. This way the complex system represented during the interteam meetings is not the international one usually referred to in this book, but rather a single actor with an introspection of its composing units.

Policy formation is usually characteristic of state actors, but it is applicable and important for other simulation teams as well. All entities, states, nonstate actors, international organizations, and media actors have (1) values to defend/promote, (2) goals to reach, and (3) plans to formulate. All teams have to discuss and decide on these matters in order to construct a collective feeling of "we" versus "them" and to formulate their strategy toward other teams. Yet, the specific values, goals, and policy plans are likely to differ from one type of actor to another. For instance, in world politics, states and many nonstate actors typically negotiate, make concessions, issue threats, and implement many other moves characteristic to political actors. Their policy planning includes the consideration of many available tools for cooperation by diplomatic and economic measures or for confrontation by use of coercive diplomacy. By contrast, media teams use other tools: they "fight" with words, specialize in the selection of pictures, and set the agenda for the public and for the decision-makers. Media teams can interview political leaders and need to decide what to publish in breaking news items or how to shape political developments. Policy formation must take place, but the contents of values, goals, policy plans, and choices differ from that of political teams. In the description of policy formation, this chapter refers to all types of actors and when relevant it explicitly distinguishes between political and media teams.

Policy Formation Plan

To become an effective and enjoyable teaching tool, simulations require careful planning and creativity on your side. Entering your class with a call to "Let's start the simulation!" may be exciting, but more than that is needed to make the simulation successful. When it comes to policy formation, your tasks as an educator involve (1) planning the initial scenario, (2) preparing assignments for students, (3) providing them with detailed instructions, and (4) observing their progress. All these activities are intended to make it easier for students, individually and as a team, to build a coherent policy toward other teams in the simulation.

During the setup preparations, addressed in chapter 4, you have already made several decisions on the teams and roles for the simulation, assigned your students to their political or media teams, and allocated them to specific roles. You have also introduced the simulation topic and schedule, so all participants are familiar with the idea of the simulation and its empirical setting. Now it is time to plan and present your students with an initial scenario for the simulation in order to begin the policy formation process.

Simulation Topic and Scenarios

A *simulation scenario* is a short story that describes a real or fictional situation with triggers for participants of all teams. It provides information on issues and events related to the simulation topic, within a specific time frame that serves as a common theme for students to study and discuss. Any simulation scenario is designed to set immediate activity in motion among participants. A good scenario should be (1) informative, revealing the story on stage with core information on who, what, where, when, and, sometimes, why; (2) relevant to all actors in the simulation: political and media, state and nonstate ones; (3) challenging and sometimes even provocative, so as to require a thorough decision-making process during policy formation and sophisticated implementation of that policy during world politics interactions; (4) flexible, so as to leave room for students' imagination, some interpretation, and innovative additions; (5) short, so as to enable immediate comprehension and frequent reference to its details when needed; and (6) accessible, so even if one lost the printed version, the scenario should always be available, on the simulation website, social network, or other virtual platform.

A simulation scenario can be written in a plain text format. Yet, with a little effort you can enhance the scenario considerably by transforming it into a theatrical element that adds to the atmosphere of the simulation, such as (1) an invitation, (2) a political document or resolution with an official letterhead and signatures of the leaders involved, (3) an intelligence or commission report, (4) a satellite image with explanatory interpretations on findings, (5) a WikiLeaks file, (6) a newspaper front page, or (7) a printed or video news release, a short interview or breaking news items. By using any of these formats for a scenario, you add an authentic hue to the simulation and make it easier for your students to step out of the academic setting and enter the stage of the past, current, or imaginary world they will soon engage in. Such opening formats tend to add drama, trigger creativity, and motivate students.

There are several ways to reveal the scenario to your students. In a face-to-face simulation, you can distribute printed copies to participants and screen it with a projector in class. The lecture slot confines the timing of the publication as it is the only occasion for all participants to gather together. So, the scenario is usually published at the start of a face-to-face meeting, leaving very little time for the participants to get familiar with it. Instead, you can choose to publish the scenario during a preceding lecture, but be aware that the time interval between lectures may reduce the element of drama and surprise, thus students' enthusiasm to take an active part in the simulation may decline somewhat. With online tools it is easy to overcome constraints of time and space and detach the publication of the scenario from the lecture slot, even when you plan a face-to-face simulation. The cyber platform comes in handy so you can publish the scenario on the simulation website or social network, or even send it by e-mail, a short time before the scheduled date for the beginning of policy formation discussions. Virtual platforms provide an equal opportunity for all participants to access the scenario from the moment it is published, in cyber and face-to-face simulations alike.

With the publication of the scenario, your students should consider the situation it describes carefully and handle their activities effectively by communicating with other participants, first within teams during policy formation and then among teams in world politics encounters, as described in chapter 6. To distinguish between policy formation and subsequent world politics, we use two distinct but related scenarios for each of these processes, as summarized in table 5.1. The two scenarios develop different parts of the same story, but the initial scenario for policy formation introduces less acute changes, threats, challenges, and escalations than the opening scenario for world politics. While the initial scenario describes a prelude to an approaching crisis or an incipient change that signals opportunities, in diplomatic, economic, humanitarian, environmental or military spheres, the opening scenario presents a full-blown crisis situation or a drastic change that introduces a severe challenge along with new opportunities.

The *initial scenario* is designed to set comprehensive intrateam discussions in motion so as to reach a coherent policy plan. It tells a story that narrows the topics of contention, so students can deepen their knowledge and focus their discussions on a chosen time frame, specific issues, and salient events. The initial scenario is introduced a short time before or immediately as the policy formation process begins. After students are familiar with the general simulation topic, their assigned actor, and the character they represent, they have to cope with specific information and come up with policy alternatives regard-

TABLE 5.1. Initial and Opening Scenarios

Attributes	Initial Scenario	Opening Scenario
Format	A plain text, invitation, political document, resolution, intelligence report, commission findings, all with an official letterhead as decor, satellite images with interpretation, WikiLeaks, newspaper front page, news release, or breaking news. All these can be distributed on paper, as a video clip, or as a digital file	
Criteria for good scenario	(1) Informative, (2) relevant to all actors in the simulation, (3) challenging and sometimes even provocative, (4) flexible, (5) short, (6) accessible	
Publication mode	In class: screened up front, distributed in print Published online, uploaded on the website, posted on the social network, or sent by e-mail	
Prior information	Solitary learning on topic, actor portfolio, and character biography	Initial scenario and policy plans that developed during the policy formation process
Publication date	Before policy formation begins	Before world politics interactions begin
Aim	(1) Narrows topics of contention (2) Defines operational stakes (3) Challenges values, goals, and policy plan (4) Pilot for world politics	Defines crisis elements: step-level change that induces uncertainty, threat, time pressure, or an opportunity coupled with a serious challenge
New information	Moderate	Extensive
Type of change	Limited and incremental	Sudden and major
Gravity of threat	Moderate	Severe
Time pressure	Moderate	Severe
Extent of uncertainty	Moderate	High
Triggers	Policy speeches, consultations, messages and declarations, military maneuvers, refugee flows, and deterioration in economic or domestic stability including protests and demonstrations	Mediation proposal or peace plan, endorsement of plan, abrupt cancelation of long-standing agreements, breach of redline, ultimatum, unconfirmed or confirmed alarming information on intentions, deployment or withdrawal of peace forces/observers, blockade, change in status quo, shift in balance of power, leadership change, coup d'état, takeover of strongholds by rebels in civil war, massacre, terror attack at strategic or symbolic location within or outside a state, hostage taking, retaliation raid, natural disaster, health epidemic, oil spill or massive environmental hazard

ing new developments. The initial scenario defines several operational stakes, touches upon basic values, and challenges core goals and policy. As a precrisis situation, the events in the initial scenario should leave ample space for students to use their creativity, consider alternatives, and come up with coherent operational plans. So the initial scenario involves limited change and moderate levels of threat, time pressure, and uncertainty. You can choose between domestic events, like prescheduled military exercises, or international ones, like diplomatic consultations that might affect the status quo, as good triggers for intrateam discussions.

Once policy formation ends, the *opening scenario* for the simulation is added to signal a drastic change that calls for immediate reactions and provokes intensive interactions among teams, as described in chapter 6. The opening scenario builds upon the story described in the initial scenario, incorporates teams' policy plans, and specifies elements of a crisis situation or a new opportunity that also contains a dramatic challenge, usually nullifying the continuation of the domestic, economic, diplomatic, or military status quo. A good opening scenario should describe a sudden and major change that adds considerable uncertainty, presents grave stakes, and increases time pressure for most actors in the simulation. This situation can be generated by a variety of triggers: diplomatic, economic, environmental, hostile acts related to civil wars and terror, nonviolent military moves, and confined violence. At times, even massive violence that has already ended can be used as a trigger, to set the stage for a "day after" simulation, as described in chapter 6 and in the appendix on the Iran nuclear simulation. When teams face such stressful situations, they realize that communications and interactions with other teams are essential to defend and promote their team's interests within a complex system of multiple political and media actors in world politics.

Figure 5.1 illustrates the evolution of a narrative told in the simulation story, from its most general topic introduced during the setup preparations, through the more focused initial scenario that is revealed before policy formation begins, to the acute change contained in the opening scenario that triggers the activities of world politics. As you plan your simulation, you are like a professional storyteller who knows the full story but discloses the details gradually and saves some new information for each publication. Such incremental information disclosure, with its dramatic impact in the transformation from precrisis to crisis or from limited change to drastic challenge, sets a gradual learning process in motion, motivates your students to deal with more focused and operational aspects of the subject matter, and leaves ample room for practice and critical thinking on the simulation events and the teams' activities.

The following example from a simulation on the Russia-Georgia conflict demonstrates how the initial scenario fits in with the general simulation topic. During the preparations for the simulation, the educator introduced students to some basic information about the topic and actors of the approaching simulation. The students knew that they were going to play six teams in the protracted conflict between Russia and Georgia: Russia, the United States, Georgia, the European Union, Russian media, and American media. They studied the entire conflict, from its genesis to the most recent developments to gain a general overview of the topic of the simulation. Once students had become familiar with the big picture and its historical context, they were ready to handle more specific details, as illustrated in figure 5.2.

The report was designed to bring participants back in time and to reflect the tense atmosphere of July 25, 2008. It mentioned the dangers of escalation, so the teams could plan their policy to avoid violence and war. It referred to each team, political and media alike, to indicate that they have a role in the conflict and are relevant to the stability of the region. The initial scenario purposively added a hint on the possible mediation contributions of the United States and European Union teams, to trigger some diplomatic initiatives. As planned, this scenario led to immediate discussions within all teams, who weighed diplomacy and military tools to promote their goals.

Other examples of initial scenarios illustrate the wide range of possibilities you have, in formats and triggers, when writing a narrative that will set policy formation

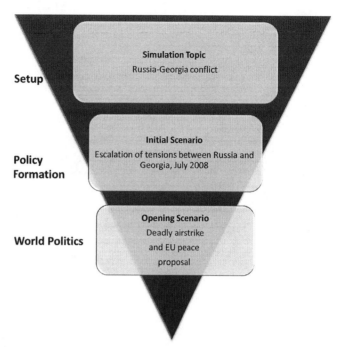

Fig. 5.1. Gradual disclosure of information

Independent International Commission Report on South Ossetia, July 25, 2008

Increased tensions between Russia and Georgia in recent months pose a serious threat to peace and stability in the region and beyond.

Mutual accusations, military buildups and non-routine exercises that violate the 1992 cease-fire might lead to uncontrolled escalation and even violence.

The 'war of words' in the media involves local and international newspapers.

It seems that intervention and mediation by external powers, such as the US and the European Union, are necessary to constrain further escalation by Russia and Georgia, the two bitter rivals.

Fig. 5.2. Scenario format: International Commission Report

within teams in motion. In the Middle East simulation, summarized in the appendix, the initial scenario was formatted as a newspaper regarding regional developments on the Iranian nuclear program and the Palestinian issue.

This scenario, illustrated in figure 5.3, was planned for a multi-issue simulation among ISA scholars who were assigned to three working groups in which negotiations took place. It described several simultaneous initiatives that all teams had to consider. The initial scenario requested all teams to compose opening initiatives for three working groups: a nuclear free zone in the Persian Gulf, the Palestinian quest for statehood, and an economic cooperation forum. As a result, all teams had to decide what trade-offs they could offer in the negotiation process and publicize some of their positions in the media. The scenario mentioned February 6, the prescheduled date for the beginning of the world politics round, as the deadline for completing all policy formation activities, press releases, and opening initiatives. To illustrate the impact of a newspaper format for atmosphere and decor we published the scenario as a front page, displayed in figure 5.4.

The initial scenario of another simulation on the Arab-Israel conflict in 2012 was published as an intelligence report. Like previous examples, this scenario, illustrated in figure 5.5, contained information relevant to all teams in the simulation, including the United States, Israel, and

---

Middle East Tribune, December 23, 2011

Quartet members are formulating a draft resolution to enforce a nuclear free zone in the Persian Gulf. They will convene on February 6, 2012 to vote on the resolution.

US secretary of state invited Israeli and Palestinian delegations to Washington on February 6, 2012 to continue talks on the Palestinian quest for statehood, that are currently taking place in Jordan.

The UN secretary general is finalizing a plan for an economic cooperation forum in the Middle East. He requested all parties to propose topics for the meeting in Washington.

The media welcomes updated press releases from all parties for a breaking news publication on February 6, 2012.

Fig. 5.3. Scenario format: *Middle East Tribune*, Dec. 2011

Middle East Tribune

No. 1
January 20, 2014

Palestinian Abbas to speak at the Israel Knesset

Kerry: The Leaders Need to Take Bold Decision

Washington. The talks between the Israeli Prime Minister Benjamin Netanyahu and Palestinian President Mahmoud Abbas have reached a critical point after intensive negotiations led by US Secretary of State John Kerry which included more than ten visits to the Middle East and endless rounds of talks in Jerusalem and Ramallah. Kerry praised the willingness of both leaders to confront core issues and take bold decisions towards compromise.

Secret Talks in Spain

Unofficial sources in Jerusalem and Ramallah said that "Oslo style" talks were being held between Israeli Foreign Minister Avigdor Liberman and the Palestinian chief negotiator Saeb Erekat in Toledo, Spain. According to these sources, the Toledo talks are held under the auspices of Catherine Ashton, the European Union Foreign Affairs High Representative. The borders of Palestine, the status of Jerusalem and the Jordan valley, as well as the Israeli settlements and the Palestinian refugee problem are among the core issues considered by the parties.

Israel to recognize independent Palestine

Jerusalem and Ramallah Sources revealed that Israeli Foreign Minister Liberman is considering a proposal to recognize an independent Palestine by January 15, 2015. As part of the deal, Israel will support the acceptance of Palestine to the UN and pass a bill in the Knesset, the Israeli Parliament, to secure the status of Arabs in Israel as a minority with equal rights in a Jewish state. In return, President Abbas will formally recognize Israel as a Jewish state. The sources emphasized that to legitimize the agreement, President Abbas is planned to come to Jerusalem on March 25, 2014, to meet Israeli President Shimon Peres and to make an official visit to the Knesset.

EU officials and sources in Washington, Jerusalem and Ramallah refused to comment on the news.

ISA 2014 World Politics Simulation Project
Hemda Ben-Yehuda. Luba Levin-Banchik. Chanan Naveh

Fig. 5.4. Scenario format:
Middle East Tribune, 2014

the Palestinians, represented by rival factions of Hamas and the Palestinian Authority.

The scenario combined military, diplomatic, and humanitarian triggers presented from the perspective of the United States. It was designed to offer participants a choice between diplomatic cooperation and further escalation. This required an overview of various policy al-

---

U.S. Intelligence Report, 2012

In Gaza the warring Palestinian factions continue to 'one up' one another by shelling Israeli towns across the border. So far Hamas is unable to impose an agreement among them.

Gaza is on the brink of a humanitarian crisis with shortages of fuel, basic daily products and medicine. Israel has agreed to a schedule for allowing supplies to enter but Hamas leaders are reluctant to accept the Israeli offer which would mean, to them, cooperation with an occupying force.

The United States finds the status quo untenable. It is determined to act decisively to reduce the likelihood of another round of fighting across the Gaza-Israel border. It seeks to advance Israeli security and to ensure the well-being and peace of Israeli and Palestinian civilians.

US President Obama believes that restraint and mediation can break the current deadlock, achieve Palestinian statehood and bring positive change to the region.

Fig. 5.5. Scenario format: U.S. Intelligence Report

Official Israeli News Release, June 15, 2013

The Israeli press highlighted that the new Iranian president-elect Hassan Rouhani poses either a threat or an opportunity for Israel and the world, depending upon his policy choices.

Israel calls for increased media openness in Iran and hopes that the international media will play a constructive role in preserving stability in the Gulf.

Israeli Prime Minister Benjamin Netanyahu warns that international appeasement of Iran, like the European policy towards Germany before World War II, endangers peace and stability in the Gulf and beyond.

Israel will continue to cooperate with its allies from the region and without to halt the Iranian nuclear project.

Israel calls upon the US and the European Union to enforce stricter sanctions on Iran in the immediate future.

Fig. 5.6. Scenario format: First Israeli news release

ternatives, taking into account the values and goals each team had defined. Though the scenario raised the prospect of an American-sponsored peace initiative, it was flexible enough to accommodate various plans offered by other teams. In reaction to this scenario, the teams had to come up with detailed plans for action to be implemented during the subsequent world politics round.

A simulation on Iran's quest for nuclear status after the leadership change in 2013 opened with an initial scenario in the form of an Israeli press release that analyzed the consequences of the new Hassan Rouhani presidency, portraying it as a possible opportunity coupled with threats.

The initial scenario illustrated in figure 5.6 deliberately showed that leadership change in one country affects all others in the region and in the world. It highlighted the Israeli point of view to promote a discussion within all teams on how to handle Iran and what the Israeli reaction might be. To trigger a thorough debate, we added a hidden dilemma regarding policy planning toward old rivals who, with new leaders, offer a genuine or maybe a fake readiness to compromise. If Iran cheats, all actors become even more vulnerable. Thus, each team had to decide to take a risk or perhaps to miss a groundbreaking opportunity to settle the nuclear issue and stabilize the region. The initial scenario also added a challenge for Iran: if leadership change means genuine policy transformation, Iran must allow greater freedom of the press as a first step toward transparency in other fields. But such moves might impinge upon fundamental religious and institutional values. In reaction to this scenario all teams had to consider the gap between the declarations and the deeds of the newly elected President Rouhani in the domestic and international spheres.

All initial scenario examples presented herein provide some new information and events related to the simulation topic. These developments are designed to help participants move from the big picture contained in the simulation topic to particular aspects they now have to deal with during policy formation.

Simulation Rules

All simulations have *rules* that guide the interaction process and shape its outcomes. You create these rules according to the specifics of the planned simulation, in order to clarify when and what is to be done, what is permitted and what is forbidden. Making the rules explicit reduces students' uncertainty about how to behave during the simulation and shapes their decisions and moves.

In our simulations we use nine core rules related to (1) proper conduct, (2) paradigms and theories, (3) empirical topics, (4) use of violence, (5) teamwork, (6) media exposure, (7) platforms, (8) the backup process, and (9) the schedule. You can add other rules, from your own experience, to suit the simulation you run.

Rule 1: All interactions must follow proper modes of conduct. In their communications participants must use appropriate language, show mutual respect, avoid privacy violations, refrain from personal attacks, and exercise self-constraint in extreme situations. While the simulation makes learning informal and fun, it is important that students remember it is still primarily an academic project with diplomatic exchanges, so students must follow the protocol of civilized and polite conduct. In simulations on social networks this rule is especially crucial, as students may unintentionally use offensive language toward fellow students, just as they may do in personal exchanges toward their friends on the network.

Rule 2: Adhere to assigned paradigms and theories. In simulations that are designed to teach paradigms and theories, students must explicitly integrate theoretical concepts into their discussions. The choice of language, values, and policy tools should stem from the assigned paradigm. For instance, if you assign the realist paradigm to a team, then teammates should integrate concepts such as balance of power, military pacts, conflict of interest, anarchy, and other terms into their decision-making process. If you assign a liberal paradigm, then the team should talk about economic interdependence, resources, growth, and welfare. They should stress the importance of international institutions and cooperation, and aim to spread democracy, establish open markets, protect human rights, and promote environmental issues. When this rule is violated, the simulation can't serve its purpose as a learning exercise. So along with a designated actor and a role, each participant has to adopt the specific paradigm or theory and act, as closely as possible, according to its stipulations. Then, during the debriefing session, all participants can assess the ways in which the core concepts of a theory have shaped the conduct of actors and the outcomes of political interactions.

Rule 3: Act in accordance with the details and logic of the empirical topic. In their interactions participants should follow the logic of the events in the scenario and the empirical topic they have learned and are implementing in detail as they practice policy formation and world politics. Although simulations enable students to create a new reality or to revisit a past one, all interactions should be based on students' knowledge of the empirical topic.

Their activities should make sense with the political environment, context, and actor constraints. Thus, it is possible for Iran and Israel to take part in back-channel diplomatic negotiations, as happened in the 2012 Middle East simulation, but it is unlikely that the rivals would immediately reach a long-term formal compromise on all aspects related to the nuclear issue. The line between real and fiction may be blurred in simulations, but even in the most creative and breakthrough turning points, some basic logic should apply to behavior choices in order to convey the empirical topic of the simulation, along with its inherent constraints and opportunities for all political and media actors.

Rule 4: Any act of violence must first get the consent of the educator. This rule is common to all diplomatic simulations described in this book, which focus on a wide range of foreign policy tools short of full-scale war. Promises and threats, negotiations and the conclusion of agreements, even ultimatums and other modes of coercive diplomacy and brinkmanship may be used. But since the cost of violence in simulations is much lower than in reality and students do not conduct real military operations or calculate gains and losses, violence is not allowed as a central tool. Diplomatic simulations are not designed to integrate field activities like in war games. When a participant or a team violates this rule, you should announce that no violence has occurred and instruct all participants to disregard the illegitimate activity.

Rather than use violence, we urge students to consider the cost of such options and come up with effective nonviolent alternatives. When a team insists on the use of violent tools even after consideration of other alternatives, you may decide to approve an announcement on a short violent event that is limited in scope as we did in the Gulf nuclear simulation, when the Israeli team declared a preemptive strike on Iran and the Iranian team got permission to "use" diversionary force through armed nonstate actors against Israel. In such cases, you must make sure to explain that the major activity among teams will focus on the "day after" the violence and coach students to move on from hostilities to diplomacy and work out poststrike realities.

Terror involves threat and violence, but is a relevant and important topic for diplomatic simulations. It can be introduced in the scenario or develop as an act initiated by a nonstate actor who got your consent during the simulation. Unlike full-scale war and massive violence, terror is an act of violence confined in time and space. It is coupled with diplomatic activities, ethical dilemmas, the paradoxes of soft versus harsh reprisals, and the difficulty of striking back against an elusive target at the risk of the deterioration of relations with host states.[2] Yet, as with other acts of violence, participants that represent violent nonstate actors and terror groups must get your consent before they decide to use terror attacks.

Rule 5: Adhere to policy decisions reached by the team when interacting with other teams. Teammates must stand together as a cohesive team. This rule is especially relevant during world politics interactions when students represent their political or media actor and implement policy plans in negotiations with other actors. When representatives of a team apply contradictory positions and inconsistent policy, the team loses its credibility and quality of negotiations as a whole is considerably diminished.

Rule 6: All negotiations or other communications cease during the breaking news session. This rule is meant to provide the media teams some prime time within world politics rounds during which all teams consume media products. This rule is essential because participants who are immersed in intensive interactions tend to disregard the media, just as often happens in the real world. However, media teams invest considerable effort to produce their coverage of the simulation, and it is necessary to establish a designated session when all attention is dedicated to the media, as explained in chapter 6.

Rule 7: In cyber simulations, one primary platform is where all activities take place. The platform can be Facebook or a different social network but students should not roam to alternative routes of communication. It is easier to follow this rule in an online course as participants rarely meet in person, if at all. However, during an on-campus course, some players may opt to meet face-to-face in conjunction with the times for interactions on the virtual platform. This can be allowed if the entire class is situated in a computer lab and plays against a distant campus. But most often, ad-hoc meetings or the resort to other channels of activity, such as text messages by phone or e-mail, make it hard for all participants to follow simulation developments and reduce the teams' ability to build a cohesive policy. Activities beyond the primary platform also make it hard for you to supervise and coach students. Participants should be aware that such use of alternative platforms may add disorder and uncertainty, nullifying many advantages social networks offer as a major platform for academic simulations, as detailed in chapter 1.

Rule 8: Back up all communications that occur outside the primary simulation platform, to share them with your team, educator, and other participants at a later time. This rule supplements the previous one and indicates that sometimes alternative applications do take place as necessary exceptions, like a social network chat between leaders that is meant to be secret, or e-mail and Skype to allow for bilateral contacts. Such exchanges may be needed to coordinate final agreements between top decision-makers or between opposition members within a team. The backup of these secret contacts makes it possible for all participants to use them during debriefing and research, as detailed in chapters 7 and 9.

Rule 9: Strictly adhere to the schedule, instructions, and rules. For the simulation to become an efficient and enjoyable learning experience, all participants should make sure to meet all deadlines for assignments because the simulation is based on gradual learning and step-by-step preparations that must be completed on time and coordinated with other participants. The schedule and rules apply to all students, so those who violate them damage the learning experience of their fellow students and impinge on the quality of the simulation as a whole.

The simulation rules are usually created and presented during setup preparations on the simulation website or the social network platform if you run a cyber simulation. But you will need to highlight their importance again before policy formation begins. It is best to introduce and explain the rules in advance and to revisit them as you publish the initial scenario. You can also bring hard copies of the rules to class or screen them up front during a face-to-face simulation.

Beyond defining the rules and distributing them, your task is to enforce the rules once the simulation begins. This can be done when (1) students sign a digital form stating that they have read the rules and accept them; (2) an explicit note on the website warns that rule violation would be reflected in the grade; and (3) on the social network, you can easily detect and omit messages that violate rules and send a personal note to the student by chat on social networks to warn against such behavior. In the Palestinian statehood simulation, for instance, one student continuously uploaded an alarm sound from YouTube announcing that Israel had been bombarded by missiles. This activity, without our consent, was a violation of rule 4, on the need to get approval before the use of any violence, so we deleted these messages immediately and notified students about the violation. While such violent developments did happen in reality, we prohibited them in the simulation, since the time for negotiations was short and we wanted to give diplomatic endeavors a chance. A burst of violence could have totally undermined the fragile cooperation moves, the evolving peace process, and the simulation as a whole.

Policy Formation Process

The *policy formation process* necessitates an active dialogue between all teammates on the team's values, immediate goals, and policy plans in reaction to the initial scenario. The process involves an action-reaction exchange, verbal in case of a face-to-face meeting and written in cyber simulations. One student, possibly at the request of the head of team, initiates discussions by expressing views on the values related to the events in the scenario, points to the goals the team should pursue, or suggests a plan for activity in the immediate future. Others react to these views by clarifying or challenging them. After cross-examination by all team members, a joint team position should be chosen by a vote or by a decision of the leader.

Planning strategy toward the media is also important and requires teammates of political actors to debate the public image they want to create for their actor. Political teams can use the media to maximize their goals, but they can also become a subject for manipulation by the media. In order to gain media coverage each team can publish press releases and get interviewed. The text of press releases must be short and contain sound bites that are likely to be published by the media networks. When an interview is planned, potential questions with answers should be outlined in advance. Teamwork on strategy toward the media increases the chances for a successful public diplomacy campaign when world politics interactions begin.

Media teams are usually organized hierarchically with a chief editor as the head of the team who decides on the orientation and the agenda of the media agency, its values, goals, and means. The regime of the country the media organ represents also affects media ideology, the freedom to report, and competition with other media organs. In line with these constraints the editor reaches decisions on publications but should take into account the opinions of other members in the team so as to ensure their cooperation and the efficient functioning of the media team as a whole. In simulations with several media actors, members in each media team need to discuss and decide how to introduce and brand their actor so as to appear attractive to others. Otherwise, the media organ risks being overshadowed by competing media teams or becoming disregarded by the political ones.

The chief editor can be the first to present some views on values, goals, and means the team should follow to create the simulation news agenda. Other members can then comment on these suggestions and discuss them. The media team also has to plan who in the political teams to

approach for an interview and how to distribute the task of covering the simulation developments among its reporters. Editors may assign correspondents to seek information on specific issues or to contact specific actors once world politics interactions begin. Some reporters may be assigned to handle each political team or a group of them. Reporters should also follow core topics of the simulation with specialized coverage of diplomatic negotiations, prisoner swaps, economic sanctions, or other issues that appear in the initial scenario.

During policy formation, media teams have to discuss the products they will publish and decide on their contents. They can schedule when to publish interviews, breaking news items, single article reports, op-eds, newspapers, and audio or video reports. The team has to plan which of these products will be published at the beginning of world politics and which would be presented, with some adjustments, during the breaking news media session. So the preparation of high-quality media products during policy formation helps the media teams cope with time pressures and reporting challenges during intensive world politics negotiations.

A good way to illustrate the importance and contributions of the policy formation process is to revisit examples from simulations we ran in the past. Policy formation in the Middle East simulation, summarized in the appendix, started after each participant was allocated to a specific team and assigned a role within the team. All participants began to interact, logging in to their Facebook groups at flexible times, to conduct within-team negotiations and formulate their policy goals on two core topics: first, Palestinian statehood, where a negotiation process was scheduled to resolve the current Israeli-Palestinian impasse, and second, Gulf nuclear development, where the Iranian quest for nuclear weapons was handled, as illustrated in figure 5.7. The political teams also planned specific policy initiatives, illustrated in figure 5.8, and discussed them before approaching other teams including the media.[3]

To pinpoint the most important aspects for policy formation within political teams, an initial scenario was posted on the Facebook wall with specific triggers for each team. The initial scenario required students' attention and focused their practical planning of behavioral responses. It also left space for diplomatic initiatives and negotiation proposals to be developed by the players in their political roles. The different teams discussed their national goals, how to implement them, and various alternatives designed to achieve the most important objectives within the time range of the simulation. We made it clear

Fig. 5.7. Iranian policy formation in the Middle East simulation

to all participants that the precondition for success was to come up with well-defined and operational plans that will be placed on the negotiation table once the synchronous processes start.

In many ways, cyber exchanges of policy formation were a sort of relatively low-speed pilot run before the two rounds of world politics. They included flexible, asynchronous sessions within Facebook groups. Simply put, each player joined the group at different times and posted a comment that was later addressed when others read it and reacted. So the intensity of interactions at this stage depended on each participant's time allocation, motivation, and actual availability in terms of time zones across the global village. The policy formation process also served as a training period for individuals who were less familiar or comfortable with Facebook procedures and allowed each team to create its collective identity based on the personal traits of each participant, accounting for creativity, leadership, negotiation skills, and decision-making abilities.

During this early simulation stage, the media teams carried out Skype video sessions to coordinate their coverage responsibilities and to build their media strategies. These exchanges provided individuals who played media professionals with encounters online as surrogate for face-to-face encounters. They also facilitated some coaching needed for players who were in the media team but

were not familiar with media theories or actual conduct techniques.

Within the Iranian team, debates took place on how to cope with the Nuclear Free Gulf initiative and all the while continue at full speed with the nuclear buildup. The team had to discuss the issue of continued support for Hamas, especially given Palestinian aid to the rebels in Syria. Another core topic was how to manage the growing pressure of the sanctions imposed by the Western powers.

Within the American team the question of an active U.S. role in the region and its specifics were debated and the measures necessary to make the United States an effective mediator were considered. In the Israel and Palestinian teams core national interests and redlines were defined. At the same time, the alternatives open to negotiation and compromise were weighed. The Israeli team had to cope simultaneously with two adversaries, Iran and the Palestinians, in two overlapping conflicts, to safeguard American support, and to stabilize a region in which Fatah and Hamas had reached a reconciliation agreement and dangerous radical forces were operating all around Israel.

At the end of the policy formation process, we posted an announcement about the upcoming synchronous world politics encounter on Facebook to remind players they should get ready for intensive synchronous negotiations. Clearly, the most exciting part of the Middle East simulation was about to begin. Some teams even set up a short Facebook meeting before the synchronous run, to coordinate strategy and make last-minute arrangements.

Creating an authentic atmosphere on cyber simulations is important, just as it is in face-to-face ones. To transform the social network into a stage for the regional conflict, the team members used national emblems and flags to decorate their group wall and changed their personal profile photo to those of the leaders they played for the two hours of synchronous interactions. This way all participants were always recognized by their real name but were also visually connected to the character they represented. The atmosphere was further enhanced by ethnocentric rhetoric typical to the characters and orientations of each actor.

By contrast, during the Gulf nuclear simulation, the policy formation process was brief as it often occurs due to time constraints in face-to-face simulations. The teamwork was usually confined to class time, and beyond that few discussions took place. When world politics began, teammates split into distinctive working groups, and the intense and accelerated pace of international negotiations pushed domestic politics aside.

Some additional intragroup contacts became easier and more relevant toward the end of the world politics round when players of the Iranian team, for instance, consulted carefully before each statement they made and reached joint decisions on cost and benefit calculations for each of their moves. At the same time the media players prepared reports with a "leak" on an upcoming Iranian offensive against Israel, although the Iranian team had really only chosen to approve some confined violent action by non-state actors and had no intention of using an all-out offensive against Israel.

When these media reports were published, during world politics interactions, the Iranian team felt betrayed as their plans were revealed and exaggerated. Through

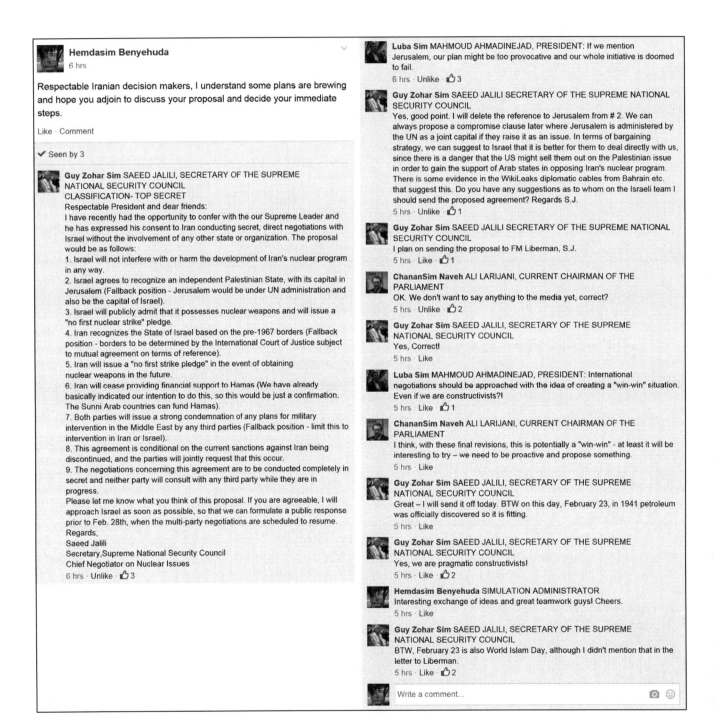

Fig. 5.8. Initiatives in the Middle East simulation

practice of decision-making and frustration regarding the difficulties of operating with the media, the students learned the importance of public diplomacy and media management as well as the active and at times manipulating role of media organs in world politics.

The hybrid Palestinian statehood simulation involved cyber policy formation with voluntary face-to-face meetings between teammates before and after regular classes. During setup preparations, separate Facebook groups were set for each political team and media organ, allowing participants to interact within the groups, to formulate their policy, and to instruct the media reporters on how to cover the events by video clips and newspapers.

After the initial scenario was published, participants joined the simulation groups on Facebook. The initial scenario was based on actual events in the region so the Israeli students that were familiar with them were motivated to act fast and find solutions, even though the process of political decision-making and policy formation was a new experience for most of them.

Immediate activity began within each team and teammates discussed the developments and their reactions. They logged in to teams' Facebook at flexible times, and posted offers, positions, reactions, and all sorts of expressions related to the initial scenario. All teams put the Palestinian statehood issue at the top of their agenda, trying to resolve the current impasse, and discussed initiatives before approaching other teams or revealing these initiatives to the media.

In such current events simulations, participants also need to follow developments that occur in reality as the simulation project unfolds. The initial scenario of the Palestinian statehood simulation, for example, coincided with elections for parliament in Israel and presidential elections in the United States; both were important inputs for all teams. The simulation also involved a kidnapping event of Israeli citizens including a women soldier, while Gilad Shalit, an Israeli soldier, was held captive in Gaza and on-and-off negotiations for his release were held. Participants in the simulation had to be aware of major real-life events relevant to the simulation topic to plan their activities in the simulation world, parallel to actual changes in the outside world.

Another example of the inclusion of real-life events along with fiction during team discussions was evident in the Palestinian statehood simulation, when the Israeli team discussed a scenario-based proposal for a deal on the exchange of prisoners, particularly the United States freeing Jonathan Pollard and Israel freeing 1,000 Palestinians. The team was faced with a heavy ethical dilemma

and debated it intensively before deciding what to do with the prisoner swap deal. One of the Israeli participants compared it with the release of the Israeli soldier Gilad Shalit in return for Palestinian terrorists and attached a link on the Facebook wall with a speech of a representative of the terror victims' families, who criticized the deal. Another participant replied with a link to an article where Pollard's wife claimed that her husband is against freeing any Palestinian prisoner in return for his release.

After policy formation ends, it is usually helpful to announce that once the opening scenario is disclosed, events in the outside world will no longer matter for the simulation world. This declaration on the separation of real events and simulation realities helps participants focus on the story in the opening scenario and makes it possible to apply the plans they had made collectively for interactions with other teams. If turmoil and change are intensive, as in Arab Spring events, it is good to start this separation even earlier, such as in the middle of the policy formation process, to reduce the task of updating with constant changes in current events.

When making decisions, teammates must be ready for compromise after intensive debates. It is important that they understand that all decisions represent the team as a whole. How each team makes decisions depends on the type of regime characteristic of each actor and on intra-group dynamics. Political teams representing democratic states are likely to decide by voting, while in the teams that represent autocratic states and terror organizations the leader is likely to impose his decision. Media teams also have structured constraints, so the editor and all reporters should conform to the media regime that characterizes their network.

Political teams have to distinguish between policy planning toward other political teams and toward the media. In planning toward political teams all means of foreign policy are valid, including political offers, direct and public diplomacy, mediation proposals, coercive diplomacy, economic sanctions, military threats, and even the use of confined violence you have approved. The teams have to discuss and decide which of these means are most appropriate to reach their actor's goals. Participants should be aware that other political actors are also considering the full range of policy means and should evaluate how to react when different contingences develop.

The examples discussed above indicate that policy formation in simulations evolves through a similar scheme. It is triggered by the initial scenario, requires teammates to communicate and collectively build a policy plan, and ends with policy choices toward other teams. In the next section we detail the necessary procedures on your side to make the policy formation process a successful exercise.

Policy Formation Procedures

During policy formation each team has to discuss and decide (1) who the actor is, (2) what it wants to achieve, and (3) what activities and policy plans are useful to reach these goals. To enhance the learning process and to motivate students to engage in this discussion, we integrate the use of four assignments from solitary preparation as a starting point for the joint creation of a collective actor portfolio, values, goals, and policy plans. By transforming the individually prepared assignments into a single document the team agrees upon, each team makes progress with its policy formation and increases its identification with the actor it represents.

Collective Actor Portfolio

The *actor portfolio* contains all the relevant information the students had collected on their actor, be it a political or media team. This task begins with solitary learning in the setup preparations detailed in chapter 4 and continues with intensive teamwork during policy formation when students are required to discuss and integrate individual actor portfolios into a joint one for the entire team. By doing so, all team members learn new facts about their actor from peer students, review and internalize acquired knowledge, and collectively construct their actor identity. When participants play an actor other than their own country, especially an enemy, this task becomes a challenge that is likely to contribute greatly to empathy, on the one hand, and to critical thinking, on the other. It forces players to set prejudices aside, penetrate the minds of others, and act as if they are the adversary.

The collective actor portfolio contains an actor's profile and all biography brochures. An *actor's profile,* as noted in chapter 4, involves a relatively short textual and graphic description of the actor in its various attributes: the type of regime and decisional hierarchy, power elements, allies and rivals, previous involvement in and core events related to the topic of simulation, as well as other elements you choose and specify. During policy formation, students are required to share, compare, and discuss their findings so as to reach a consensus on the most relevant information to include in the final version of the collective actor portfolio. This document will then guide the team throughout the simulation.

Character biography involves a list of all team characters and their short biographies, with a special focus on each character's role with regard to the topic of simulation. Sometimes, especially in media teams, a fiction character is made up by participants as a cover story for the personality they represent. Otherwise, students need to take into account and follow the worldview of the specific character they are assigned to represent in the simulation. Each participant had already composed a biography of one's own as a solitary task in the setup phase. Now it is time to introduce the character to teammates and assemble all biographies into a single file.

Once all teams finish their collective actor's portfolio, the portfolios of all simulation actors are placed on the website or social network platform so that all participants can get familiar with other actors involved in the simulation. You should make sure to notify your students that the public version of the portfolio should exclude secret information, such as content and rank of values, goals, and some of the plans the team had agreed upon during the policy formation process.

Values

Policy formation develops gradually as a three-step process illustrated in figure 5.9. Each step in this process requires a closer focus and becomes more tangible, from the definition of core values, via the clarification and ranking of goals, to the formulation of policy plans with specific means to reach them.

In many past simulations we noticed that when the task of defining team values and clarifying goals was not made explicit enough, students regularly moved directly from the initial scenario to policy planning. Yet the same policy choice may serve different goals and have different implications for each one of them. Resort to coercive diplomacy and the use of violence may enhance one goal at the cost of another, so it may not be the ultimate policy tool. For example, Israel in the Gulf nuclear simulation chose to attack Iran without consideration of the costs of this option in terms of its relations with the United States and without taking into account the implications of such activity on the core goal of continued American supply of advanced military aid. Similarly, if a media team decides to publish strictly unbiased products, their choice may serve the goal of becoming a reputable and reliable source of information for international audiences, but it may hamper the goal of mobilizing support for the local government. Thus, one basic lesson to be learned from participating in a simulation is that before one plans policy, the values and goals must be addressed.

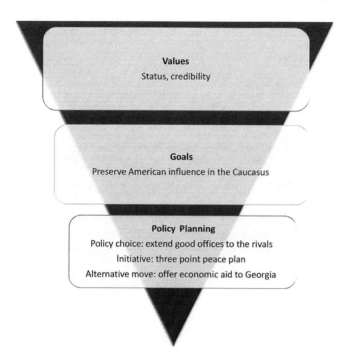

Fig. 5.9. Gradual policy formation

Values are core beliefs that shape the actor's world-view.[4] They include the fundamental ideological and normative precepts that guide the actors, and are usually not forsaken. Survival, security, and power are among the primary values of all states. Human rights and liberal freedoms are common values of democracies. Strong leadership and control are characteristic of autocratic states. Media actors, too, have core values, such as freedom of speech, professionalism, credibility, economic profit, exclusivity, and rating.

The fundamental values of an actor usually remain intact for generations. But in different situations some values become more important and relevant than others. In the 2008 Russia-Georgia tensions, for instance, American status and credibility were of much higher significance to the United States than economic well-being and gains. Awareness to these priorities should guide the choice of goals and lead a debate on the trade-offs one makes when a policy plan is adopted.

Once students are familiar with the specific situation described in the initial scenario, ask them to (1) define their actor's most crucial values that need to be promoted or defended in the given situation, limiting the number of values so the debate is practical and time efficient, and (2) rank the chosen values and discuss the relationship between them in order to understand value trade-offs. As different students are likely to have views of their own,

this task may lead to intensive debates till teammates agree. From a learning perspective, such discussions are valuable as they provoke students to think analytically, lead them to continue the exploration of their actor, and increase their identification with it. In some cases, especially in acute situations when the actor faces an imminent threat, the students may easily and quickly agree on the content and rank of values. In other situations they may engage in provoking moral deliberations that require analytical skills, sensitivities to intercultural diversities, and even empathy with the actor they represent. The discussion regarding values is an introduction to the debate on political goals.

Goals

Goals are the operational stakes an actor wants to reach and is ready to allocate resources immediately in order to promote them. They stem from core values and are closely related to events that appear in the initial scenario and in the case that was chosen for the simulation. For instance, the value of power was selected as first priority by the U.S. team in the 2008 Russia-Georgia simulation. But *what exactly* did the team want to promote? One goal was to preserve American status and influence in the Caucasus, but another one with very different implications was to strengthen the American position, as the sole superpower, against Russia. While each of the two goals was linked to the value of status, the team also wanted to avoid a violent confrontation with Russia, linked to the value of a peaceful orientation characteristic of a democracy. The team's activity followed the latter at the expense of the former.

After students define and rank the values of their team, ask them to (1) clarify a limited number of most important goals their actor wants to achieve regarding the situation detailed in the initial scenario, and (2) rank the chosen goals according to their importance and address the issue of conflicts between goals. Opposition and coalition members are likely to disagree on the content and rank of many goals. The more students discuss and debate goals the better, because through such discussions they learn more about their actor, experience group dynamics in decision-making, and understand how difficult it is to reach an agreement on the fundamental elements of the policy formation process.

Some teams may avoid serious discussions in order to quickly complete their assignments. This happens because participants may be wrongly impressed that the outcome of intrateam discussions is more important for their grade than the process itself. Ad-hoc appointment of dominant members in the team to take the role of "devil's advocate," who will deliberately disagree and advocate opposite claims, can encourage students to reconsider goals and initiate debates. In face-to-face simulations, where all deliberations are verbal, it might be extremely difficult to detect teams with poor participation in such discussions. Even if you move from one team to another, you have little control over the participation and quality of conversations once you leave a team. In such cases it is useful to introduce a *policy formation summary form,* which the head of team completes. It contains some information on the main ideas that were discussed and the final decision reached on them by team members, with details on the contributions of each team member. This summary is obviously less detailed than the data on the social networks, but it helps the team act collectively in the world politics process. In simulations on social networks all deliberations are automatically saved so you can easily evaluate the contribution of each participant and the team as a whole after the simulation ends or add encouraging notes, provide guidance, and sometimes even post a warning during policy formation debates.

Policy Plans

Once each team agrees on its core values and immediate goals, it is time to discuss and decide how to reach them and what policy means to use. The *policy plan* depicts the chosen way of action to be implemented in interactions with other teams. It involves the most suitable policy measures and initiatives related specifically to each of the goals from the perspective of the team. For example, in the Russia-Georgia simulation the goal of the U.S. team was to preserve American influence in the Caucasus, so teammates suggested that the United States (1) offer its good offices and mediate between Georgia and Russia, (2) grant economic aid to Georgia, or (3) threaten Russia to stay out of Georgia. Each of these policy moves was related to the initial scenario and had an expected impact on the team's goals. The team decided that an offer of its good offices to Georgia and Russia was the best choice as it entailed the lowest cost and highest benefits of maintaining regional status. It also demonstrated a balanced position in the conflict and made it possible to continue ties with a relatively weak Georgia as a U.S. ally and at the same time to prevent the deterioration of relations with a powerful Russia.

To implement their policy choice effectively the team had to translate its decision into an operational initiative. By *opening initiative* we mean a short proposal in the form of a three-to-five clause document with offers or threats for immediate consideration by other teams. The team prepares, discusses, and agrees on the contents and wording of the document and then presents it to other actors as a proposal for negotiations when the world politics interactions begin. Peace offers and agreements from past cases in real life can be useful as examples for the formulation of core points in such an initiative. But these documents must be very brief and concern the immediate time frame in order to serve as a practical policy tool for the simulation. In the 2008 Russia-Georgia exercise, the U.S. team drafted a three-point plan for the immediate reduction of tensions: (1) a commission with representatives from both sides will investigate the roots and immediate sources of the conflict; (2) both sides would meanwhile avoid and condemn any use of violence till the publication of the full commission report; and (3) both sides would avoid and condemn propaganda through the media. These points were supposed to trigger complex bargaining and lead to an agreement among actors in world politics after reformulation and adjustments.

What would happen if Russia or Georgia, or both, declined the American offer? How would the U.S. team adjust its policy to advance its goals? The team also has to be ready for such unfortunate developments. *Alternative moves,* which may cover a range of activities, are the second-best choice to reach goals and should be prepared as a backup plan. For the American team, offering economic aid to Georgia rather than threatening Russia was chosen in advance as the alternative move because it safeguarded American involvement in the regional conflict without elevating hostilities to a global level.

To help students create an efficient policy plan and sophisticated alternative moves, it is useful to provide them with preformatted forms that contain open spaces to fill in, or structured questions with multiple-choice answers to choose from.

In the open form, ask your students to (1) specify at least three possible means of policy for each one of their actor's goals. It is preferable that these means span diverse options available to the actor: diplomatic, economic, military nonviolent, and military violent. There could be many options for policy moves, so students' applied knowledge, imagination, and creativity would be reflected in this assignment; (2) evaluate the costs and benefits of the suggested moves relative to the goal; (3) decide which of the policy moves is the most cost-effective and choose it as the team's policy plan; and (4) pinpoint a second-best alternative in case the first policy option fails. These tasks induce students to think analytically and teach them that any decision, even an optimal one, has its price.

In the structured form, first list several policy statements that you want your students to discuss. Each policy statement should be brief, rely on real information, and be somewhat provocative, such as a claim that "the UN will be the exclusive mediator" or that "the use of war contradicts the UN charter and will not be used as a means in conflict resolution." We recommend that contents of policy statements remain the same for all actors so as to create a joint framework for all participants. The structured format touches upon core topics that you want the teams to address in preparation for world politics interactions but may be overlooked in an open format form. Second, request that students discuss their actor's attitude toward every given statement, expressed on a 1–5 scale from "disagree" to "agree" and consolidate their joint position. Such discussions are designed to increase students' familiarity and identification with the policy orientation of their actor. For instance, the U.S. team may become more ready to consider mediation and evaluate its efficiency after it discusses a policy statement on the UN as the sole mediator in the Russia-Georgia conflict. Discussions on policy statements that were written by the educator enhance the range of choices and trigger in-depth policy planning by students.

As illustrated in figure 5.10, you may decide to use both types of forms in the same simulation to encourage students' creativity and at the same time to direct them toward specific issues you want to stress in the learning process.

To make the forms user-friendly, accessible, and easy

American responses: open form

Initial scenario:
Increased tensions between Russia and Georgia in recent months pose serious threat for peace and stability in the region and in the entire world. Military buildups, parallel military exercises and mutual accusations on violation of 1992 cease-fire are only few of many demonstrations of the hostility and antagonism between the states that might escalate to full-scale war at any moment. The 'war of words' had already begun in the media, and it is extremely difficult to find unbiased reports in these days, even in international newspapers. It looks like the two bitter rivals, Russia and Georgia, are on the path to real war and without the intervention and mediation by the external powers, such as USA and EU, the war would become the inevitable outcome.

Actor: *USA*

Core values*:
1. *Credibility*
2. *Status*
3. *Sovereignty*
4. *Human rights*
5. *Political freedom for minorities*

Goals & means*:
1. *Preserve American influence in Caucasus*
   a. *extend good offices to the rivals*
   b. *offer economic aid to Georgia*
   c. *threaten Russia to stay out of Georgia*

2. *Prevent escalation to violence*
   a. *stress American commitment to Georgia's security*
   b. *offer to mediate the conflict*
   c. *make ultimatum to Russia if intervenes to Georgia*

3. *Avoid confrontation with Russia*
   a. *keep secret talks with Georgia on NATO membership*
   b. *use media to emphasize neutral position in conflict*
   c. *send diplomatic envoy to Russia*

4. *Become an effective mediator in the conflict*
   a. *offer to mediate the conflict*
   b. *suggest peace offer*
   c. *call for a peace conference*

5. *Protect the existing status of all minorities in the region*
   a. *offer collaboration to the EU on the issue of minorities*
   b. *extend economic aid to minorities*
   c. *support democratic representation of minorities*

Policy choice:
Diplomatic activity: extend good offices to Russia and Georgia, emphasize American commitment to Georgia's security and Keep covert all talks on Georgia's NATO membership.

***Ranked from the most important to the least important. May differ from reality. Script fonts illustrate the answers students are supposed to add.**

Combined response form: structured and open

Mediation: The U.N. will be the exclusive mediator *
Mark your position on a scale from 1 "disagree" to 5 "agree"

1 2 3 4 5

○ ○ ○ ○ ○

Your exact position on the issue *

Diplomatic Recognition: All parties recognize one another's right to exist and exchange diplomatic envoys *
Mark your position on a scale from 1 "disagree" to 5 "agree"

1 2 3 4 5

○ ○ ○ ○ ○

Your exact position on the issue *

Fig. 5.10. Values and policy

to grade, you can design them as a digital survey. With an application like Google Forms, for example, it is easy to formulate such a survey and make it available to students at a click on a link. Survey responses are visible only to you and are automatically saved on your Google Drive on the web. Once you create the survey, you may use its contents repeatedly, with some adjustments, for other simulations by different students in future runs.

After the simulation is over, you can make the responses public for all participants to enhance postsimulation debriefing and research. You can explore the contents of these forms during the debriefing session and analyze them with your students in various output formats, including a graphic display of answers. Making policy forms public after the simulation ends lets students enter the minds of their allies and rivals and reconsider the world politics interactions from other's perspectives. When students compare their own beliefs with the contents in the forms of other actors, the meaning of values, misperceptions, prejudices, and expressions of empathy becomes clearer and more tangible. Students may be surprised to find that their rivals share similar values to their own and even have common goals that actually remained unnoticed in the context of growing tensions and animosity. This comparison also helps students understand the meaning of interdependence in world politics, when goal realization and the implementation of one's policy plans depend on what other actors do. Postsimulation debriefing and research on these and related topics can greatly benefit from a digital survey with your questions and students' responses, which are accessible online and saved as an archive for research.

Coach Participants

Any student, even the best, may encounter difficulties in preparing assignments and participating in policy formation with teammates. These may relate to incorrect implementation of a theory, incomplete understanding of methodology, or inaccurate presentation of empirical facts. There is also a problem of free riders who remain aloof during most of the teamwork, increasing the burden on fellow teammates. Other problems may emerge due to tense interpersonal relationships between several students, which may lower the prospects of a successful simulation experience for the class as a whole. All these and related problems require your attention and sensitive intervention to coach participants who need assistance or seek an advice.

It is preferable to coach students on an individual basis

to avoid embarrassment. Social networks enable covert contacts even during the most intensive discussions. Without changing physical location, you can follow discussions between teammates on Facebook, send messages to individual students that need assistance, or coach them by Skype. At the same time, you can keep updated with ongoing discussions to see if you missed something, since all conversations are constantly available on the social network.

Together, the intrateam discussions and decisions on the collective actor portfolio, values, goals and policy plans trigger a gradual learning process and a sense of what real decision-making is all about. Thoughtful preparation, careful evaluation, and strict adherence to deadlines for assignments reduce time pressure and lessen the student's dependence on teammates when it comes to the implementation of the policy during the world politics interactions.

After you complete all preparations related to the (1) initial scenario, (2) simulation rules, and (3) contents and forms for the assignments on values, goals, and policy plans, it is time to instruct your students so they can start the policy formation process.

Instructions for Participants

This section on instructions for participants summarizes the main points, described in the chapter till now, in a concise form. It is designed as a quick checklist you can present to your students, especially the instructions table, which you can hand out in class or upload on the simulation website; post on the social network platform; or send by e-mail. The brief explanations provided in this section assume that the reader is familiar with the details provided in the previous sections of this chapter and especially on the policy formation process, which you can assign as an elective reading requirement for your students.

A constructive debate on the actor's policy must take place within teams. The main purpose of such activity is to create a cohesive policy and to consolidate each team so it would act as single unit during world politics interactions. Table 5.2 summarizes policy formation instructions along four core tasks: get familiar, study, participate in intrateam policy formation, and follow instructions.

When you give specific instructions to individual participants or to the team as a whole, avoid direct interventions in an ongoing debate that are likely to disrupt the flow of communications and bring participants back

TABLE 5.2. Policy Formation Instructions for Participants

Task	Details
Get familiar	Read and assess initial scenario
Study	Conduct research on the values, goals and policy plans of the actor and character you represent Instructions and submission dates for assignments appear on simulation website or other platforms used in your course
Participate in intrateam policy formation	Share, discuss and decide: - Collective actor profile - Values - Goals - Policy plan Practice decision-making and reach a viable decision within the domestic context
Follow instructions	Abide by simulation schedule and rules Hand in assignments on time

from the simulation reality to a formal top-down academic hierarchy.

To preserve the advantages of learning with simulations, provide your instructions before the discussions begin, and if further guidelines are needed, add them on the simulation website, write them as new posts on the social network, or summarize them during the break between rounds in a face-to-face simulation. Major interference by you during team discussions becomes problematic as the interactive exercise is designed to give participants a sense of independence to develop the team's identity, to shape developments, and to lead the course of action.

Individual Tasks

To increase the contribution of each team member, design policy formation assignments as individual tasks to be completed before the policy formation process begins. All participants must remember that personal commitment, individual efforts, and meaningful involvement in all tasks are crucial to ensure the successful performance of the team as a whole.

Get Familiar

To start policy formation, participants have to get familiar with the situation described in the initial scenario and assess its positive and negative meanings from the perspective of their team and from the point of view of the character they represent. If the situation described in the initial scenario is based on an empirical setting, historical or current, this task requires participants to search out and learn additional details on the events. When the initial scenario describes a fiction narrative students should look for historical analogies as a useful way to get familiar with

the situation at hand. Participants must understand that information is power and that the more they know about a particular event and the actors involved, the better their chances are to assess it correctly and to reach constructive and innovative policy solutions. As participants get familiar with the events described in the initial scenario and enrich their knowledge with video clips, newspaper articles, and official documents, the atmosphere brings the given situation to life and the team becomes a cohesive group that is ready to act in a coordinated way.

Study

Learning in simulations evolves through all its phases, as described in chapter 1 and detailed in figure 5.1. Participants begin the policy formation process after they have already studied the simulation topic, the actor, and the character they are assigned to, on an individual basis, as described in chapter 4. With the publication of new details in the initial scenario, participants can deepen their knowledge by focusing on specific elements. They must further their research to learn about the values, goals, and policy plans of the actor and character they represent. This is a precondition for their next task of completing the open or structured policy forms, which is designed to help participants identify with their roles in the simulation and practice decision-making. Individual study to prepare for discussions with teammates reduces the risk of free riders and the frustration they trigger for active teammates.

Participate in Policy Formation

Active participation in intrateam discussions is crucial for the success of the policy formation process and the simulation as a whole. Each team member has an individual responsibility to present and discuss relevant findings on the actor profile, values, goals, and policy plan. This means that every participant should initiate a dialogue with teammates and comment on their remarks. You should remind your students that the contents of these communications are just as important as the intensity of participation. In face-to-face simulations it is difficult to follow the contributions of each participant, but on social networks all conversations are available, even after the simulation ends, with the identity of the person who uploaded them and the exact time they were written.

During policy formation, each participant gets a chance to look at things from the point of view of others, such as opposition members, representatives of ethnic minorities within the team, or ideological rivals. Internal debates teach participants the importance of compromise and the difficulties of reaching a viable decision within a domestic context. The internal debate also indicates that turmoil and changes must be taken into account even as policy is planned.

Follow Instructions

Simulations develop through consecutive phases with preset dates, assignments, and activities for all participants. The schedule obliges all students to keep up with gradual learning and the preparation of assignments as the simulation proceeds, even if some participants miss a fixed deadline. Assignments that are handed in late become irrelevant because other participants who prepared them on time have already shared them with all teammates. When someone violates schedule deadlines, all the others are affected. Even when there is a real excuse for being late, the student who did not adhere to the collective timetable provides fewer inputs to the team's activities at the next stage of activity. Policy suggestions and choices that such students offer and share may be at odds with the knowledge other students had gained during solitary preparation.

Teamwork: Discuss and Decide

Teamwork during policy formation can be summarized by two core tasks: (1) discuss and decide and (2) formulate opening initiatives. At the start, teamwork involves the choice of a collective logo or a flag and a discussion of the main characteristics of the actor. The debate on the contents of a joint actor profile, values, goals, and policy plan transforms individuals with personal views into a team with a collective identity of a political or media actor. During policy discussions teammates should explicitly evaluate, comment, and argue with each other on their findings and suggestions. They should integrate several personal assignments into a single document that represents the team as a whole. This task requires participants to consider information provided by each teammate and choose the best formulation of facts for their collective documents. Sometimes the intrateam deliberations may result in true breakthroughs and give rise to absolutely new ideas that no one thought about during solitary learning.

As the policy formation process ends, each political team has to prepare initiatives in the form of short proposals with main points for interteam negotiations for world politics interactions. The formulation of such opening documents enables each team to highlight the main principles and issues it wants to address. When a team succeeds in drawing other teams to negotiate on its opening initiative, it often increases its chances to lead the talks and reach its goals.

Media teams must discuss several products they will publish during world politics and decide on their contents. They should plan a schedule for interviews, breaking news items, single article reports, op-eds, newspapers, and audio or video reports. The team also has to decide what to publish as their opening product at the beginning of that world politics round and what products they will add later with some adjustments during the breaking news session described in chapter 6. The preparation of high-quality media products during policy formation helps the media teams cope with the time pressure and reporting obligations that characterize intensive world politics interactions.

Summary

Policy formation is an essential part in simulations. It enables students to practice decision-making processes and illustrates how these processes may be affected by personal prejudices and group dynamics. It increases awareness of diversities and teaches that things that seem self-obvious to one may have many different interpretations. The policy formation process helps students to step into the shoes of others, sometimes even of enemies in real life, and try to find the most effective ways to maximize their goals. The incorporation of media requires students to plan media strategy and focus on public diplomacy, which is an inevitable part of international relations in the global information age. All these make the policy formation process a valuable learning exercise and an efficient pilot toward the world politics experience of intensive interactions between different actors.

This chapter explains the rationale for conducting policy formation activities even as the main purpose of the simulation is world politics. It then outlines the plan for policy formation by addressing simulation topic and the scenarios, rules, and activities of the policy formation process. To implement policy formation we offer a set of operational measures and procedures, such as preparing assignments for teams, observing students' progress, coaching them, and explaining instructions for participants. These instructions summarize the chapter from the point of view of your students based on four individual tasks: get familiar, study, participate in policy formation, and follow instructions, as well as a central teamwork undertaking to discuss all matters and decide on a collective plan.

Policy formation may last several weeks, depending on your choice. During this period participants build themselves as a team, create a collective identity, and formulate a cohesive policy toward political and media teams. At the end of the process, each team member should be able to represent the actor and implement its policy autonomously during intensive world politics encounters with other teams.

The policy formation process does not end with the beginning of world politics interactions. Some intrateam consultations continue as teammates brief each other on the ongoing negotiations. Yet the extreme pressure during the world politics process makes such intrateam contacts difficult and leaves only short breaks for team reassessment. Quality policy formation is crucial because it gives all participants enough time to create a solid basis for interactions with other teams.

CHAPTER 6

Playing World Politics

Intensive interactions among teams are the culminating point of world politics simulations. In communicating with others, state, nonstate, and media teams implement knowledge gained and consolidated from setup to policy formation in order to influence other actors in the conduct of world politics. With each team wishing to maximize gains for its actor, conflicts of interests are inevitable. Interactions between all actors, allies and adversaries alike, are needed to manage conflicts, avoid escalations, and find solutions if violence occurs. Such communication is the core component of diplomacy in world politics simulations.

In face-to-face simulations, the entire world politics process usually takes place during an on-campus encounter of several hours. In cyber and hybrid simulations, social networks overcome constraints of time and space and enable protracted interactions among teams. This makes it possible to organize several world politics rounds, face-to-face or online, or both, so participants can experience and practice diplomatic exchanges and international negotiations over a long time period. The optimal choice is to run the first round on social networks to get activities among teams started and as a pilot toward a face-to-face round on campus. This sequence maximizes the benefits of virtual and physical platforms and lets you and your students enjoy the benefits of both high-tech and human experiences.

This chapter describes world politics interactions among teams and suggests how to enhance them with hybrid learning on social networks. First, the chapter addresses the options for a plan of world politics encounters. Second, the chapter details core procedures that are essential for an efficient flow of the world politics process.

The chapter ends with a concise outline of instructions for simulation participants and pays special attention to the different roles of political and media teams.

World Politics Plan

The *plan* for the world politics encounter is the heart and soul of a simulation. It builds upon and follows earlier developments described in chapters 4 and 5 on implementation. During setup and policy formation you have already decided on the simulation type, topic, teams, rules, assignments, and initial scenario. Now you need to decide on four core inputs to set the simulation in motion and guide its course: the opening scenario, ad-hoc events, the process of world politics, and the schedule.

Opening Scenario

A simulation scenario presents activity triggers for all teams and is designed to catalyze intensive communications among participants. In chapter 5 we have addressed several criteria of a good scenario, described various format options, and suggested efficient ways to present it to your students. We also explained why there is a need for an initial and an opening scenario. The *initial scenario* marks the beginning of the policy formation process, describes changes that characterize a precrisis situation, or is an opportunity with a moderate challenge for all teams. It leaves ample space for dialogue between teammates and sufficient time for the practice of decision-making. The latter, an *opening scenario* of world politics, marks the onset of a crisis situation or a drastic change coupled with diplomatic opportunities and an extreme challenge that requires hard choices. Such situations are at the heart of this chapter.

An *opening scenario* of world politics presents an acute crisis situation designed to spark immediate reactions by teams and interactions between them. It introduces (1) a sudden and major change to create an atmosphere of urgency and draw attention; (2) severe gravity of threat or a striking challenge to mobilize teammates to act as a single unit in order to defend and promote their team values, goals, and plans. Situations of threat and challenge signal an opportunity for a diplomatic turning point. This is true whether or not the scenario hints at the dangers of escalation or involves an option to move toward dramatic agreement and increased cooperation among some or all teams; (3) high time-pressure to urge teams to react quickly and to act intensively; and (4) high uncertainty to motivate all teams to communicate with each other and with the media in order to acquire more information about the situation.

All four elements together pit the teams against each other, even as they struggle to transform the dramatic changes in the scenario into assets for their own actor and to settle disagreements in a diplomatic mode. A good opening scenario presents a major turning point that can change the course of events. It could signal a unique opportunity for an agreement or a grave deterioration with prospects for major escalation, even to the brink of war. For instance, the 1977 announcement by the Egyptian president Anwar el-Sadat of his intention to come to Jerusalem created an outstanding offer for peace between long-time rivals, but if it failed, it could also lead to further worsening of the conflict between Egypt and Israel. Some even thought that the initiative was a deception, meant to gain time in preparation for violence, like the 1973 surprise attack against Israel. Another example is the 2011 International Atomic Energy Agency (IAEA) report on the Iranian activities toward the development of nuclear weapons that could trigger a preventive Israeli airstrike and lead to all-out war. When we used this case in the opening scenario of our simulation, it challenged all teams, including Israel and Iran, to seek alternatives that would preserve international stability in the Gulf and beyond.

To enhance the feeling of real challenge and an impending sense of crisis, you can use several formats, like an official invitation to attend a UN Security Council meeting or a newspaper front page, discussed in chapter 5. By using special formats rather than a simple text, you

add theatrical atmosphere and help your students enter the simulation stage. It is also helpful to enrich the text of the opening scenario with official logos and emblems, to add pictures of decision-makers and photographs of core events, and to incorporate graphic illustrations and maps.

A good opening scenario should enable teams to implement their policy plans. For this, it should purposely leave space for initiatives and proposals that were brewing during the intrateam discussions. You may choose to integrate several points from each team's proposal and present it as a plan for mediation by a third party offered in the opening scenario. If you find that the teams' plans are overwhelmed with military options, the opening scenario can contain a military action that had just taken place and lead the teams to engage in coercive or constructive diplomacy of a "day after" the violence. This type of scenario can reflect students' choices and at the same time preserve the diplomatic nature of the simulation. We illustrate these and other options in several examples of opening scenarios.

A wide range of triggers, like those noted in chapter 5 for policy formation, can stimulate teams to react immediately and communicate intensively: (1) diplomatic moves, negative such as an abrupt cancellation of long-standing agreements and an ultimatum, or positive such as an offer of a peace plan, a mediation proposal, a summit meeting, or an alliance proposal; (2) economic measures such as a decision on or cancellation of sanctions, a dramatic fall of world's major stock markets, a meaningful change in trade agreements, an unexpected economic pact among actors, or a decision on new economic regimes; (3) environmental hazards and natural disasters, such as a tsunami, earthquake, or outbreak of an epidemic, which are likely to trigger direct contacts even between vicious rivals; (4) hostile acts related to civil wars and terror, such as the takeover of a strategic or symbolic stronghold by rebels or government forces, hostage-taking events and terror strikes, especially outside the target country, so many parties are forced to confront its consequences; (5) nonviolent military moves such as the deployment or withdrawal of peace forces, a change in their mandate or composition, movement of military forces, or a blockade; (6) confined violence, such as isolated airstrikes and escalations short of war, with which teams have to cope to avoid the brink of war by diplomatic measures; and (7) massive violence that has just ended, to set the stage for a "day after" simulation designed to deal with defining a new status quo and a working relationship between warring parties after violence ceases. These and related triggers indicate step-level change from a routine state of affairs or a precrisis situation presented in the initial scenario and create an atmosphere of emergency, with grave threats, high time-pressure, and extreme uncertainty, that drives teams to interact with each other.

Any opening scenario, especially those describing violent escalations, such as brutal civil war massacres, the takeover of a significant stronghold by rebels, or military retaliations to terror, should direct participants of political actors toward diplomatic talks. For this to happen the scenario should explicitly address the need for diplomacy among teams and schedule a date for an international event at the time the world politics round opens. It is also useful to offer a few points for discussion in the scenario so students can focus on similar topics as they revise their plans for world politics. Even if the simulation narrative is nonmilitary in type, such as a natural disaster, an economic crisis, or an integration offer between states, a turning point event in the opening scenario is necessary to create a tense, urgent, and acute atmosphere. These situations usually motivate teams to reach a compromise. In the course of such extreme events the participants can understand how difficult but still important it is to use diplomacy in world politics, to take advantage of opportunities, and to prevent escalation to violence.

To illustrate several story lines and formats of opening scenarios and to show the wide range of possibilities you have, we present examples from our own simulations. Each opening scenario builds on previous developments contained in the narrative of the initial scenario, discussed in chapter 5. You can adopt ideas from these stories for the simulations you plan or develop new ones that serve your curriculum and learning goals.

In the 2008 Russia-Georgia conflict simulation, each of the political teams—Russia, the United States, Georgia, and the European Union—prepared a three-point plan for the reduction of tensions in the Caucasus region. To maximize the participants' role in constructing the story of the simulation, we integrated the best points from each team's plan into a six-point French mediation proposal as an opening scenario, as illustrated in figure 6.1. We took into account that both Russia and Georgia considered military tools as a second-best alternative, so military triggers in the form of a limited airstrike also appeared in the scenario to lower the chances of all-out war by highlighting the dangers of escalation.

The missile strike in this scenario was designed to set the agenda for diplomatic talks set for 8:00 p.m. Saturday evening, when the synchronous world politics round was to begin. Together with the offers for mediation and warnings against further violence, it was designed to com-

---

From the Office of the European Union President

At least ten Georgian soldiers and three Russian citizens were killed last night in a missile attack in the separatist region of South Ossetia, close to a Georgian military base. The European Union condemns the attack and criticizes the biased media reports about the incident that could incite further provocations.

The European Union is concerned about US statements in support of Georgia and the commitment to back its ally in case of a Russian attack.

The European Union is also aware of a conflicting statement by an anonymous US official, who warned that America would not support Georgia if it decides to retaliate against Russia.

The European Union calls all parties to refrain from violence and schedules a summit meeting for 8:00 PM Saturday evening. It welcomes the Russian agreement to participate. It also extends an invitation to the US so as to meet the Georgian request that the US co-chair the negotiation.

To prevent further escalation the European Union offers a six-point plan:

1. Georgia and Russia will refrain from any use of violence against each other.
2. Georgia and Russia, jointly, will investigate the events related to the missile strike and offer measures to prevent attacks in the future.
3. Both sides will cooperate to prevent separatist violence in South Ossetia.
4. Both sides will coordinate preparations for an immediate referendum on the future status of South Ossetia.
5. The Russian Federation will immediately reduce the number of Russian peacekeepers in South Ossetia.
6. Georgia will postpone its plans to join NATO.

Fig. 6.1. Scenario format: French mediation plan

---

pel all actors to join the negotiations. The unidentified attack was purposively described in order to add uncertainty and leave ample space for creative initiatives to restore stability. The detailed mediation plan touched upon the core stakes of all actors to shape the dialogue between them. At the end of the scenario we added some preliminary demands that would have to be met before the meeting could happen, to make compromise a bit harder so as to highlight trade-offs. In reaction to this opening scenario, all actors tried to bypass the risk of tit-for-tat

---

February 5, 2012

Middle East Tribune

DEAD AND INJURED FROM GAZA ROCKET

Jerusalem: 3 Israeli were killed and 10 wounded yesterday in a rocket attack from Gaza. US secretary of state Clinton met Israeli foreign minister Lieberman and expressed her deep concern. She urged restraint on both sides on the eve of the forthcoming Israeli-Palestinian talks in Washington.

Unofficial US sources: major topics for the coming Israeli-Palestinian talks

1. Immediate 6 months cease fire (HUDNA) between all parties.
2. All Palestinian factions will disarm, and Hamas will be the only military power in Gaza.
3. Israel will enforce a complete freeze on the settlements in the contested territories.
4. The Palestinians will cease their anti Israeli propaganda campaign.

US TO DEFEND ISRAEL FROM IRANIAN MISSILES

Israeli sources in Washington: "What is on the table in the nuclear talks with Livni in the US?"

1. Early Israeli notification to the US before an attack on Iran.
2. US will offer its support to Israeli or Iranian moves.
3. US will immediately post anti-missile defense systems and personnel to defend Israel.
4. US will support the nuclear free zone initiative.

Israeli Leader Heads for Nuclear Talks in DC

Israeli opposition leader Livni and US officials will hold talks on the nuclear free initiative. Before leaving for Washington Livni announced that her activities are fully coordinated with the Israeli government.

Fig. 6.2. Scenario format: *Middle East Tribune,* February 2012

---

counterstrikes that could escalate to war and opted for a diplomatic solution.

In the Middle East simulation, the opening scenario offered two plans for a summit in Washington, one on Israeli-Palestinian issues and the other on Israeli-U.S. coordination regarding a nuclear Iran. During policy formation we noticed that Israel has taken a much softer stand than in the real world, so we added details on a fatal rocket strike at Israel from Gaza to remind all participants that all negotiated accords must contain operational safeguards against provocative violations.

The opening scenario, illustrated in figure 6.2, for a simulation among ISA scholars combined terror and diplomacy to spark an emotional debate and a strenuous negotiation process. Presented in the form of a breaking news publication, it involved high uncertainty, questions of trustworthiness between rivals, and concerns regarding fragile diplomatic solutions. Under severe threat and extreme time pressure it challenged the teams to take risks or face deadlock. In reaction to this scenario, an acute crisis developed, which almost led to the collapse of negotiations on both issues, but eventually resulted in groundbreaking initiatives and the signing of historic accords.

In another example for a simulation among students on the Arab-Israel conflict in 2012, we emphasized the complexities of a turbulent Middle East politics by coupling three invitations all at once, each by a different initiator on a specific issue of contention. This opening scenario, illustrated in figure 6.3, was designed to have students work in three separate working groups. Each invitation required a particular actor to prepare a short opening document for discussion with others.

These invitations described acute military events between states and nonstate actors and hinted at the dangerous consequences of spillover from regional to global confrontations. All invitations, from U.S., UN, and Arab League leaders, emphasized grave stakes to compel actors to join the talks. The request for an opening document intentionally left space for creative initiatives and decisions on the specifics of the negotiation agenda. In reaction to these invitations all parties joined the diplomatic process in an attempt to reach working solutions on each of the contentious issues and prepared opening documents as requested in the scenario.

In the 2013 simulation on the Iranian quest for nuclear weapons, the opening scenario, like the initial one, took

Multilateral Negotiation Invitations, November 2012

First Invitation, Washington

Given the recent escalation between Hamas and Israel and fragile ceasefire between them, President Barack Obama invites all parties to an urgent meeting of the Gaza working group, on November 28, at 11:00 PM, US EST.

The President requests that Jerusalem submit a six-point document to which Russia, the Arab countries, the Palestinians and the European Union will respond as the negotiations begin.

Second Invitation, New York

UN secretary general Ban Ki-moon invites all UN members to an emergency UN working group meeting in New York on November 28, at 11:00 PM, US EST.

The parties will discuss the Palestinian request for full UN membership and their quest for independence.

Secretary Ban asks the representative of Jordan to prepare a six clause draft that will guide the session.

Third Invitation, Cairo

In light of the deadly terror attacks in Lebanon, Arab League Secretary General Nabil Elaraby calls for an emergency meeting of the Lebanon and Syria working group in Cairo on November 28, at 11:00 PM, US EST.

In the two massive explosions in Beirut yesterday, ten American tourists, an unknown number of Russian citizens and a senior Syrian intelligence officer were killed. The Arab League sends condolences to the US, Russia and Syria. The secretary general rejects the Israeli and European allegations that Hezbollah and Iran were behind the attacks.

The meeting, to which the Quartet members are also invited, will deal with terror-driven escalations in Lebanon and Syria. Elaraby requests the Quartet and Lebanon, each separately, to submit six-point proposals on ways to stabilize the tense situation.

Fig. 6.3. Scenario format: Multilateral negotiation invitations

the form of an official Israeli news release and deliberately highlighted the Israeli point of view. This opening scenario, illustrated in figure 6.4, confronted all actors with the possibility of an impending agreement that overlooked some core interests of the adversaries and could lead to countermeasures, even violence and war. It described an opportunity to settle the long-standing nuclear issue that involved high stress for all actors who were uncertain of Iranian credibility. The conditional Israeli

willingness to join the negotiations, a fiction element at the time of the scenario, was designed to make the rivals aware that, if a viable accord is the aim, regional actors who were left outside the negotiation process must also be taken into account. In reaction to this opening scenario, all teams addressed major dilemmas real leaders face when they need to coordinate conflicting interests between multiple actors. It made participants realize that risk-taking, openness, and compromise are essential to prevent radicalization of foes and at the same time to preserve good relations between allies.

When you design a simulation with several rounds of world politics, an opening scenario for each one of them is necessary, with an introduction of new developments. Just like the first opening scenario, each additional scenario builds upon events from the previous round with some step-level change, a new challenge, threats, time pressure, and uncertainty for all actors. For example, if the first round ended with stalemate, you may introduce a dramatic mediation proposal to foster communications. Conversely, if teams reached an agreement in the first round, you may add a mass-casualty terror attack, which challenges the agreement and calls upon the teams to confirm their mutual commitments.

The opening scenario can be presented shortly before world politics interactions begin or immediately as they start. To publicize the opening scenario, in cyber and face-

Official Israeli News Release, June 15, 2013

Israel is determined to clarify its positions on the Iranian nuclear program, in light of the forthcoming talks scheduled for next week in Geneva and the uncertainties regarding the French position.

Israel disagrees with US President Barak Obama, who sees the Iranian initiative as a promising turning point to solve the nuclear issue without use of military force.

Israel rejects the idea that all military intervention would be postponed as long as negotiations take place. It warns that it will act independently if necessary.

Israel promises to come to the negotiation table if it receives serious indications from the European Union or the US regarding an Iranian willingness to compromise.

Israeli diplomats called on Russian President Vladimir Putin to intervene immediately and convince Iran to accept international observers to monitor its nuclear sites.

Israel threatens to disclose intelligence information on Iranian military facilities to the media if the diplomatic negotiations end in deadlock.

Fig. 6.4. Scenario format: Second Israeli news release

to-face simulations alike, you may use online tools, such as the simulation website, the social network, and e-mail. In addition, you can distribute it on paper to the heads of teams as the face-to-face simulation starts and screen it up front as the world politics round begins.

The opening scenario enables you to shape the direction of events before each world politics round you conduct. But what if you want to direct activities that take place during the rounds? The best way to intervene without disrupting the ongoing flow of interactions is by introducing ad-hoc events, which are like mini scenarios that you had prepared in advance for insertion when deadlock or agreement are immanent or when you want to change the course of events.

Ad-Hoc Events

Planning ad-hoc events for world politics rounds can help you manage the pace and direction of ongoing interactions among teams. By an *ad-hoc event* we mean a new development that is presented to participants after the publication of the opening scenario. The introduction of ad-hoc events during negotiations is especially useful in case of deadlock, when the new information creates a common theme for talks and brings about new offers and fresh initiatives. Alternatively, when teams are ready to compromise everything simply in order to quickly reach an agreement, an ad-hoc event, especially a hostile action, can force participants to reconsider their offers and willingness to compromise.

It is preferable to frame ad-hoc events as news flashes to mask your direct intervention in activities among teams. Most of our simulations on current world politics in Middle East region contained some of the ad-hoc events presented in figure 6.5.

We presented these news flashes at different points of the world politics rounds to challenge the sincerity of the talks that were taking place and to test the attention span of the leaders who were deeply involved in strenuous negotiations. In times of stalemate, ad-hoc events accelerated the pace of interactions among teams by the introduction of new topics. However, when intensive talks were taking place, teams often ignored most news flashes, with the exception of extreme ones like those on chemical, biological, and nuclear weapons. This means that during negotiations teams chose which events require immediate reaction and set the unimportant ones aside.

Ad-hoc events can also be used to direct negotiators toward specific issues, such as refugees, weapons, borders, internal instability, and other topics relevant to your cur-

Gaza: Iranian intelligence reports indicate that non-conventional warheads have been smuggled from Sinai to Islamic Jihad militants, Hamas rivals, located near Rafah.

Cairo: Last night security forces in Egypt arrested five major opposition leaders, their whereabouts are unknown.

Jerusalem: A noon explosion in an open air market in the capital has left ten people dead and thirty severely injured. Israeli police have arrested two Arab at the scene.

Jerusalem: the Israeli secret service arrested ten Israeli Arabs, alleged members of a Muslim Brotherhood terror network in Nazareth.

The West Bank: According to Palestinian sources, an Israeli was kidnapped early this morning, but as of now Israel still remains silent on the issue.

Moscow: A Russian delegation of nuclear scientists has arrived this morning in Tehran for an unscheduled visit.

Washington: On a nationwide broadcast at 11:00 PM US President Obama announced that he will offer a 'New Deal' to Iran in exchange for a freeze in their nuclear program.

Washington: A White House spokesman confirmed that in ten minutes President Obama will present his new 'Roadmap for Palestine' at the UN general assembly.

Amman: Upon his arrival in the Jordanian capital, for security and counter-terrorism talks with King Abdallah, Prime Minister Netanyahu's car was fired upon by unknown assailants. The car raced to a nearby military compound with a Jordanian army escort; casualties, if any, are unknown.

Damascus: Alleged CIA agents were brought to court this morning on charges of smuggling weapons and equipment to anti-government rebels and training them to use advanced transmission methods.

Beirut: Future Party sources claim that an unmarked convoy of non-conventional weapons crossed the border between Lebanon and Syria just before sunrise.

Riyadh: The Saudi Arabian radio announced the arrest of ten foreign reporters on charges of espionage.

Fig. 6.5. Ad-hoc news flashes

riculum. But the contents of such events must be brief and very challenging to capture the attention of leaders and drive them to react.

Once you have prepared the opening scenario and ad-hoc events you are ready to begin the most intensive, exciting, and important part of any world politics simulation.

The Process of World Politics

Many rapid action-reaction exchanges between all teams, including states, nonstate actors, international organizations, and media teams, build the *process* of world politics. It begins after you present an opening scenario and your students briefly adjust their team's policy plans according to the situation described in it. The simulation reaches its apex with one or several rounds of intensive synchronous interactions between all teams and ends with a conclusion of agreement or the formulation of a summary document on the disagreements among teams. This scheme is common for all world politics simulations suggested in this book: face-to-face, cyber, and hybrid.

In face-to-face simulations the entire world politics process takes place in a physical setting on campus. You present an opening scenario in class when all participants gather together during a lecture before the interteam meeting or just at its beginning. Teammates must stay close, so they can quickly and covertly coordinate their immediate reactions to the opening scenario and jointly adjust policy plans. Then, intensive encounters among teams begin, when representatives of different actors sit together in the meeting room and talk to each other. These face-to-face interactions involve multiple forms of communication, when teams present their positions and react to initiatives and arguments by others with words and with vocal intonations, facial expressions, and body language. At the end of the world politics process, all participants must jointly formulate a text of agreements and disagreements, as they are unlikely to have a second chance to do this after the face-to-face meeting ends.

In cyber simulations the entire world politics process takes place on a virtual platform. You present an opening scenario on the simulation website, upload it on the social network, or send it by e-mail on a date you choose, regardless of your lecture slot. Teammates can easily access the opening scenario online and adjust their teams' policy asynchronously within their closed groups on social networks. Each team member should react to the opening scenario by posting messages at any convenient time without the need to meet teammates in person. Intensive interteam encounters begin when all participants meet in a joint group open for all participants on the network at

a scheduled time. This is when all students synchronously communicate by writing messages and posting comments. To attend these meetings, there is no need to change physical locations; any team representative can join the network from any place through various electronic devices with Internet connection. If teams were unable to reach an agreement or formulate a document of disagreement during the time of intensive negotiations, the use of a virtual platform enables you to extend the time frame and allow participants to finalize all documents asynchronously after the end of the synchronous meeting.

You can also integrate both platforms to take advantage of the flexibility introduced by social networks and the human touch embedded in face-to-face encounters. One option is to present the opening scenario online but have the rest of world politics process in a face-to-face manner. Another option is to use the social network for publication of the opening scenario and for asynchronous communications between teammates before the face-to-face meeting, so when participants gather in class they can immediately begin interteam engagements. In a third option, you can further extend the salience of social networks and ask students to negotiate online, leaving only the final aspects related to the formulation of an agreement and handshake ceremony to the face-to-face meeting. These different options are examples of how you can enhance face-to-face simulations with cyber tools and social networks with different weight and points of time during the world politics process.

In all simulations genres, teams interact with their allies and foes and use a variety of policy means, short of war, to defend and promote their values and goals. Political teams may (1) initiate diplomatic moves, participate in negotiations, offer to serve as mediators, suggest topics for discussions, and draft, challenge, accept, sign, reject or modify diplomatic offers, treaties, alliance proposals, or peace plans; (2) grant or halt economic, humanitarian, or military aid; (3) threaten to use violence or other forms of coercive diplomacy, issue an ultimatum, declare a state of emergency or high alert, move forces or order military buildups; and (4) engage in limited violence short of war.

The use of violence requires the team to ask for your permission, as noted in chapter 5 with regard to the simulation rules. In such cases you first instruct participants to consider nonviolent alternatives in order to preserve the diplomatic nature of the simulation. You should also immediately weigh the impact of violence on the process of world politics. Sometimes you may authorize limited violence if it fits the unfolding narrative and your goals, as detailed in the appendix on the Gulf nuclear simulation.

When it comes to the conclusion of an agreement or to

the formulation of a document on disagreements, the precise wording becomes the core topic of negotiations. To persuade the other side to accept one's version, a team can use all policy tools short of war, but teams quickly realize that without mutual compromise it would be impossible to reach an agreement.

World politics also involve interactions between political and media teams. These interactions take place parallel to diplomatic and other encounters and during the breaking news session. To promote public diplomacy campaigns, build a positive image for their team, and set the news agenda, spokespersons of political teams can address the media teams by (1) publication of press releases with official positions on certain issues; (2) interviews with media professionals; (3) reaction to media publications by approving, criticizing, or rejecting reports; and (4) circulation of spin and leaking information to the media.

A press release publicizes official positions and viewpoints of the actor and increases its chances to shape the flow of information available to others. The text of these releases is discussed by members of political teams during policy formation, but political leaders should be aware that they may be edited by media professionals to reflect the language, goals, and agenda of the media organ. With regard to interviews, all political actors should prepare for their meeting with a press representative, request to get some core questions ahead of time, and remember to share some information but keep the teams strategy secret.

Political teams should follow media publications closely, react when needed, and try to avoid manipulation by the media or by other actors who use the media as a tool to advance their own policy. They may impose censorship or use other impeding techniques to restrict the flow of information to the media, as a form of "negative" media strategy characteristic of nondemocratic actors or even democracies in time of crisis. The information that an actor wants to share with the media should be carefully formulated, with a choice of suitable sound bites to fit the targeted audience and the media organ orientation, for example, Western, Arabic, international, economic, religious, and so forth. Once the information is sent to the media, it spreads throughout the simulation arena, whether it is accurate or not.

Media teams become influential actors in world politics when they set the simulation agenda and shape the activity between political teams. Media teams should cover simulation developments by regular publication of media products, framed as short but salient breaking news items, with sensational facts, colorful sound bites, and emotional pictures. Media reporters should maintain ongoing contacts with political actors to get exclusive press releases, timely interviews with high-ranking leaders, and provocative leaks, just like media professionals in the real world.

Media products may take the form of a short report, a front page, a news bulletin, a full newspaper, or a video clip. All these items can be prepared during policy formation, adjusted to the developments between actors and published during the world politics round, preferably in the breaking news session when the simulation stage belongs exclusively to the media. The media teams can get immediate feedback, high rating, and positive evaluations of their work during this session, indicated by applause in a face-to-face setting or by comments and frequent "*likes*" to the media products on Facebook.

Media products add an authentic atmosphere to the world politics process, elevate the students' understanding of the links between the media and the political world, and enhance the learning experience of all participants. They add considerably to the development of critical thinking skills and empathy because they offer multiple perspectives, often very different from those discussed by teammates in the formulation of policy.

The synchronous rounds of world politics may take place is several formats: (1) One or more working group(s) that focuses on a specific issue raised in the scenario, for example a single working group designed to coordinate measures toward an immediate referendum on the future status of South Ossetia or three working groups designed to solve the humanitarian crisis in Gaza, decide on the borders between Israel and Palestine, and coordinate security measures between the two states. By use of several working groups you can let students negotiate in small groups and focus on specific aspects in great detail; (2) an international conference, with a designated chair or mediator, in which all parties participate, with or without a media presence. You may design an open conference with media participation like the opening or conclusion of the talks between Iran and a group of six world powers including the United States in the fall of 2013, or closed to the media like the Camp David peace process; (3) bilateral negotiations, like the 1969 U.S.-USSR Strategic Arms Limitation Talks or the 2009 U.S.-Russia talks on disarmament; (4) a news conference at the conclusion of an international agreement in which leaders offer opening speeches and address questions from the media; (5) an international organization assembly to vote on a resolution, like the Arab League decision to request that the UN Security Council impose a no-fly zone in Libya in March 2011 or the UN General Assembly vote on granting the Palestinians observer status in November 2012; (6) a session at the International Court of Justice handling war

General Assembly of the United Nations

67th regular session of the General Assembly

All members of the United Nations are represented in the General Assembly. Each nation, rich or poor, large or small, has one vote

Work Program of the 67ᵗʰ Session

10:00 – Opening speeches
10:30 – Multilateral negotiations in working groups, 1ˢᵗ session
11:15 – Coffee break
11:30 – Media releases
11:45 – Multilateral negotiations in working groups, 2ⁿᵈ session
12:15 – Plenary meeting and vote on resolutions

Fig. 6.6. Gulf nuclear simulation schedule

crime cases with states and political leaders testifying; and (7) ad-hoc summits for coordination in cases of terror attacks, hostage takings, natural disasters, or environmental hazards.

Examples from past face-to-face, cyber, and hybrid simulations we have conducted illustrate the many options you and your students have in shaping the process of world politics.

Process in a Face-to-Face Simulation

The Gulf nuclear simulation took place during a half-day face-to-face meeting. It was designed as a multitopic diplomatic simulation primarily on the Iran nuclear program but also on the Palestinian issue and other current affairs in Middle East politics. The simulation opening announcement and work plan, illustrated in figure 6.6, was presented to teams in class at the beginning of the face-to-face meeting. Once the world politics process began, we took a step backward and students became the main driving force.

The UN General Assembly session on the Gulf nuclear issue began with opening speeches, prepared ahead of time by representatives of each team. The media attended the session but did not participate in its discussions. Some speakers were better than others, but given the short time assigned for each participant, the stage was immediately set for multilateral negotiations on the key matters that each team had placed on the agenda.

After the official gathering and opening speeches, multilateral negotiations took place in the Gulf nuclear and Palestinian working groups. Participants in each group

had to prepare a short document of agreement on three major points we had set in the opening scenario. The goal of reaching an agreement, despite the gaps in national interests and under extreme time pressure, was designed to capture the essence of crisis decision-making in world politics.

During synchronous face-to-face interactions, bilateral secret talks behind the scenes were coupled with formal multilateral negotiations that were open to the media. A notable example of the secret activities was a move made by the U.S. president who asked the Egyptian president to meet outside the negotiation room once the talks had reached a deadlock. A few minutes later, both players were back at the negotiation table with the Egyptian leader cooperating more closely with the United States. As it later became evident, the Egyptian team was promised specific rewards for their support of the American side. Another interesting example is the behind-the-scenes information the Israeli prime minister acquired about the Iranian plan to strike first through the diversionary use of a nonstate actor. This information was leaked by media reporters, showing the crucial role the media may play in shaping the process of world politics.

According to the simulation rules, both the Iranian and the Israeli leaders requested permission to use military force almost simultaneously and their requests were approved after the multilateral negotiation efforts had failed. Our consent to these requests shifted the topic of the simulation to the "day after" diplomacy, an interesting turning point that we had not planned. Amazingly, the two media teams had anticipated military strikes and the films they had prepared in advance blended well with the ad-hoc developments. The third hour-long session of world politics began with the announcement of military strikes by Israel and Iran and a breaking news broadcast. The media teams had also conducted a few interviews during the negotiations, and these too were screened in the breaking news session.

The violent developments made the continuation of routine multilateral negotiations irrelevant. To meet the challenge of a new poststrike reality, we called an emergency UN Security Council meeting with all actors attending. All participants understood that the acute crisis situation required immediate reconsideration of values, goals, and plans. The spontaneous discussion that developed during the emergency meeting included reactions by each actor to the "day after" situation and dynamic deliberations between all of the teams on how to stabilize the situation. Only the Palestinian team remained aloof in the discussion, frustrated that their core interests were set aside due to the violent escalation between Israel and Iran. Participants from the Iranian and Russian teams decided to sit next to each other and coordinated their reactions. The same was done by members of the Israeli and the U.S. delegations. Though the Jordanian and Egyptian teams condemned all violence, they were subjected to intensive U.S. coercive diplomacy and in the end decided to support a U.S.-led resolution. During the entire emergency meeting, the UN secretary-general played a crucial role and creatively contributed to the postsimulation wrap-up session. This role was given to a student who spoke English fluently and used theatrical skills well on stage. With formal rhetoric, decisive intonations, determined facial expressions, and restrained body language by the secretary-general, the atmosphere was set for a genuine summit gathering to reach agreement and vote on the clauses of the emerging resolution. To bridge the gap between adversaries the UN secretary-general offered creative suggestions to sidestep deadlocks and urged the teams to vote on a document that was amended in real time during the concluding session as a provisional UN resolution. The world politics process ended with a vote and a short debriefing on the implications of all the events for the stability of a poststrike Middle East and Gulf region.

Process in a Cyber Simulation

In the Middle East simulation between ISA scholars, the process of world politics developed in a very different way and even led to an agreement on the nuclear issue. Two rounds of synchronous negotiations on Facebook were scheduled for confronting and resolving two main topics:

stability in the Gulf and the Palestinian quest for statehood. In the first round on the Gulf nuclear topic the situation mirrored the real world affairs between adversaries. A slow start of mutual accusations between Israel and Iran signaled to all parties that negotiations were deadlocked and fruitful results were not forthcoming. Events developed initially along the path we planned for the simulation in the opening scenario. However, during the interim break between synchronous rounds on Facebook, the political leaders in Iran debated the strategy of direct contacts with Israel, decided to propose secret negotiations to the Israeli foreign minister, and indicated that they were willing to make serious compromises, which eventually led to a breakthrough in the second round of world politics negotiations. Israel reciprocated with a risky decision of her own and agreed to join the back-channel we opened on Facebook to host secret negotiations. Both teams were truly apprehensive to see if their moves would lead to a breakthrough or end up exposed to the media as another spin in the protracted conflict. Once the negotiators built basic trust in the new approach, the remaining bulk of the second round of talks on Facebook contained a practical tone among negotiators, very different from that in the formal adjoining working group that was open to the media. So, while the media professionals were actively building up a "clash of civilizations" agenda between Israel and Iran, top decision-makers behind closed doors in "virtual rooms" were bridging gaps and implementing a mixed-motive bargaining reality.

At the same time, the participants involved in the negotiations on the Palestinian statehood issue were busy with the task of formulating an accord that would follow the idea of two-state solution to the conflict. Major developments here followed the track paved in the scenario but the specifics of the actual document were a result of heated confrontations and nerve-wracking efforts to bypass critical stumbling blocks. Because both the Israeli and the Palestinian teams had built-in opposition players, with Fatah and Hamas factions representing the deep cleavage in the latter group, the road to compromise was not an easy one to travel. Overall, the negotiations on Facebook involved near collapse of the entire process, anger at one another, ineffective U.S. mediation efforts, frustration, and finally a deep sense of achievement, reward, and commitment to compromise when the accord was completed toward the end of the simulation. With some U.S. assistance to overcome core obstacles met during the negotiations, the Israeli and Palestinian rivals agreed on a four-point plan that contained the principles of the agreement and left the disagreements open for later negotiations.

In this simulation the *Global Crescent* was the only media actor, designed as an equivalent to *Aljazeera*, the major network in the Arab world. Like the real *Aljazeera*, the *Global Crescent* developed an "Arab-centric" orientation, used a language that was fit for portraying their agenda, and chose to highlight certain events over others. The *Global Crescent* reporters produced several original video clips, newspapers, and short breaking news posts in two synchronous rounds. The short media clips, headlines, and photos were a creative way to gain political leaders' attention and to shape news agenda. While the clips were placed as a link on Facebook to YouTube, the newspapers and breaking news were posted directly on the Facebook wall of the joint social network group where all participants met. The clips and written material reflected the diversity of media functions that can be used during reporting on simulation events: coverage, interpretation, mobilization, and heritage embedding, making players aware of the impact the media has and the need to plan their strategy toward the press and to keep in touch with the media professionals in order to gain soft power. Yet despite the considerable efforts of the media and their creative contributions to the unfolding events, the political teams found it hard to follow the news in real time, especially during intensive synchronous interactions. Moreover, when a real breakthrough occurred in the Israel-Iran secret back-channel, reporters still focused on the traditional tit-for-tat exchanges that took place in the formal negotiations, which were open to the media. Since no information on the back-channel was leaked to the media, they were utterly surprised with the Israel-Iran handshake that took place at the ISA panel in San Diego, representing a turning point and an entirely new agenda not predicted by the press.

Process in a Hybrid Simulation

The Palestinian statehood simulation took advantage of both physical and virtual platforms with two synchronous rounds among teams on Facebook, followed by a face-to-face meeting on campus as a third round. To host the international negotiations on a virtual platform, a joint Facebook group was created, visible to all simulation participants and only to them, as a closed group for educational purposes. It served as a place where all teams met to attain their goals and manage the conflict in the region. Communications were posted on the joint Facebook wall according to five relevant topics—terror, regional cooperation, Palestinian elections, mutual Israeli and Palestinian recognition, and public opinion debate—so that interactions can be easy to follow in a systematic manner.

Interactions also took place between political teams and media professionals and resulted in the publication of media products, such as video clips, photos, newspapers, and news flashes, and a discussion about them during a breaking news media session in the midst of the face-to-face round that concluded this hybrid simulation.

Intensive negotiations took place especially between Israeli and Palestinian teams with the United States active in all rounds in an attempt to promote a plan of Middle East Reform that was proposed by the U.S. president. The plan was debated intensively in the cyber rounds and made the U.S. team the major actor and important mediator in the simulation. This role continued and intensified later, in the face-to-face round, during a secret tripartite international summit. While the Americans demonstrated creativity, the Israeli and Palestinians teams were somewhat less flexible and found it hard to initiate moves beyond their traditional positions. During the cyber round they did not try out new political ideas or activities to solve the issues at stake. They only modified their attitudes in the face-to-face meeting, after intensive U.S. mediation.

The face-to-face round started with an opening ceremony, in which a representative of each team delivered a policy statement from the podium while the other teams and players watched from audience seats in the lecture hall. The familiarity gained by the previous rounds on Facebook made it quite easy to start intensive negotiations on all issues. After the ceremony, participants of all teams met to discuss issues and reach agreements. Negotiations took place in different parts of the huge hall and its surroundings. The atmosphere during the on-campus meeting became an important feature with real decor for the simulation, signs, flags, and costumes, as well as ethnocentric terminology, rhetoric, body language, gestures, and intonations, all contributing to a theatrical event with students deeply embedded in the roles they represented. A simulation cocktail for diplomats and media professionals that was prepared during the break between sessions added an informal hue to the intense bargaining that was going on. Some high-tech touches also contributed to this typical face-to-face setting, like continuous voluntary interactions on Facebook even during face-to-face talks and links to YouTube clips prepared by the media.

The scenario for the face-to-face round described contacts between Israeli and Palestinian leaders, talks between the United States and Israel, developments regarding Palestinian prisoners held by Israel, and a news flash about a missing Israeli soldier held in Gaza. The scenario was published in the format of a news items collection. The secret breakthrough tripartite summit between the United States, Israel, and the Palestinians culminated by a public conference in which the Palestinians, with tacit American approval, surprised Israel and declared statehood.

At the end of the negotiations all students reassembled in the hall for media updates and concluding speeches by team leaders. When the plenary conference was over, the Israeli prime minister claimed he had been deceived, not knowing that the U.S. president had supported the Palestinian move. This led to a heated debate and ended the simulation with a burst of misunderstandings and mutual accusations. The drama at the end of the face-to-face round indicated the depth of the learning process, which allowed the Palestinian team, played by Israeli students, to overcome major prejudices, express a better understanding of the enemy, and show some empathy when the Palestinian leader declared statehood.

Three media teams were active in the simulation, created as equivalents to real organs: (1) the *Global Times*, an international newspaper with a *CNN* ideology, (2) *Our Israel*, an Israeli newspaper, with strong ethnocentric perspective, and (3) the *Global Crescent*, an Arab news organization, inspired by the *Aljazeera* network. During all rounds of the simulation, cyber and face-to-face, all media teams covered simulation developments and competed with each other to publish exclusive items and at the same time to keep in touch with the political leaders and interview them. The formats developed for the cyber rounds involved breaking news, newspapers, and impressive video clips posted on YouTube. The media teams tried to keep up with their creative contributions during the face-to-face round but quickly discovered they were unable to draw attention at the height of the negotiation process. To prevent frustration, we dedicated a special time slot for a media conference that run "live" news and screened the newspapers, video clips, and other media products up front. However, the event took place parallel to the secret tripartite summit, so unfortunately the top decision-makers were not available, as often happens in real situations.

The Israeli and Palestinian reluctance to change could have been a true reflection of the realities in the region and the hardships of reaching an accord nowadays. But it also shows the added value of combining simulation rounds on social networks as a pilot for face-to-face negotiations. The fact that the cyber rounds ended in an impasse may have reflected inadequate negotiation experience at the early stages of the political process, so perhaps the breakthrough during face-to-face talks and the declaration of the Palestinian state were a result of better negotiation practices. This ending of the hybrid simulation symbolized that change in the regional politics of the Middle East could maybe take place and left all players with food for thought.

All these examples illustrate that the process of world politics in simulations evolves through a similar scheme. It is triggered by the opening scenario and requires teams to interact in order to conclude an agreement or otherwise reach the most favorable outcome possible for their actor. These examples also show that while face-to-face and cyber world politics encounters have unique advantages, each one of them can be supplemented by theatrical elements and creative media products to improve simulations and offer participants an exciting experience.

Schedule

Careful planning of the time element adds considerably to the success of the simulation experience, so schedule considerations should be part of your decisions on what type of simulation to run, how long it will last, and other aspects summarized in table 6.1. For the proper flow of all simulation processes it is essential to introduce the schedule to all teams before their interactions begin and to post it on the website, social network, or hall where interactions take place, to remind all players of time constraints for their activities.

In setting the schedule core decisions are needed on the (1) timing for presentation of the opening scenario, (2) number of sessions in each round of world politics, (3) timing and duration of the breaking news session, and (4) duration of the interim break between synchronous world politics rounds for policy readjustments and additional learning of empirical and theoretical topics related to the simulation.

In face-to-face simulations, the physical setting imposes spatial and temporal constraints and dictates reduced time for each session. It especially restricts the options of waging consecutive rounds separated in time from one another. This is usually true unless you run the simulation in your own classroom and during the time slot of your lecture. But face-to-face encounters usually last longer than a regular lesson, and you must give up some lectures in favor of simulation rounds. It is much better to schedule them for an intensive single-day meeting.

You can present the opening scenario at the beginning of the meeting when all participants gather together, like most face-to-face simulations do, or during the lecture before the meeting. In the former option, you leave too little time for reassessment of policy plans before the syn-

TABLE 6.1. Schedules for World Politics Interactions

Schedule Aspect	Plan 1: Face-to-Face	Plan 2: Cyber	Plan 3: Hybrid
Rationale for choice	Time for on-campus meetings is limited Preference for a face-to-face simulation	Consecutive rounds provide time and opportunity for progressive acquisition of knowledge, better practice, development of skills, and attainment of deeper understanding of the topics involved	An attempt to maximize the benefits of both cyber and face-to-face platforms to advance the learning experience of simulation participants Diverse consecutive rounds provide even more time and a variety of opportunities for progressive acquisition of knowledge, better practice, development of skills, and attainment of deeper understanding of the topics involved
Number of rounds	Single round	Two rounds The schedule is identical for each round	Three rounds: two on a cyber platform and one face-to-face The schedule for the cyber rounds is identical to plan 2 in the table The schedule for the face-to-face round is identical to plan 1 in the table
Duration of each synchronous round	Up to six hours	Two and a half hours	Cyber round: two and a half hours Face-to-face round: up to six hours
Duration of the interim break between rounds	A single round with no break	Two weeks or more	One month or more
Number of sessions within a single round	Two	Two	Two
Duration of break between sessions	Half an hour	Half an hour	Half an hour, for both cyber and face-to-face sessions
Duration of each session within the round	Two and a half hours	Two hours	Two hours for cyber rounds Two and a half hours for the face-to face round
Timing of breaking news session	After the first session	After the first session within each round	After the first session within each round
Duration of breaking news session	Half an hour	Half an hour	Half an hour

chronous world politics round begins. In the latter, there is a risk that the long interval between the lecture and the simulation date would erode the momentum of the new and surprising information contained in the opening scenario. But if you rely on supplementary cyber aids for your face-to-face simulation or run world politics rounds on social networks, you can free yourself and your students from the impact of physical constraints on schedule decisions and present the opening scenario online whenever you decide. Your students can access the scenario at any time that is convenient for them and revisit their

team's plans before they act in world politics. We suggest that you post the scenario on the website or social network and send it by e-mail two days before the world politics round begins, to preserve an enthusiastic mood for the start of diplomatic and other exchanges and still leave some time for readjustment of policy plans.

Though schedule considerations allow some flexibility, you need to take the duration of your course into account before you plan your simulation, as discussed in chapters 2 and 4. The duration of world politics sessions may vary from a couple of hours to several days, depending on your plan for a mix of asynchronous and synchronous interactions. Table 6.1 presents three alternative plans to illustrate the options you can choose from.

Plan 1 for face-to-face simulations usually includes a single round of world politics that is limited most times to your lecture slot or extends to a single-day event. Beyond that, it may be extremely difficult to coordinate a time that is convenient for all students. Yet, for a comprehensive face-to-face simulation, a short meeting during a lecture slot may be too intensive and restricting, especially if you integrate a breaking news session and if students want to enjoy the theatrical aspects of being dressed up in costumes and using symbolic artifacts to decorate the "territory" of their actor. Moreover, once they depart from formal learning, your students might find it difficult to return to regular classes immediately after the simulation. A preferable option is to schedule face-to-face encounters for a day when few other classes take place, if it all. In the Palestinian statehood simulation, for example, we had to find a time that was convenient for students from two different campuses. We scheduled the face-to-face meeting for Friday, a day with very few lectures on both campuses, and extended face-to-face sessions to five hours in total.

For us this was an optimal choice, but it entailed additional costs for transportation for students from one campus to the other, arranging a conference room on campus, the diplomatic cocktail we hosted during the break between sessions, and the use of a sound specialist to operate the audiovisual systems and Internet connections that supported the simulation event. Students had to give up leisure time or to rearrange work obligations in order to partake in this onetime event. In simulations on social networks, there are no time limits imposed by platform considerations or other costs for the duration of world politics sessions. Social networks are available 24/7, so you have the flexibility to decide on the duration of interactions among teams. However, bear in mind that even though social networks can perform for an unlimited time, humans cannot. It is unlikely that negotiations can proceed for an intensive synchronous session of more than two hours. If you want world politics to go on for several weeks it is unrealistic to expect intensive negotiations throughout the entire period. Asynchronous exchanges may replace synchronous ones, and the sense of an acute crisis atmosphere is likely to fade quickly.

Since interactions among teams are at the center of world politics, their duration is a core concern. In face-to-face simulations, it depends on the time slot you have

for an auditorium or simulation lab with several adjunct rooms, as well as on students' other classes that may overlap with the meeting time. In simulations on social networks you are less restricted by such considerations, especially if you plan the simulations for the early morning or late evening when no classes are taught. You must still avoid long and inconvenient time slots for synchronous rounds, to ensure an effective learning experience. We suggest splitting a world politics round into two consecutive sessions of about 45 minutes each with a 15-minute break between the sessions or a half-hour media session. The confined duration of each session encourages intensive student participation and forces them to focus on the most important issues. The second session improves students' performance, as more practice usually makes things more perfect.

Plan 2 outlines the optimal schedule for cyber simulations. To provide gradual learning and prolonged practice, as well as the momentum, intensity, and even stress that is characteristic of many situations in world politics, we find it useful to run several consecutive rounds with a break between them. In most of our simulations on social networks, each round lasts for two hours, which is enough time for students to negotiate and conclude an agreement. The pace of interactions on social networks is considerably faster than that in a face-to-face meeting. Participants can write simultaneously when they interact on social networks without interrupting each other, but when they all talk at the same time in face-to-face meetings they cannot hear one another or understand what the others have to say.

Some consideration is also needed on the exact time for synchronous world politics sessions on social networks. We usually chose late evenings after the students end their day on campus or their workday elsewhere. If you run simulations with colleagues across multiple time zones the choice of an appropriate time for the synchronous meeting may be more difficult, but given the relatively short two-hour time frame, we find that students are usually willing to cooperate and accommodate some inconveniences in exchange for a multicultural encounter with peers from a distance.

To maximize the benefits of face-to-face and cyber simulations, you can decide to adopt the scheme in *plan 3* and combine two different platforms for consecutive world politics rounds. This way you enhance your face-to-face simulation with two preceding rounds on the social network at very low cost. When students communicate on social networks, they act on a familiar and informal platform and can hide behind screens. Your supervision of negotiations is invisible for them for most of the time, and the students can feel a real partnership in the creation of the simulation reality and a deep responsibility for its success. When students practice interactions with other teams on the social network, they come much more prepared to the face-to-face round. Moreover, as an educator, you can considerably reduce the costs of consecutive world politics rounds if you move one or more of them to the social network platform.

We find that it is preferable to begin with rounds on social networks and end with a face-to-face round because the cyber rounds provide practice and act as a pilot for the human encounter during the face-to-face round that climaxes the simulation experience. With knowledge and practice creating an enriched atmosphere based on decor, costumes, body language, eye contact, vocal intonations, and other forms of communications, the face-to-face round is a good way to end the project and to get ready for debriefing and research as discussed in part III of this book. The human touch and theatrical setting always add to the "magic" of the simulation experience and its impact on learning effectiveness.

The *breaking news session* during a world politics simulation is devoted to the presentation of media products by the media teams. It is an important episode that provides the media teams with a prime time to publish or broadcast their work in the midst of negotiations, and it increases the awareness of the political teams of the role of the media in world politics. Later in this chapter we address different formats for the breaking news session, its rules, and the tasks of political and media teams during the session. Here we only refer to schedule considerations. The timing of the breaking news session is a schedule choice open for you to consider. We have learned that the best option is to split the world politics round into two sessions, and in between them to add the media session that enables teams to get new insights and multiple perspectives from media reporters as outsiders regarding the developments that have taken place while they were busy fulfilling their own world politics plans and engagements. Alternatively, you can postpone the breaking news session to the end of the simulation and still provide the media teams with time to present their products. Such a solution, we believe, is not as efficient as the timing in the midst of world politics activity because by then the political teams may be too worm out to closely concentrate on the contents of the media coverage. Moreover, earlier exposure leaves room to readjust the team's plan if important information for the actor is revealed by the media. Thus, for the simulation as a whole and for the benefit of political and media teams, it is wiser

to run the breaking news session about halfway through the world politics round.

One of the nine simulation rules discussed in chapter 5 concerns the need to enable media exposure. So as a basic simulation rule, during the breaking news session all interactions cease. This break gives teams some time to think, to reconsider their activities and options, even as they gain more information from the media. If, for example, a world politics round lasts for two hours, we introduce a half an hour breaking news session after the first hour. A longer time would reduce the media impact, risk the loss of the news value effect, and totally divert the students' attention from world politics to the media publications. In face-to-face simulations, the breaking news session is the only way media teams can gain sufficient attention from the decision-makers who are overwhelmed with the task of implementing their plans and promoting their goals, just as often happens in real-life situations. During the media session the editors and reporters present their products: video and audio clips, interviews, public opinion polls, and newspapers. In simulations on social networks, the media teams can publish their products online at any time, and teams, especially their media spokespersons, can study these products and update their leaders on information and new perspectives presented in these publications. This continuous flow of information from the media to the teams and back is hard to implement during intensive face-to-face encounters, and reporters may find themselves rather frustrated. The breaking news session is designed to overcome this problem, at least partially, giving media players in the simulation a time slot toward which they need to direct most of their efforts and even work under considerable pressure to be ready on time for the deadline with the most updated reporting as possible. Given the versatility in schedule options you can also use media groups on social networks to enhance a face-to-face round, either as open channel broadcasts or as updates screened up front during the breaking news session. Such incorporation of a cyber platform makes it easier for the media teams to get ready for their prime-time presentation and use the time allocated to them in the most effective manner.

The last schedule consideration you should take into account is the duration of the interim break between world politics rounds. The period may range from several days at one extreme to several months at the other, depending on your academic setting, discussed in chapter 2, and on the type of simulation you run—face-to-face, cyber, or hybrid, as discussed in chapter 4. The purpose of this interim break is to let teammates discuss and evaluate the outcomes of the first round of world politics, to reassess their policy, and to plan moves for the forthcoming round. To be efficient, the interim break should give students enough time for serious intrateam discussions and a reassessment of their activities in light of their achievements. But if it is too long then the momentum of the previous round and of the simulation as a whole is lost under the pressures of daily student obligations and other social activities. We find that an interim period of several weeks seems to be the best choice. In face-to-face simulations, the dates for consecutive rounds and the duration of the interim break are often affected by the lecture time slot, availability of a conference room, or a date free of other lectures the students need to attend. Unless you teach an entire course on the use of simulations, it might be extremely difficult to devote many lectures for the world politics encounters at the expense of teaching curriculum topics. An arrangement for a conference room for multiple rounds at separate times may lead students to feel overwhelmed and frustrated with a simulation that comes at the expense of their free time. You can easily overcome these constraints by moving some of the rounds to the social network, as described in plan 3, or give up the face-to-face simulation and run a cyber exercise as outlined in plan 2. Any way you decide, social networks come in handy to increase the time available for world politics processes, advance an effective breaking news session, and enable teammates to use the same platform to discuss and revise their policy.

After you have made all decisions related to the schedule for the world politics rounds, you need to make it known to all participants, preferably by posting the schedule on the simulation website and on the social network you use as a primary or supplementary platform for your simulation. Here, too, the social network is useful as each student can easily access the schedule at any time and from anywhere. In this respect, as in many others to which we point throughout the book, social networks and other cyber tools are likely to considerably enhance your simulation, face-to-face and cyber alike.

World Politics Procedures

Your role in the world politics process resembles that of a referee in a soccer match. You must carefully observe participants' performances, enforce simulation rules, keep track of the schedule, and make sure interactions follow the path you have paved. Like a referee who remains on the field over the entire game but should never kick the ball, you have to minimize your intervention and let the participants be the central players who shape the interaction process. But just like the referee on the field, your presence is necessary to ensure that if problems occur they are solved and all goes well.

In operational terms, we highlight eight core tasks designed to direct the interaction flow and guarantee its effective progress: (1) present the opening scenario; (2) declare the start and the end of each world politics round; (3) follow the interaction process closely; (4) encourage participants; (5) input ad-hoc events; (6) establish the breaking news session; (7) make sure participants adhere to the schedule and the rules; and (8) summarize participation for grading. Each of these tasks are explained below with an emphasis on how they affect the quality of face-to-face and cyber simulations.

Present the Opening Scenario

Your first task is to advertise the opening scenario to signal the transformation from intrateam policy formation to world politics interactions. It might be useful to remind participants a few days ahead of time about the approaching date for the publication, which was already scheduled as early as you have completed your setup preparations, described in chapter 4. The publication date is important for all teams as it is when new and highly relevant information will be revealed. Since information is power, the teams that study the scenario on time and complete their policy adjustments as early as possible can gain time and present better initiatives compared with others who are slower in this revision procedure.

In face-to-face simulations, the opening scenario can be presented to participants during the lecture that precedes the synchronous world politics meeting. It may be useful to devote that lecture or part of it to intrateam discussions. This will ensure that each team gets a chance to reassess and adjust its foreign policy plans to take into account the new developments. The virtual platform frees you and your students from the lecture slot constraint. Accessibility of social networks 24/7 enables you to upload an opening scenario online, on the website or on the social network, at any convenient time, and it increases the time available for individual participants of all teams to contribute in the final discussions before intensive cyber or face-to-face interactions begin with other teams.

Declare Start and End of Each World Politics Round

The declaration of the beginning and the end of the rounds may seem a technical matter to be made by announcement in face-to-face meetings or by posting a written message on the social network. But actually it is an important role of yours because it assures that you maintain order, control interactions, and keep some flexibility for unplanned developments. You must keep in mind that during quality simulations, all participants are engulfed in their activities, and most of them tend to lose track of time. So you not only declare the start time but should also remind players that time is running out and the session is coming to an end. You may decide to make team leaders aware of the time shortage a bit earlier than other participants to allow for final considerations regarding the last activities of the session or round. At times, you may decide to be flexible and add few minutes to a breaking news or negotiation session. A bit more time may allow rivals to reach a compromise or bypass deadlocks and make the simulation a success for all sides. Act with caution, however, and be aware that time changes may shift the balance of achievement among teams in the simulation, at the expense of one or the other team. More time may add too much pressure on participants who thought the end of the simulation had arrived, force teams to give in despite their inclination, and result in players who end the simulation feeling frustrated or even betrayed. So, remember to keep close track of time and make team members aware of it also. From the start, remind your students that you are an objective authority and the only one who indicates the beginning and end of the world politics sessions and rounds.

Follow the Interaction Process

To follow participants' interactions you need to look at and listen to debates among teams in a face-to-face meeting or read the messages and watch video clips posted on social networks in a cyber meeting. When you take the role of an observer and let your students become the driving force in shaping the learning material, you can watch the "show" and enjoy the benefits of active learning. The intensive pace of exchanges among participants makes the follow-up task an exciting challenge as it demands that you stay attentive and watchful at all times to immediately identify arguments that may violate simulation rules, contradict assigned theoretical or methodological approaches, or be at odds with basic empirical details. The follow-up is an important task that helps you identify

problematic situations as early as possible and intervene in order to redirect interactions by ad-hoc events or brief remarks to diffuse tensions or clarify misunderstandings.

Encourage Participants

Positive feedback motivates participants. You are likely to increase participants' confidence and stimulate active and thoughtful involvement in negotiations when you show support and appraise (1) comprehensive theoretical implementation, (2) empirical accuracy, (3) creative ideas, and (4) sophisticated formulations. Such encouragement also signals that you constantly and carefully follow interactions among teams and evaluate all players. This is especially essential because the motivation and contribution of students is never identical. Those who really invest more should get immediate recognition and those who bandwagon at the expense of others should be carefully reminded to be more active in order to gain a better status in their team and a more effective learning experience.

But even positive feedback may become counterproductive when it distracts participants from the ongoing process of world politics. Save your encouraging statements to the break between sessions and add a smile, applause, symbolic gestures, and body language in face-to-face encounters. In cyber meetings, one of the most popular Facebook settings, the "like" function, provides immediate encouragement while negotiations unfold. Each message on the Facebook wall may receive a "like" from any person involved in simulation. When you click on the "like" button, you express positive feedback to the player who wrote the message and encourage other participants to do the same, all without disturbing negotiations. Other digital tools substitute the human touch with icons of a smile, applause, and symbolic gestures that may be effective in signaling your approval of activities, initiatives, and media products.

Input Ad-Hoc Events

During the entire world politics round, you should act from a background position and minimize direct intervention. However, there are occasions when you must redirect the flow of events. If there is a deadlock in talks, for instance, or if the conflict gets too intense and at times offensive, you must step in to help the parties overcome difficulties and make progress. The input of ad-hoc events, described at the beginning of this chapter, lets you lead from behind and shape the course of the simulation flow without breaking the theatrical setting.

In face-to-face simulations, it is useful to screen ad-hoc

events up front with a projector, though you may also distribute printed versions of the additions you introduce, so participants may read them carefully. In simulations on social networks, it is easy to copy and paste the text of ad-hoc events you have prepared in advance to the social network, as a new message or as a comment to existing deliberations among teams. The addition of provocative photos is especially useful to catch the attention of participants that are in the midst of negotiations. Make sure the additions are brief and sometimes repeat them if you really want to make sure they are noticed by simulation participants who are busy interacting with one another.

Establish a Breaking News Session

The fast pace of exchanges during synchronous rounds makes it difficult to follow the media reports in real time, especially for the leaders of political teams who take an active part in diplomatic talks. A formal breaking news session gives the media teams a better opportunity to present their creative products and makes all participants more aware of the media's inputs.

Breaking news sessions can be arranged in different ways. In a face-to-face meeting media teams can use the main auditorium stage to (1) screen video clips, (2) announce breaking news, (3) show pictures of events from the simulation encounters, (4) report on developments, (5) host decision-makers for real-time interviews, and (6) distribute newspapers, or otherwise publicize their networks and its products. This way the media teams can reach all participants at once for a short period, because the prime time is allocated to all media teams who compete with one another.

Another option is to organize media "studios" at different parts of the conference room and let participants choose what station to watch or switch between studios during the break. In this case, each media team has more time for exposure, but can reach only the decision-makers that physically approach the studio.

In simulations on social networks the constraints of time and space diminish considerably. Different media teams can simultaneously use the same stage, such as a wall of a Facebook group, without interrupting one another. We suggest creating a separate group on social networks for media publications, parallel to the one where all interactions between political teams take place. In this group media teams can upload their products and summarize developments. In fact, this is the place where the media can broadcast video clips and post breaking news, photographs, and newspapers, just as they would do in a face-to-face meeting. Participants of political actors can

visit this group anytime in the midst of their activities. During the fixed time for a breaking news session all participants are instructed to discontinue their activities, watch the media products during prime time, and readjust their policies if needed.

To motivate teams to follow the breaking news session in a simulation of any type, you may prepare a few questions on the media products and its role in politics and let your students know they will have to address these questions at the end of the breaking news session. You may ask three general questions: (1) To what extent did you follow the media products and when did you do so? (2) In your opinion, to what extent was the media biased in its reporting? (3) To what extent do you feel the media enhanced your team's status and supported its policy? As detailed later in table 8.5, you can formulate these questions in a digital form or as a poll on social networks and use the information to assess the media-politics link during the debriefing session. These and related questions are designed to stimulate participants to follow media reports and increase their awareness of the media and its role in world politics. You may also add some questions on the media in the registration form, basic knowledge quiz and policy formation form, and repeat them after each round of world politics to assess change in the role of the media over time, as described in chapter 8.

Make Sure Participants Adhere to the Schedule and Rules

Simulation schedule and rules obligate students and educators alike. They were planned and presented in setup, published during policy formation, and should remain intact over the entire world politics process in all rounds and simulation types. It is important to adhere to the original schedule and rules and to verify that all teams and students do the same. With regards to the schedule, this means that the world politics process as a whole, its rounds and sessions, should begin and end on the dates and times announced, with as little variation as possible. A major and sudden change in schedule and rules is likely to confuse participants, reduce students' confidence, and impinge upon their efficient performance. If a time change is needed it should be confined to no more than a few minutes of synchronous activity or possibly a longer time for nonsynchronous interactions.

With regard to the rules, you should verify that all activities follow the formal content and implied meanings of the preset regulations, discussed in chapter 5. All students should know that activity at odds with rules will be stopped immediately and those participants who are rule breakers and cause repeated abuses will end up with a lower grade. If, for example, you set the rule that an act of violence must first get the consent of the educator, but during negotiations some students declare a war without your approval, you should immediately announce that this action is illegal and hence should be disregarded, as if it had never happened. In a simulation on a social network you can also delete the message on a declaration of war and send a separate message to the students involved, reminding them of the simulation rules.

Summarize Participation for Grading

Grading participation in world politics interactions requires careful follow-up and evaluation of each student's contributions, relative to others. In chapter 10 on assessment we look closely at grading-related issues. Here we provide a short overview of this task. In face-to-face meetings the bulk of the follow-up for grading has to be done while encounters take place. Otherwise, it is extremely difficult to remember who said what to whom. You may refresh your memory based on video clips, but these often do not present the big picture accurately. Moreover, the cost of professional equipment may be high and amateur devices may provide poor quality recordings. In simulations on social networks, all conversations are automatically recorded and saved. You can review the activity of each and every student at any time during world politics process and after it ends. This can be supplemented with activities during the policy formation process to give a wide perspective and to show progress and improvement over time. Revisiting the contents of encounters in a calm atmosphere makes it easier to differentiate between the quality and quantity of statements made by each student.

Grading of participation in the world politics process should reflect whether a student attended an international meeting and was present and contributed during each of the rounds and the breaking news session. Furthermore, the grade should reflect the quality of a student's contributions. Students that suggest creative and innovative ideas, demonstrate understanding of theory and empirical knowledge, adhere to simulation rules, and lead should receive a higher grade than others who bandwagon and just add superficial posts to the negotiation process.

Instructions for Participants

This section on instructions for participants is designed to increase students' contribution to simulation, elevate the quality of the joint exercise, and improve the learning experience. It summarizes the main points, described in this chapter, in a concise form. Instructions for participants can serve as a quick checklist that you can present to your students, especially the tasks in table 6.2, which you can hand out in class, upload on the simulation website, post on the social network platform, or send by e-mail. The explanations provided in this section assume that the reader is familiar with the details and analysis in all previous sections of this chapter and especially on the process of world politics, which you can assign as a reading requirement for your students.

During world politics interactions the simulation stage belongs to students. You, as the simulation administrator, take a step backward and your students become the primary driving force in the creation of a simulation reality. In the role they are assigned within a political or media actor they intensively communicate with others to reach their team's goals. Such transformation in the learning experience, from a top-down structure to vertical interactions among peer participants, gives your students a unique opportunity to get a feel of what world politics are all about, to have hands-on practice of the learning material, to shape the outcomes of their activity, and to contribute to the collective construction of knowledge within a learning community. In essence, students combine individual responsibility with quality teamwork. Table 6.2 summarizes world politics instructions for participants along four core tasks: (1) get familiar with the opening scenario, (2) participate in interactions among teams, (3) keep updated, and (4) follow instructions.

During world politics, each student represents a team and should follow its cohesive policy decided upon earlier, during policy formation, as described in chapter 5. The atmosphere of a turning-point event disclosed in the opening scenario, the extreme challenge and at times even severe crisis situations characteristic of the world politics process, encourage participants to apply the knowledge they have gained, be creative, improvise, think critically, act effectively as a team, and lead in their specialized roles to increase their chances of success.

Get Familiar

At the beginning of world politics interactions, participants should get familiar with the opening scenario. Members of all teams should (1) read the scenario carefully, (2) assess its positive and negative meaning from the team's perspective, (3) search for additional details on the situation described or find relevant historical analogies to relay on, (4) adjust decisions and plans from the policy

TABLE 6.2. World Politics Instructions for Participants

Task	Details
Get familiar	Read and assess opening scenario, adjust policy plans accordingly
Participate in interactions among teams	Play the game of world politics: initiate, react, and promote the team's goals, cope with uncertainty and frustration, try out theories in actual negotiations, practice different tools of foreign policy, use soft power, and engage in public diplomacy
	<u>Political teams</u> Initiate diplomatic moves, participate in negotiations, serve as mediators, offer a peace plan, sign agreements, or summarize disagreements in a formal concluding document Grant economic, humanitarian, or military aid Issue an ultimatum, declare a state of emergency or high alert, threaten to use military force, or other forms of coercive diplomacy Impose a blockade, move forces, order military buildups, or use other forms of nonviolent measures With consent by educator, announce the use of terror, hostage taking acts, reprisals, and other limited violence short of war Implement a public diplomacy campaign in the media: publish press releases, get interviewed, and react to media publications
	<u>Media teams</u> Set the agenda, gain exposure and rating, interact with political teams, publish products during ongoing interactions, prepare for the breaking news session, and make sure to lead the agenda and capture the attention of political teams during prime-time media exposure in the simulation
Keep updated	Share and discuss communications and media publications with your team
Follow instructions	Abide by simulation schedule and rules

formation dialogue to fit the new situation, and (5) define the appropriate media strategy and public diplomacy campaign to affect the ways the media will set the simulation agenda.

The opening scenario builds upon the main simulation story line, embedded in the simulation topic and the initial scenario published at the beginning of policy formation discussions, so teams that followed instructions accurately all along, as detailed in chapters 4 and 5, will be able to catch up with developments quickly, even with the most surprising events. In essence, the first three get-familiar tasks required of all participants are similar to those detailed in chapter 5 on policy formation, but now the challenge students face is considerably greater because the opening scenario introduces a more drastic change and, often, an acute crisis situation.

Adjustment of policy plans requires that teammates reconsider previous decisions on content and ranking of actor values, goals, and alternative moves, reassess policy plans, and reevaluate the relevance and cost efficiency of their opening initiative. Such adjustments by joint brainstorming provide gradual development of creativity and critical thinking that will enable participants to represent their teams accurately as they join the synchronous activities of world politics.

Participate in World Politics

To take an active part in world politics and promote the team's goals, all actors should (1) initiate discussions with representatives of other teams and (2) react to comments, arguments, and proposals. This means that each participant now performs as a political leader or media professional and leads in a specialized aspect of the scenario, even as all teammates follow the cohesive plan their actor had decided on earlier during policy formation.

Political teams should implement policy plans by using a variety of foreign policy tools: (1) diplomatic ones including negotiation and mediation; (2) economic means like aid or sanctions; (3) military tools of coercive diplomacy, (4) nonviolent military activity, or (5) violence, short of war, which according to the simulation rules requires the consent of the educator; and (6) communicate with media teams to brand their actor in the news agenda and implement their public diplomacy campaign.

Media teams should (1) interact with political teams, (2) report on salient events, (3) set the simulation agenda, (4) gain attention, (5) compete with other media organs, and (6) increase their rating, all through the world politics encounters and especially during the prime-time breaking news session. After you notify students about your plan to conduct a poll on the contents of the media products, on exposure to the media, and on its impact during the simulation, the motivation for professional reporting is likely to increase.

During world politics interactions adversaries and allies alike should communicate intensively with one another to express their demands, explain their positions and find mutually acceptable solutions. Each of the political teams should strive to reach an agreement with the most favorable conditions for their actor, so a conflict of interests is inevitable. To settle these conflicts and avoid extreme escalations, all actors must consider compromise, though some may do so less than others. In case productive negotiations unfold, when teams reach an agreement they should draft a formal document that outlines the specific points of agreement. However, if negotiations fail, teams should formulate a summary document on their disagreements as a map for future talks among teams.

The media teams follow all these developments, report them as they occur, offer interpretations from different perspectives, and frame the simulation reality in the creative products they prepare. During intensive world politics interactions media teams may find it hard to get attention from political leaders who are busy implementing policy and promoting their goals. When a dedicated breaking news session takes place in the midst of the world politics round, some prime time for media reports takes place. At that time all negotiations and other activities come to a halt and the attention of all participants is directed to the media products.

Keep Updated

It is important for participants of each team to share and discuss the outcomes of all developments and of media publications with other teammates, update one another, and coordinate their reactions as a routine process coupled with world politics encounters. But this is a hard-to-implement requirement in short and intensive sessions. An update and quick consultation is especially needed when there is an unexpected breakthrough proposal, a serious threat, an ultimatum, or a provocative media publication. During the interim break between rounds, teammates have adequate time to fully update one another and reassess their team's strategy.

Follow Instructions

For the simulation to become an efficient and enjoyable project, participants must follow instructions and abide by the simulation schedule and its rules. If, for example, members of a team are absent from some encounters, join late, or leave early, they increase the burden on other teammates and weaken the ability of their actor to function with allies or fight against foes. When a member of a team violates simulation rules, others can attribute this to the entire team, questioning its credibility. Similarly, if the media teams are not ready with their products till the breaking news session, all other actors miss the opportunity to gain exposure to new information and are affected by the lack of an overview of the simulation encounters based on multiple perspectives. Participants that disregard instructions reduce the quality of the learning experience of all fellow students and undermine the success of the simulation as a whole. To help avoid such situations, the simulation schedule and its rules should be handy at all times, on paper or online.

Summary

World politics encounters make learning an enjoyable and efficient process. Paradigms and theories come to life and orient students' positions in interactions. Students learn to manage conflicts, face complex issues, cope with interdependence, and realize the important role of the media and its implications in world politics. The simulation project interrupts the routine of passive learning and leaves its imprint on participants. Active participation pays in the long run as it enables students to internalize experiences related to learning the material and retaining it long after the simulation ends.

The chapter addresses the plan and procedures for world politics rounds. To shape the plan we suggest you decide on an opening scenario, ad-hoc events, various activity types for the process of world politics, and a detailed schedule. World politics procedures translate the plan into operational measures as you present the opening scenario, declare the start and end of each world politics round, follow the interaction process closely, encourage participants, input ad-hoc events, establish a breaking news session, make sure participants adhere to the schedule and rules, and summarize participation for grading.

Along with the educator's outlook, the chapter adds instructions for participants with four verbs that focus on the perspectives and activities of students: get familiar with the scenario, participate in world politics, keep updated, and follow instructions.

Intensive encounters among teams, irrespective of the simulation genre, are at the heart of the world politics rounds. Taking part in negotiations helps participants step into the roles of decision-makers and media professionals and deal individually and collectively with the challenging opportunities and grave crisis situation detailed in the opening scenario. Communications among teams, allies and adversaries, with each one aiming to conclude agreement on the best terms for the respective team, teaches students how difficult and still important it may be to compromise. The breaking news session emphasizes the role of the media in setting the world politics agenda and demonstrates how decision-makers use the media to create a positive image and send signals to other actors. Coordination among teammates during and between world politics rounds teaches students about the linkage between domestic and international politics. All in all, participation in the world politics process gives students a chance to encounter and confront multiple viewpoints in conjunction with a unique opportunity to practice, experience, and understand politics from the perspective of an active insider.

PART III

Analysis

CHAPTER 7

The Simulation Overview

A simulation project is never really complete without an overview conducted in retrospect after participants remove their masks and look at the simulation world they have entered and developed, from the outside as observes. The *simulation overview* consists of three activities in which you and your students take part: (1) feedback, (2) debriefing, and (3) assessment. Together, the simulation overview activities enable you and your students to see the big picture of the simulation project, to draw conclusions, to evaluate what happened, and to try to understand why. This chapter clarifies the three basic concepts that form an overview of the simulation project, explains the rationale for conducting all three of them, and ends with a brief discussion on the contributions of the simulation overview to research.

Concepts

The literature on how to draw conclusions from simulations as a method of study and produce a comprehensive overview of a world politics simulation project is vast.[1] It covers feedback, debriefing, and assessment based on different definitions, perspectives, and emphases. By developing these outlooks the literature contributes insights regarding the need for a dual perspective: first, from the simulation stage as participants step into the shoes of a character, and, second, from the seats of an audience, as you and your students exit the stage, step out of the character costumes, and look back at all that happened.

Most scholars focus on the process of how to conduct feedback, debriefing, or assessment and pay less attention

to conceptual definitions and to the important links and overlap among them. Feedback is commonly understood as an activity, loop, or cycle, directed by the educator and performed by the students to summarize the results of a simulation and advance knowledge.[2] Debriefing is viewed as an activity, occasion, or process in which participants share reflections and emotions in a discussion on the simulation experience to advance learning.[3] Assessment is considered as the stages and techniques designed to determine what students had achieved during the simulation, grade them, and find out whether the simulation was useful to promote course objectives.[4]

This chapter addresses and clarifies the meaning of each of the concepts and highlights the areas where they intersect. Table 7.1 compares the three concepts as distinct activities that together provide a comprehensive overview of the simulation.

We regard *feedback* as a learning activity in which each participant submits information and evaluations on topics related to the simulation. Feedback covers details on cognitive aspects and knowledge acquired during the simulation, as well as on affective aspects experienced in the simulation and skills practiced, such as empathy, coping with frustrations, creativity, critical thinking, leadership, and teamwork.

During the feedback process, students follow guidelines provided by their educator to build an individual overview of all simulation encounters. The educator decides on the plan for the feedback activities, but the students are those who are active in the process, and it is their perspectives that form the contents of the feedback inquiry and the data derived from it.

Shifting from the individual participant to the students

TABLE 7.1. Simulation Overview

Attributes	Feedback	Debriefing	Assessment
Who	Students Participants step out of their roles and look back at the simulation encounters as an attentive audience from outside, in hindsight	Students and educator Collective and interactive, participants step out of their roles and collectively with the educator appraise the study experience in retrospect	Educator Solitary activity to grade students and appraise the simulation project
What	Information and evaluations Self: student and character Simulation: teams, policy formation, world politics, breaking news, consecutive rounds Learning efficiency: cognitive, behavioral, affective	Information and evaluations Insights, critiques, and ideas for adaptations, mainly spontaneous during the interactive session Self: student and character Simulation: teams, policy formation, world politics, breaking news, consecutive rounds Study efficiency: cognitive, behavioral, affective	Grade students and appraise the simulation project Students: assignments and participation Simulation: feedback from students and educator's perceptions of the entire project Teaching efficiency: cognitive, behavioral, affective
When	Ongoing, before, during, and after the simulation	Ongoing, during, and mainly after the simulation	Ongoing before, during, and mainly after the simulation
Tools	Registration form and knowledge quiz before the simulation activities begin Policy formation and breaking news activities during the simulation World politics form after each round of interteam encounters and as final feedback after the simulation ends	Preparation and opening: (1) topics for aggregate summary of feedback data, (2) theme questions, (3) guidelines for team presentations, (4) elements of opening statements by heads of teams Collective brainstorming Concluding remarks and implications	Rubrics to grade students and appraise the simulation project

and their educator as a learning community, we see *debriefing* as interactive debates on the main topics of the simulation, the experiences it produced, and the study efficiency of the project as a whole. During debriefing, the individual perspectives of each participant mingle with collective insights of players as teams and the inputs of the educator as an active moderator who lets various voices be heard. At the end of the encounter, the educator leads the task of joining all parts of the simulation puzzle together to form a comprehensive picture.

Shifting once more, this time from students to dedicated teachers at the heart of the learning process, we consider *assessment* as summing up activities in which the educator grades students, revisits simulation goals, and evaluates the study efficiency of the simulation project as a whole. Assessment is also the best time to validate research-oriented issues, confirm hypotheses that shaped the plan for the simulation from the start, and verify goal attainment at different stages of the course.

Any educational experience needs some way of closure, to draw conclusions. The overview usually starts with the feedback process by looking back at the simulation experience to bring together reflections and evaluations that serve as raw material for debriefing and assessment. The conceptual definitions summarized in table 7.1 indicate that these three activities are not confined to a postsimulation time. They occur before the simulation, throughout its activities, and after it ends, whenever and as often as you plan. This way, the information and evaluations provided by students as feedback can be compared over time, as table 8.1 on the feedback schedule outlines. Similarly, debriefing is not a onetime event. Different encounters may be planned for joint brainstorming between students and their educator, as table 9.1 on the debriefing schedule suggests. While assessment is a necessity for grading students as the course ends, a gradual appraisal of the simulation process lets you cope with the need for adaptations to improve students' performance. For example, you may underestimate the workload or the difficulties students have with decision-making and policy planning. When you get systematic feedback early on, you can adjust the pace of events, add coaching if needed, provide more detailed guidelines, and make sure the simulation process fits your students as best as possible.

Without conducting a progressive simulation overview, before, during, and after the simulation ends, the learning

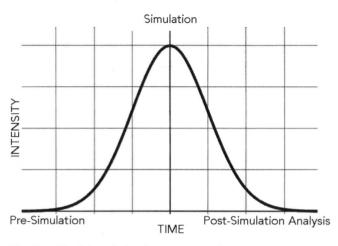

Fig. 7.1. Traditional simulation project learning curve

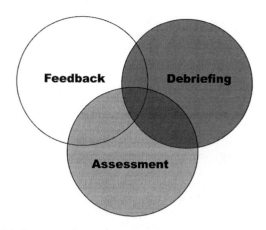

Fig. 7.2. Integrated simulation overview

cycle will be incomplete. Figure 7.1 describes a traditional learning curve of courses that employ simulations as a supplementary tool, where the simulation encounters are the peak experience with little or no ongoing overview.

We suggest a blend of feedback, debriefing, and assessment as an ongoing practice to reduce the steep decline from peak to routine and prevent a learning curve where the simulation encounters diminish other modes of study. In doing so, you can transform the simulation into a synergetic experience that overlaps with all other activities in the learning cycle detailed in figure 1.4, and complements them. Such periodic overview can tighten the links between the topics of your curriculum and the cognitive, behavioral, and affective outcomes of the simulation as a multifaceted process.

Rationale

As a teacher with many constraints that shape your choices, you may decide to engage in a full simulation overview with equal emphasis on each of its three parts. Or you may skip feedback and debriefing and go directly to assessment, which is usually a must in academe. But we believe that the distinct components of the simulation overview overlap and contribute to one another, creating an integral whole that is more meaningful than its distinct parts. Figure 7.2 presents the three concepts and the areas of overlap between them.

First, without feedback the debriefing encounters lack a detailed and well-thought-out student perspective that contributes to a rich dialogue between students and edu-

cators. If you skip feedback or reduce its weight, you drop important events that embody the transformed learning structure presented in figure 1.2 where students are more equal contributors to the study in the learning community you create. When you integrate feedback with debriefing, you not only guide your students through an extensive introspection but enable them to see points of view raised by their peers and recognize important nuances they might have otherwise overlooked. For example, during the feedback activity, participants may revisit their own contributions to their team and the collective behavior of their actor in the simulation. But what about the contents of the values, goals, and plans of other actors, allies or rivals? An effective way to practice empathy and to increase the awareness of complexities in world politics is to place one's own policy formation in comparison with that of others. This occurs during debriefing encounters and helps bring self-centric approaches, misperceptions, and mirror images to light. Long-lasting empathy with the "other" is also related to attitude change as a result of cognitive, affective, and behavioral learning. During different stages of feedback activities and debriefing processes one can pinpoint baseline attitudes and hidden assumptions and then revisit these positions during and after the simulation.

Second, without feedback, assessment lacks the inputs of a detailed and well-thought-out student perspective that contribute to a systematic introspection of the simulation project by the educator. The development and application of rigorous rubrics for grading students and for appraising simulations as a teaching tool necessitate the integration of data from students' self-reflections, with all voices being heard. Table 10.5 summarizes a possible rubric for aggregate assessment of the simulation project that takes into account differences between students' evaluations and educator's assessments on goal attainment. It is useful to plan the feedback activity thoughtfully and integrate its data into your own comprehensive overview of the simulation project.

Third, without debriefing, both feedback and assessment remain solitary activities that lack the impact of collective debates, conflicting points of view, and the insights of joint brainstorming within a learning community. Such interactions add new insights and are likely to evoke critical thinking by students and educators alike. During debriefing the links between the different aspects of policy formation and world politics come to life and put to the test a variety of hidden assumptions that shape theories and may trigger hostile positions.

The overlap between the three parts of the simulation overview indicates a gradual buildup of study efficiency. The first step involves solitary work by students in feedback and by the educator in assessment. Then, during debriefing, students and educators get a chance for a second look within a frank, dynamic, and open dialogue that is designed to summarize, add insights, criticize, and improve simulation procedures.

To benefit from these overlaps we suggest that you engage in all three overview activities even as you give them a different emphasis depending on your needs and choice. Each of the overview parts can have a different weight, but all of them are necessary to produce an integral whole.

Feedback, debriefing, and assessment activities can be done on a solitary or interactive basis through the use of physical platforms or virtual ones, as detailed in chapters 8 to 10. Irrespective of the core platform you choose, the introduction of supplementary tools from both platforms can increase the efficiency of data creation, management, and analysis. The best practice is to perform feedback, debriefing, and assessment progressively, as long as the information is fresh and alive in the memory, close to the simulation events and experiences. Postponing these activities may lead to forgetting facts, details, and recollections at the cognitive level.

Stepping into the role of a character on the stage of a simulated world is likely to trigger emotions as participants identify and empathize with roles, teams, and actors that in real life may be unfamiliar or even one's own enemies. At times, contradictions may arise between one's personal ideologies or beliefs, the role represented in the simulation, and the occurrences that take place, particularly during intensive debates over values and goals.

Overview activities help reduce emotional complications and bring to light many affective aspects. As the simulation progresses, a change from being participants to becoming an audience adds considerably to resolution of the gaps between one's personal life and that of the character represented in the simulation. This transformation also involves a change from a practical viewpoint during an evolving process to a comprehensive analysis in retrospect. Feedback and debriefing in the midst of an ongoing simulation triggers the temporary removal of costumes and decor to confront and resolve difficulties and contradictions.

Research

We believe scholars who use simulations should share their experiences, adjustments, and solutions as part of an ongoing dialogue between colleagues to improve teaching and to advance the quality of simulations as a more sophisticated tool in academe.[5] This dialogue can proceed in several avenues: (1) informal cooperation between colleagues who share an interest in innovative learning; (2) participation in conferences where a more formal exchange of experience takes place; and (3) publication of research in professional journals. Beyond a dialogue between scholars, this path can considerably aid faculty in ways advantageous to obtaining professional credit by generating pedagogical research and publications in journals such as *International Studies Perspectives*, the *Journal of Political Science Education*, or *Simulation & Gaming*. To considerably advance this option, scholars need detailed logs of their past experiences; access to extensive databases on simulations processes captured by written, photo, audio, and video formats; reputable methods; and rigorous tools allowing them to conduct comparative research. If simulations are to become a real political research lab, we must advance our tools, improve our methods, and share experiences so that joint progress can be made.

Current research on simulations is reviewed in chapter 3 with an emphasis on publications since 2004 on simulations of world politics. The paths for future research may include research by students after they take part in a simulation or by scholars who run simulations or use materials generated during the simulation and after it ends.

Feedback-based research, described in chapter 8, can be deductive, when you plan ahead of time and design the feedback forms to fit your research design, or inductive, when you look at the wealth of aggregate findings to investigate characteristic attributes and highlight links between variables. All forms include a wide array of questions that produce a rich foundation of information for quantitative and qualitative research. Each feedback question is a variable that can be probed alone or compared and correlated with others. For example, you can look at expectations, familiarity with the case, and previous experience with simulations and test results in knowledge gain and skill development. The breaking news poll, described in chapter 8, is a useful tool to generate findings on media consumption in routine and crisis situations, depending on the simulation topic you have chosen. Together, the feedback forms are a descriptive treasure for summing up and comparing simulations, over time and across topics. It is also an indispensable foundation for deductive explorations of theories and inductive tests on the core effects variables have on one another.

Debriefing-based research, described in chapter 9, utilizes the products of brainstorming sessions as ideas for research. These can be the result of a deductive investigation led by the educator or teams who look at assumptions and hypotheses anchored in theories from various fields. Serendipity is another way ideas can emerge, when spontaneous insights and confrontations among participants highlight interesting findings that are worth further investigation.

Beyond feedback and debriefing, the products of the simulation, like individual and team assignments described in table 4.3, can serve as major inputs for research on simulations as a teaching tool. An inquiry into activities can lead to a systematic exploration of platforms in face-to-face and cyber rounds. The basic knowledge quiz can add findings and insights on knowledge development and its retention by looking at regimes, leaders and roles, minorities, nonstate actors, crisis, mediation, agreements, and media in distant regions. Topic-specific feedback questions and others on the impact of different platforms in consecutive rounds can also lead eventually to the development of more rigorous tools to assess simulations. When you conduct an intercampus simulation or cooperate with colleagues in distant states the results may highlight intercultural differences and communalities.

Student research in the form of proposals or full research projects has a value for knowledge development and may trigger advanced work if the findings are convincing and worth further inquiry. Some of the many topics covered by our students include (1) a comparison between a current or historical case study and its counterpart in a simulation

to understand the meaning of events in the simulation and in real life; (2) a comparison between simulation media and real media to investigate procedures and inquire into the roles and impact of media strategies; and (3) the use and analysis of interviews with simulation participants to learn from their experience about the impact of a theory, event, or media product on the contents and salience of activity within and among teams.

To conclude with a personal note, this book as our research product owes much to our students and to the colleagues with whom we have conducted simulations over the years. They have contributed greatly to the way we plan and run simulations. Without their insights, suggestions, and critiques our research could not have progressed as far as it has and the contents of this book would not have been the same.

Summary

The simulation overview is an integral part of the learning cycle. It transforms the simulation from a theatrical stage where interactions occur to a serious teaching tool and an analytical device to study world politics. In this chapter we review three elements that jointly provide a broad outlook of the simulation project: (1) feedback is an essential student activity that sums up information on the participants and their simulation experience and provides evaluations of their learning progress, from an individual perspective; (2) debriefing is an interactive process in which both educator and students discuss cumulative data produced during the simulation, exchange ideas, provide insights, and offer critiques about the simulation project as a whole; (3) assessment is an educator activity focused on the individual learning achievements of each student and on the effectiveness of the entire simulation project as a teaching tool. In this chapter we highlight the differences between these three overview concepts, present the rationale for including all of them in an overview, and discuss the links and overlaps between them. We conclude this chapter with a discussion of the links between the simulation overview and research activities, as a dialogue between colleagues, designed to enhance the use of simulations as a teaching tool and gradually develop into a more professional research lab of world politics. The next three chapters provide a close look at each of the three overview activities.

CHAPTER 8

Feedback

Feedback is a learning activity in which each student submits information and evaluations on topics related to the simulation. It requires students to think about matters you raise, evaluate their contributions, as well as those of others, and consider their goal attainment in order to gain a comprehensive overview of the simulation. Feedback activities are important in face-to-face and cyber simulations alike. Unless we mention specific details, the discussion of the feedback plan and procedures covers all types of simulations.

The Plan

Feedback takes place when students follow your guidelines for an individual inquiry into their expectations, roles, activities, and achievements. As a result, feedback involves a rich pool of systematic data that you can use for diverse purposes, such as (1) administration of the simulation project, (2) practical adaptations throughout the simulation, (3) inputs for the debriefing and assessment, (4) refinement of plans for future simulations, and (5) student and faculty research projects. Since feedback is guided by instructions from an educator, careful planning serves a dual purpose: first, it makes feedback a meaningful inquiry for the students, and, second, it generates a source of valuable findings about the simulation project.

Guided feedback conducted periodically requires decisions on focus, method, and schedule. Proper planning of feedback also makes simulations a major source for research by using information, evaluations, insights, and critiques provided by students, as discussed in chapter 7.

Focus

Feedback contents reflect your curriculum and the simulation you have planned. Sometimes, students provide feedback on their own initiative, like a request to be assigned on the same team with a friend, a call for help to solve difficulties, or a spontaneous appraisal or critique of the simulation. Such occasional feedback may help you address immediate concerns as the simulation unfolds. But comprehensive feedback covers a variety of cognitive, behavioral, and affective elements about the (1) participants and their evaluations of themselves, others, and the simulation as a whole, (2) simulation platforms, (3) assignments in preparation for the simulation, (4) policy formation activities within teams, (5) world politics interactions among teams, (6) links between media and politics, and (7) theoretical, empirical, and methodological expectations and gains from the simulation.

You can choose to emphasize one or more of these elements as you guide the feedback inquiry of your students and shape the contents of the data you get in return. Just keep in mind that feedback is a solitary activity, so it must be short and well defined. Periodical feedback as the simulation evolves with repetition of identical queries over time makes it an in-depth comparative investigation.

An emphasis on *participants* obtains information and evaluations about individual students and their views of others. Such feedback may involve their previous knowledge of the simulation topic, experience with simulations, habits of using social networks, preferences of team and role, areas of interest, and expectations. Inputs from this personal introspection make it easier for you to adjust the simulation to your student body. For instance, many participants who registered for a simulation among ISA scholars in 2014 requested to play a role in a European Union team, so our plan built on a strong team for European Union members and began the simulation with the publication of the *Middle East Tribune,* displayed in figure 5.4, as the initial scenario, to reflect the European importance in the Arab-Israel conflict.

Information on role preferences is also useful to pinpoint motivated individuals who are willing to lead their team. Other issues, such as workload, involvement relative to others, and feelings regarding the intensity of the project, let students review their simulation experience and enable you to track the learning process and adjust the tempo of the simulation.

An emphasis on *platforms* looks at the physical infrastructure and virtual environments of the simulation. Students are the main users of social networks as a simulation platform and have an inner perspective on its advantages and shortcomings. As you guide them to look back at their experiences you gain valuable information and evaluations on the best-fit platform for your student body. Thus, feedback on student familiarity with social networks and other cyber tools, digital habits, and readiness to coach hesitant peer students is an important input for immediate adjustments in your lecture plan and simulation schedule. Feedback on the advantages and disadvantages of social networks and face-to-face meetings encourages your students to think and offer insights on the ways a platform shapes activity. As the core users, they are a good source for ideas on how to improve the use of digital platforms, such as Facebook, for the purpose of cyber or hybrid simulations.

An emphasis on *preparation* focuses on solitary work within the learning cycle. It helps students see how the different assignments, together with other simulation activities, advance their knowledge and overall experience. Feedback on preparation probes many aspects of learning, such as the (1) use of traditional and virtual resources, (2) duration of solitary study, and (3) expectations regarding grades, knowledge gain, and fun during the simulation experience. The inquiry about preparation helps students evaluate their learning habits and adjust them as the simulation unfolds. As an ongoing activity this feedback allows you to see how your students cope with the assignments. It is also a core input to the assessment of students and the simulation project.

An emphasis on *policy formation* highlights teamwork and the contribution of intrateam discussions for knowledge gains. Through such feedback, students look back at their decision-making process on values, goals, and policy plans and provide reflections on the benefits and difficulties of group dynamics, time pressure, and distribution of workload among teammates. Here students are guided to consider theoretical and empirical topics related to intrastate occurrences, political pressures, and public opinion that later might have affected world politics activities and outcomes.

An emphasis on *world politics* concentrates on interactions among teams. It broadens the range of considerations about actors, events, and interactions that students have to take into account in hindsight. To guide this overview, you may focus on the opening scenario as a trigger for activities among teams, the buildup of stress, the intensity of the interactions, and outcomes, as well as satisfaction with achievements.

An emphasis on *the links between media and politics* deals with the role of the media and its products from the perspective of students as members of political or media teams. Through this inquiry you highlight the importance of a media strategy, the use of text or photos, the consequences of media bias, and ways to handle it. The introduction of media teams enables all participants to cope with issues of quality reporting versus media orientations driven by ideologies. These matters are especially important in the digital information age where technology makes it possible to spread information at low cost and extremely fast speed.

An emphasis on *theoretical, empirical, or methodological expectations, and gains* requires students to evaluate their achievements at different times during the study cycle. By looking at simulation developments in light of theoretical assumptions, arguments, and critiques, students learn to test the validity of theories against an empirical reality they have created. When you repeat this practice several times during the simulation you help students cope with abstract concepts, engage in activity that applies complex models, and understand competing paradigms. By highlighting theoretical matters before, during, and after the simulation, you can demonstrate how theories may shape activities and how sometimes different theories may lead to similar outcomes despite their contradictory assumptions.

Feedback inquiry that focuses on expectations for empirical gains and results derived from practice as the simulation evolves demonstrates how information availability affects behavior. It also shows how practice extends one's knowledge and advances long-term retention of information.

The use of feedback to review simulations as a methodology that generates data is useful in graduate courses, mainly ones that deal specifically with simulations as a scientific method and as a research lab. Such feedback can also trigger seminar papers and dissertations on issues and aspects that students become intrigued with during the feedback inquiry you request and revisit later during debriefing. You may ask students to figure out how to test certain hypotheses and come up with operational measures for variables they plan to use in their own research projects. The need to apply qualitative and quantitative techniques to cope with simulation-generated data brings together course curriculum, assigned reading requirements, and a protracted experience the students had participated in. It makes them think creatively, review various methods, and choose proper ways to validate theory or employ empirical data. In professional training programs, simulations are a practical tool to test out and master skills and to get feedback from participants on their own performance and that of others.

All in all, feedback requires students to consider the simulation experience from four different perspectives: (1) as an individual participant, (2) as an assigned character, (3) as part of an assigned team, and (4) from an objective outlook on the simulation as a whole. With careful planning you can make the feedback activity a meaningful process for your students without overloading them with unnecessary work. Such planning depends on the methods you choose and the ways you formulate your questions.

Method

After setting your feedback plan you have to decide on a way to implement it. *Method* translates the feedback plan into a practical tool that guides students, directs their inquiry, and affects the quality of answers. Here, you have two choices: (1) traditional or cyber tools for feedback, and (2) direct or indirect feedback questions.

The use of *traditional* or *cyber tools* involves the platform and applications that suit your academic setting and serve your needs. It defines where you provide feedback guidelines and questions and how your students respond. Any contents you have chosen for the feedback inquiry can appear on paper or online, with each method having its advantages and disadvantages. You can also combine both types of tools to maximize gains. Traditional ways to distribute and collect feedback on paper involve a relatively low time investment to produce and hand out forms, but they may require extensive efforts to follow up, collect, save, and analyze responses. In the traditional manner, all you need to do is to print hard copies of the

forms with questions you create and bring them to class. Moreover, during your routine time slot you can have your students complete the feedback questions and then you can move on to the lecture you have planned. But you have to devote some lecture time to the feedback questions if you want students to fill out the forms right then and collect all the forms at once. This mode leaves little time for extended thought on feedback matters. Some students may need more time to complete the feedback questions, and others may be absent. But at least you can get hold of most forms, all at once.

Backup and analysis are the greater problem and a costly matter, especially in courses with many students. First and foremost, you need to back up the original forms, by duplicating or scanning them, so you can refer to them when you need to in the future. This is especially true when you plan to conduct comparative research on multiple simulations over a few years' time. To carry on a systematic analysis of all feedback responses in a qualitative or quantitative manner, you will need to store the data on your computer and make it compatible with additional feedback forms from one simulation to another. You will need to convert the information you have received to a data format, taking into account that some forms contain unclear handwriting and questions with no answers.

Many difficulties are solved by cyber tools, though you have to invest more in the preparation of the feedback forms before you publicize them. On cyber platforms you can employ a digital survey and reduce the costs of distribution and analysis considerably. You can also recycle your forms time after time with some adjustments from one simulation to the other, thereby reducing most of the preparation costs after the first simulation.

To create an online digital survey, you can use any application designed for this purpose, such as Google Forms, which is free and user friendly. Your first survey may take a few hours to prepare, but everything goes much faster after you master the technique. In an online digital survey, you can decide which questions are optional and which are required, so unlike traditional forms on paper, students will have to answer all required questions before they can submit their forms.

The digital survey gives you flexibility on the time of distribution and the due date for submission of the feedback, free of your lecture slot constraints. Moreover, students may invest as much time as they need or want when they address the inquiry questions and think things over, so the feedback they provide is often more valuable than that produced instantly in class. Once the form is submitted by each individual student, it is recorded with a time and date, to form a database of responses from all students. By use of this or similar applications, all forms are automatically saved and stored on Google Drive or a personal computer. You can easily follow responses and detect students that have not yet submitted the feedback. A short reminder by e-mail can help you have a feedback dataset with responses from all students. To analyze the feedback, you can use built-in features to explore descriptive statistics or convert the data into Excel and other formats you are familiar with. All these features make digital surveys a valuable method for use in face-to-face and cyber simulations alike. Once you adopt an online digital submission technique for your feedback requests, it becomes easy to run feedback often at different points during the simulation and follow simulation developments from your students' perspective almost instantly.

In the Palestinian statehood hybrid simulation, which was conducted on Facebook and in a face-to-face meeting among students of two campuses, the registration form was distributed online, as our first feedback tool, and the information was processed simultaneously and immediately for both campuses. A paper version of the form would have delayed the start of the simulation, since processing the forms would have taken much longer and would have required closer coordination between participating educators.

The advantage of the computerized online format is obvious: the data is calculated immediately when the forms are submitted, providing summaries and raw material for analysis. All this is done using relevant software, with the click of a mouse. On a digital platform you can also incorporate photos and clips created by the media and ask students to answer several questions on these products. It is difficult and costly to add photos to printed questionnaires, and multimedia requires special coordination between screening the video clips and completing of forms. When using social networks you can also design some short questions as instant polls, posted during policy formation activities or world politics interactions. But these must be very short so that they do not interrupt the flow of simulation events.

The use of *direct or indirect questions* involves a dual way to guide the feedback inquiry. Most feedback responses are based on a direct question you ask, to which the student provides information or evaluations. An example of an easy direct question is What team or character do you want to represent? More complex ones are the following: Did you enjoy the simulation? How well did your team do? Do you think your head of team helped your team reach its goals? Some participants may provide distorted information, put the blame on others, or protect their teammates to ensure they get a high grade. An indirect question addresses the same issue in different formats so you can cross-check the data with the direct one. For example, to focus on team evaluation you may ask: What team achieved the most in the simulation? Would you recommend the simulation to a friend? Would you like to participate in future simulations? Are you willing to be a head of team in future simulations?

You can also combine both types of questions to validate information. In a direct question you can ask students how many weekly hours they devoted to the simulation, and in an indirect question ask them to evaluate the intensity of their participation relative to teammates. In a focus on theoretical gains, a direct question might be whether the simulation helped students understand a theory while an indirect one can request students to apply that theory to an example from the simulation.

By a combination of direct and indirect questions, you can look at issues in a cross-cutting manner and gain a more objective overview of students' self-reflection. This makes feedback a more rigorous tool and provides a better aggregate overview of the simulation.

Schedule

In planning the feedback schedule, you have to take your simulation timeline into account. You can request feedback before, during, or after the simulation, but keep in mind that if feedback forms come too early or too late, the feedback may be useless or irrelevant. Students may not know what to answer or may not remember the details you request. Table 8.1 presents a schedule that covers milestones of the simulation timeline with a specifically designed feedback form for each one of them. You can use this feedback schedule, parts of it, or an adjusted schedule that fits your specific academic setting, simulation plan, and study goals.

Feedback activity *before the simulation* includes the registration form and basic knowledge quiz. Such presimulation feedback is a useful way to learn about expectations, background, attitudes, preferences, existing knowledge, and other attributes of each and all participants. It is likely to have an impact on how you plan and run the simulation, as it helps you decide on such matters as teams, roles, and the simulation scenario. When you are familiar with your students' expectations and preferences, you become a more attentive educator. When you are aware of students' basic knowledge on the subjects you teach,

TABLE 8.1. Feedback Schedule and Forms

Attributes	Simulation Baseline			Policy Formation	Media	World Politics	
Tools	Registration form	Knowledge quiz	Policy formation form	Breaking news poll	World politics form	Knowledge quiz	
Who	Participants of all teams, individual activity				Participants of political teams only, individual activity	Participants of all teams, individual activity	
What	Preliminary information, expectations, and requests	Basic knowledge on core simulation topics	Information and evaluation of teamwork	Information and evaluation of media roles and products	Information and evaluation of interactions among teams and gains from the simulation	Basic knowledge on core simulation topics revisited	
When	At the introduction of the simulation project	Before policy formation begins	After policy formation ends	After the breaking news session	After each round of world politics	After the simulation ends	

you can decide what issues require more emphasis in your lectures, solitary preparation, and assignments. Presimulation feedback is also important because it is the only feedback that students submit before they are affected by their participation in the simulation. When you have comprehensive baseline information about your students' knowledge and expectations before the simulation starts, you are in a better position to assess study efficiency after the simulation ends.

Feedback activity *during the simulation* lets you to track the ongoing process of interactions, identify difficulties straightaway, and find solutions on time. A separate feedback form after policy formation, a breaking news session, and each round of world politics helps you isolate the effects of each one of them on study efficiency and explore gradual learning at different points of time. For example, students are likely to submit more accurate feedback on policy formation shortly after intrateam discussions when memories of teamwork are still fresh in their minds. Such feedback should come before the world politics process begins, or else interactions with other teams may overwhelm students and affect their reflections on teamwork in hindsight.

The best time for a breaking news poll is immediately after the breaking news media session, just after students were exposed to the media. Feedback after each round of world politics is based on the accumulation of knowledge, experiences, and reflections of that round. If you run a hybrid simulation, feedback after each round can shed the light on the utility and shortcomings of face-to-face and cyber simulations from the participants' perspective.

Feedback after the last world politics round, as the simulation ends, is crucial to get a comprehensive summary of the simulation as a whole. It requires students to submit information and evaluations on the simulation as a protracted experience. It necessitates an integrative outlook on different parts of the simulation learning cycle, from solitary preparation to debriefing. For example, you can ask students (1) when they learned, enjoyed, and participated most, (2) if and how policy formation had an impact on simulation outcomes, (3) whether and when the simulation contributed to greater understanding and increased empathy toward the others, and (4) whether and when the simulation contributed to skill development such as the practice of critical thinking, teamwork, and leadership. To address these issues students must revisit their entire simulation activity. When you repeat questions from previous feedback forms, you can cross-check responses, detect changes over time, and explore the progress students have made. We also recommend that you repeat the basic knowledge quiz at least twice, before and after the simulation, to detect knowledge gain after ongoing work and personal experience.

The optimal timing for postsimulation feedback is shortly before debriefing. Since debriefing is the last activity directly related to the simulation, it builds on feedback. Feedback may be used to open the debriefing session, as we discuss in the procedures section, and help participants prepare for active participation in the debriefing debates. A delay in the submission of the last world politics form may be counterproductive because students shift their efforts to exams and research papers. These tasks may bias their evaluation of active learning with simulations or even prevent them from submitting their forms altogether.

Procedures

The shift from plan to procedures means you have considered your options and made a choice regarding your strategic design for feedback. You have also decided on the best-fit plan, taking your academic setting into account. Now you need to transform your plan into operational steps. Five verbs—*prepare, create, distribute, save,* and *analyze*—summarize the feedback procedures in a nutshell.

The feedback forms are individual tasks for each student as solitary learning. After you explain the structure and contents of each form, you can let your students know that feedback is not merely a way to gather data but a process of revisiting their simulation experience and looking at it in hindsight in a comprehensive yet critical manner.

You have to construct and apply tools that guide the knowledge review your students are conducting. By doing so, students can gain the most from the feedback activity and you retrieve the most relevant information and evaluations you want. As summarized in table 8.1, we offer five feedback forms: (1) registration form, (2) knowledge quiz, (3) policy formation form, (4) breaking news poll, and (5) world politics form. You can adapt each of these forms to the specific platform you use, be it physical in class by distributing a handout on paper, or cyber by posting the file on the simulation website and mailing it to your students or by providing a link to a digital feedback form.

Prepare Questions and Create Forms

A good feedback question focuses on the topics you planned earlier and guides your students to take a detailed look at diverse aspects, to provide information or evaluation, and to explain how they have ranked their evaluations. The clearer your instructions, the more effective the inquiry process the students engage in will be and the higher quality data you will receive. So it makes sense to invest time and create well-thought-out and strictly edited documents that can later be used as a general scheme with minor adaptations from one simulation to another. Repeated use of forms saves time and effort and makes it possible to compare data across several simulations for research purposes, as explained in chapter 7.

For all forms, create a pool of possible questions and make sure to include ones that require participants to provide information and others that request their evaluations of different simulation-related aspects. Examples of such questions are provided for the five forms we offer below. It is useful to add questions on date, name, and e-mail that let you get back to students if you need to clarify some of the data.

Next, you need to choose questions you will repeat in several forms for the purpose of comparison over time on such issues as coping with time pressure, quality of leadership, extent of empathy, and more. The topics we include in our forms are suggestions you can follow, expand, omit, or adjust to your particular interests and needs. Flexibility and revision in setting the contents of forms are advised because sometimes you may need to introduce last-minute changes and new questions as the simulation develops and unplanned events occur. For example, if participants request a back-channel for secret negotiations and get permission to do so, as in the Middle East simulation, you may want to focus on both the formal negotiation process and the secret one, so you can later compare reactions to both. You may inquire about the extent of media manipulation or raise the issue of reporting accuracy during intensive negotiations. Digital online forms allow for last-minute modifications from anywhere you are and serve as handy tools when flexibility is necessary.

All forms, on paper or online, must be as short as possible and capture core aspects you planned for the form. You can use the five forms we provide as prototypes to create those that fit your particular academic setting and needs.

Like other forms, the *registration form* contains two types of questions: (1) information, as in questions 1 to 11, and (2) evaluations, as in questions 12 to 31. We use multiple-choice and text replies in the registration form. Multiple-choice answers require more planning effort and time investment when you create the form, but they can be replicated from one simulation to another and are worth the effort, especially when you use online digital tools, because the information is automatically converted to a quantitative database with options for instant analysis of results.

Sometimes we combine both multiple choice and open text, as in question 9. When students select "other" they are requested to specify the role they are thinking of in a text reply. Beyond qualitative comments in open text, the use of the multiple-choice option allows for easy aggregate summaries of quantitative data from all participants.

By adding "specify" with a text option, you open a dialogue with your students and make them feel free to express their thoughts. For example, we gained the idea

TABLE 8.2. Registration Form

Question		Reply/Values
Information		
1	Date	Month/Day/Year
2	Name	Text
3	E-mail	Text
4	Gender	Multiple choice: (1) female, (2) male
5	Level of studies	Multiple choice, e.g., (1) undergraduate, (2) graduate
6	Academic expertise	Multiple choice, e.g., (1) political science, (2) media, (3) international relations, (4) history
7	Academic institution	Text or multiple choice, add for intercampus simulations
8	Country	
9	Preferred role	Multiple choice: (1) president, (2) prime minister, (3) foreign minister, (4) defense minister, (5) spokesperson, (6) media editor, (7) media reporter, (8) other, specify
10	Type of preferred team	Multiple choice: (1) state, (2) nonstate actor, (3), international organization, (4) media organ
11	Preferred team	Multiple choice from a list of states, international organizations, nonstate actors, and media organs
Evaluation		
What is your		
12	Familiarity with the simulation topic	
13	Experience with simulations	
14	Experience with social networks	
To what extent do you expect to gain		
15	Empirical knowledge	
16	Comprehensive theoretical knowledge	
17	Understanding of alliances and special relationships	
18	Understanding of the complexities of world politics	
19	Understanding of media roles and their impact on politics	
20	Practice of empathy	
21	Experience with teamwork	Rank on a scale from high to low and explain your choice in a text answer
22	Practice of leadership	
23	Rhetoric skills	
24	Critical thinking	
25	Creativity	
26	Skills to cope with workload	
27	Skills to cope with change and time pressure	
28	Skills to cope with challenges	
29	A high grade	
30	A unique simulation experience	
To what extent do you agree that		
31	*Realism* is the leading ideology/theory in world politics	

of including public opinion representatives from the registration forms of our students and use it when we have teams with many participants.

Questions 12 to 31 of the registration form guide students to think about the simulation project upon which they will soon embark. As evaluations, these queries provide self-reflections from each participant and can later be used to produce an aggregate overview of what your class wanted at the outset of the simulation, compared with their evaluations during and after the simulation, as expressed in the policy formation and world politics forms.

Evaluation questions ask students to rank, on a scale from high to low, aspects related to their familiarity (1) with the simulation topic, (2) with simulations in general, and (3) with the simulation platform, such as social networks. These queries, as in questions 12 to 14, tell you how ready your student body is for the simulation before you start the learning cycle. They add very useful information you can immediately take into account in planning your lectures.

Students may be biased by ethnicity, race, religious, or political affiliations. Simulation activities let educators move students out of their comfort zones. In the registration form, you can determine what those zones are and what students know. Based on "trivial" questions, such as do you know foreign languages or have you traveled to the geographic areas the simulation focuses on, you can detect some hidden biases that require attention. By using responses to the survey, you can decide who plays on which team.

Questions 15 to 29 focus on the gains students derive from the simulation. By adding them to the registration form you indicate to your students that a wealth of gains are possible and that they will improve their knowledge about the case, their understanding of theoretical topics you teach, as in questions 15 to 19, and acquire skills that prepare them for professionalism in the global village, as in questions 20 to 28. Questions 29 and 30, on the importance your students attach to their final grade and to the simulation experience, are relevant inputs for the grading rubric you plan, which is discussed in chapter 10. The learning trade-offs between traditional study assignments and participation in the simulation, described in table 4.3, should be weighed carefully so students can gain the best from the active learning.

Question 31, on realism, is illustrative of a group of questions to which students provide information on political preferences, ideologies, and normative assertions of theories they support. You may design these items as direct questions or as precepts to which the students respond with agree or disagree, for example, "power is the most important element in politics," "nuclear free zones add to global stability," or "terror is a behavior of states and nonstate actors alike." Remember that all forms are submitted by individuals who identify themselves, so keep the ethical code in mind and include queries that do not infringe on privacy. You may decide to make some of your questions optional, permitting students to skip those that seem to disclose information they consider problematic.

Unlike other forms, the *basic knowledge quiz* presented in table 8.3 contains only information-type questions. Few of them are about the participant, for organization purposes, as in questions 1 to 4 and the rest to test the student's familiarity with the simulation topic. The form we use as a prototype includes sixteen questions in total, all of them designed as a text reply. You can convert some or all of them easily to a multiple-choice mode as statements related to the topics you have taught and ask students to choose if they are true and false answers. For example, to replace the text answer to question 12 you may write: "'Between Israel and Arab states there were only two major wars in the period from 1947 to 2014'. Is this statement (1) true or (2) false?" The addition of text answers, however, can reveal the nuances of knowledge students have and help you plan what to emphasize in your lectures.

Most questions in this quiz are empirical ones, on the actors involved, as in questions 8 to 11, and on events that took place between them, as in questions 12 to 14. We choose to focus on military, diplomatic, and economic events in this quiz, but depending on your topics you may ask about domestic unrest, terror, civil war, or events at the cooperative edge of the spectrum like treaties of cooperation, alliance formation, and political integration. You may decide to add questions on the theories you teach and plan the time you must devote in your lectures to each one of them based on the findings from the quiz. For a current events simulation you may ask questions on topics in the news to see whether students follow media reports on a continuous basis.

Since this is a basic knowledge quiz, we suggest that you focus on the most salient information one can expect students to be familiar with. Your goal is that your students will be able to answer at least some of the questions, or else they will be intimidated. Let your students know in advance that this quiz is part of the course requirements but does not count in the grading rubric.

The topics and questions you include in the knowledge quiz can also be used for a condensed summary in class before the simulation begins and as it progresses

TABLE 8.3. Basic Knowledge Quiz

Question		Reply/Values
Information		
1	Simulation topic	Text
2	Date	Month/Day/Year
3	Name	Text
4	E-mail	Text
Familiarity with simulation topic		
5	Relevant documents	Identify three basic international agreements relevant to the region
6		Identify three political speeches, the leaders who delivered them, and when
7	Regimes	Identify the political system of the main actors
8	Leaders and roles	Identify name and role of three main decision-makers
9	Minorities	Identify name and status of core minorities
10	Nonstate actors	Identify name and role of major nonstate actors
11	Media	Identify three main media organs
12	Developments	Identify three main military events, like wars, low-intensity conflict, terror
13		Identify three main diplomatic occurrences, like alliances, peace accords
14		Identify three main economic events, like aid transfers and sanctions
15		Identify three main threats, like nuclear proliferation and environmental hazards
16		Identify three possible opportunities, like spread of democracy and peace initiatives

to improve the empirical basis of the interactions within teams and between them. Such gradual resort to core information can help your students extend the knowledge base and retain it longer. It is useful and important to reemploy the knowledge quiz after the simulation ends to validate the added value of the interactive process and ongoing learning cycle to the consolidation and retention of knowledge.

Questions 15 and 16 in the quiz request students to put on their thinking caps and go beyond basic information to a process of using the information they have and draw some conclusions of their own, on possible threats, as in question 15, or opportunities, as in question 16. If one wants to trace the development of analytic logic, creativity, and critical thinking skills, questions like these are an indirect gauge to identify improvements over time.

Like other forms, the *policy formation form* presented in table 8.4 contains two types of questions: (1) information, as in questions 1 to 5, and (2) evaluations, as in questions 6 to 21. For example, questions 13 to 15 focus on values, goals, and plans as the core components of policy formation. In reply to these questions, students estimate team consensus and disagreements as a reflection of discussions on a scale from high to low. In the text sec-

tions they can provide examples that explain their point.

In question 16 you guide participants to think about the importance of the media in the political arena and request them to report on their discussions about how to approach the media and react to its products. The question follows the earlier one in the registration form that focused on a better understanding of the media as a possible gain from the simulation. It is later followed by questions 26 to 28 in the world politics form and in the media poll, with a detailed look at the media as an actor in politics and at its products. As the simulation proceeds, participants gradually review their knowledge about the media and develop attitudes on the topic based on facts, practice, and experiences. This introspection into topics you decide to highlight over several feedback forms can trigger revision of positions by students and help you identify change as the simulation progresses and after it ends.

Question 17 of the policy formation form focuses on the status of the actor the team plays, from the perspective of the individual participant. It is designed to measure the students' awareness of the hardships the actor they represent faces in the context of team preparations for world politics encounters. This question may also

TABLE 8.4. Policy Formation Form

Question		Reply/Values
Information		
1	Date	Month/Day/Year
2	Name	Text
3	E-mail	Text
4	Team	Text or multiple choice
5	Role in the simulation	Text or multiple choice
Evaluation		
6	Your contribution to policy formation	
7	Effectiveness of teamwork	
8	Leadership quality	
9	Impact of initial scenario	
10	Time pressure	
11	Gravity of threat or challenge	
12	Difficulties in decision-making	
13	Consensus on values	Rank on a scale from high to low and explain your choice in a text answer
14	Consensus on goals	
15	Consensus on policy plans	
16	Consensus on media strategy	
17	Actor's status	
18	Satisfaction with head of team	
19	Satisfaction with collective teamwork	
20	Satisfaction with simulation platform	
21	Satisfaction with simulation experience	

indicate fundamental prejudices that may be put to test during the simulation encounters and change over time. So it is also repeated in question 19 of the world politics form presented in table 8.6.

Questions 18 to 21 are designed to measure individual satisfaction with the head of team as a leader during policy formation, with collective teamwork, with the simulation platform, and with the simulation project as a whole at that point in time. Feedback evaluations on these questions can lead to changes and adjustments to improve the simulation during world politics among teams. Sensitive coaching on an individual basis can reveal specific problems in real time and solve them as early as possible.

The *breaking news poll* presented in table 8.5 is designed for participants of political teams only as it focuses on an evaluation of media products. If you have more than one media team in your simulation, you may instruct the participants of media teams to complete this form too, but let them know they have to focus on the products of other media teams, not their own.

The breaking news poll contains two types of questions: (1) information, as in questions 1 to 9, and (2) evaluations, as in questions 10 to 18. For example, in questions 15 to 18 participants are guided to consider the issues of media bias and the impact of the media on policy formation and world politics. For each question, students provide their reflections on these issues, which will later, during the debriefing sessions, serve as an important aggregate input for a collective dialogue on media professionalism and its role in world politics.

The prototype poll we suggest is designed for political science and media students alike, so it does not contain professional terms from media theories that political science participants may not be familiar with. Its main purpose is to measure awareness of media activities, consumption of media products, and evaluations of the

TABLE 8.5. Breaking News Poll

Question		Reply/Values
Information		
1	Date	Month/Day/Year
2	Name	Text
3	E-mail	Text
4	Team	Text or multiple choice
5	Role in the simulation	Text or multiple choice
6	Round	Multiple choice, e.g., (1) first, (2) second
7	Media products exposed	Multiple choice: (1) newspapers, (2) video clips, (3) photos, (4) short breaking news, (5) assorted
8	Timing of exposure to media products	Multiple choice: (1) during world politics interactions, (2) breaking news session, (3) assorted
9	Reaction to media products	Multiple choice: (1) none, (2) denial, (3) confirmation
Evaluation		
10	Follow-up of newspapers	Rank on a scale from high to low and explain your choice in a text answer
11	Follow-up of video clips	
12	Follow-up of photos	
13	Follow-up of short breaking news	
14	Most effective media product	Multiple choice: (1) newspapers, (2) video clips, (3) photos, (4) short breaking news, (5) assorted
15	Media bias in favor of your team	Rank on a scale from high to low and explain your choice in a text answer
16	Media bias in favor of your adversary	
17	Media impact on your team's activity	
18	Media impact on the simulation	

media's role in politics. When the simulation involves graduate students who study theories of politics and communications you may add questions that focus more closely on topics such as agenda setting, framing, or "rally around the flag."

Some of the issues raised in the media poll also appear in the *world politics form,* such as questions 26 to 28, to trigger a revision of positions over time by students as they evaluate their knowledge and experiences in the simulation.

The world politics form, presented in table 8.6, like other forms, contains two types of questions: (1) information, as in questions 1 to 8, and (2) evaluations, as in questions 9 to 48. This form is the longest of all feedback inquiries as it serves a dual task of revisiting a round of world politics and of concluding the entire simulation experience. First, any round of world politics advances the

knowledge base, practice, and experiences of participants by moving from intrateam activities to the much broader milieu of world politics where all political and media teams operate. So this feedback process lets participants reconsider their knowledge and positions by shifting from the narrower perspective of their team to an extended one of all teams after a given round. Second, after the final round of world politics, participants step out of the shoes of their character to the position of an involved audience in postsimulation feedback and debriefing. The feedback form on the last round of world politics is a summary of the entire simulation in retrospect, from the point of view of each student. To make sure the final feedback is useful, ask your students to adhere to the feedback schedule and submit their forms on time, while they clearly recall the details of what they went through and created.

The world politics form covers topics you have already

TABLE 8.6. World Politics Form

Question		Reply/Values
Information		
1	Date	Month/Day/Year
2	Name	Text
3	E-mail	Text
4	Team	Text or multiple choice
5	Role in the simulation	Text or multiple choice
6	Round	Multiple choice, e.g., (1) first, (2) second
7	Do you want to participate in future simulations?	Multiple choice: (1) yes, (2) no, and explain your choice in a text answer
8	Will you recommend participation in a simulation to your friends?	Multiple choice: (1) yes, (2) no, and explain your choice in a text answer
Evaluation		
What was the extent of		
9	Your own contribution to world politics	
10	Your team's contribution to world politics	
11	The effectiveness of teamwork	
12	The leadership quality	
13	The relevance of the opening scenario	
14	Time pressure	
15	Gravity of threat or challenge	
16	Difficulties in the decision-making process	
17	Consensus on world politics activities	
18	Consensus on media strategy	
19	Your actor's status	
20	The status of your main adversary	
21	The status of your main ally	
22	Your team's achievements	
23	Your team's policy changes	
24	The status of the mediator	
25	The effectiveness of the mediator	
26	The status of the media	
27	Objectivity in media reporting	
28	The impact of the media	
29	Correspondence between the simulation events and reality	Rank on a scale from high to low and explain your choice in a text answer
How satisfied were you with		
30	The head of team	
31	Teamwork	
32	The simulation platform	
33	The simulation experience	
To what extent have you gained		
34	Broader empirical experience	
35	More comprehensive theoretical knowledge	
36	Greater understanding of the role of alliances and meaning of friendship	
37	Better understanding of the complexities of world politics	
38	Increased empathy	
39	Practical experience in teamwork	
40	Practice leadership	
41	Better rhetoric skills	
42	Advanced creativity skills	
43	Better skills to cope with workload	
44	Better skills to cope with time pressure	
45	Better skills to cope with challenges	
46	Improved critical thinking skills	
47	A unique simulation experience	
To what extent do you agree that		
48	*Realism* is a leading ideology in world politics	

introduced in earlier feedback forms, but this time with an emphasis on the simulation process and its implications. It focuses on individual and team activities, as in questions 9 to 12, together with characteristics of the simulation from the perspective of the individual participant, as in questions 13 to 28. The form inquires into the correspondence between the simulation and reality, as in question 29, and requests participants to summarize their attitudes in terms of satisfaction with their head of team, collective teamwork, simulation platform, and overall simulation experience, in questions 30 to 33.

In relation to gains acquired from the simulation, the form provides information about empirical and theoretical knowledge, as in questions 34 to 37, and about the practice and development of skills, as in questions 38 to 46.

The evaluations from students are an important contribution to the assessment of simulation projects, as explained in chapter 10. As the final form for the entire simulation, the world politics form is an asset when you want to gauge the use of your simulation as a method of teaching. Together, the wealth of feedback data provides valuable insights and an ability to conduct in-depth comparisons of aggregate data over time as the learning cycle progresses. By fulfilling all feedback tasks, your students can slowly gain a comprehensive overview of their activities and of the progress they have made. But feedback is an individual activity, and thus contains personal points of view and depends on the willingness of each student to think about matters in a cumulative, creative, and critical manner. The debriefing sessions, addressed in chapter 9, supplement this process with the views of others and with your active role in a collective brainstorming dialogue.

Though rigorous debriefing and assessment tools are yet to be developed, detailed feedback forms improve your ability to pinpoint gaps between the way you look at the simulation project and how your students see, feel, and remember it. As such, all feedback forms and especially the ones on world politics may contribute to cumulative research on simulations and hopefully lead to better simulations as a research lab in social science.

Distribute Forms

You can distribute the forms as (1) a paper version handed out in person, filled out and submitted back individually, (2) a digital form placed on the virtual platform of your choice that the students print and hand in or send as digital files they have filled out, or (3) a link to an online digital form on any application you choose, as discussed in the methods section. You can employ online features to accomplish a comprehensive overview of the simulation project even when you conduct face-to-face simulations. We regard this as the best way to handle all forms as it ensures a well-organized process to post, fill, submit, save, and analyze all the data you need.

Back-Up and Analyze Data

Once you gather all the submitted forms, you may be amazed by the wealth of information the feedback process generates. The information you have obtained includes quantitative data and basic statistics if you employ online applications that immediately convert data into aggregate descriptive output. It also contains qualitative expressions provided in text replies, which are essential contributions to the big picture of the simulation project. This information indicates that your students have completed their individual overview, and now you need to record all the data you have obtained in computer-friendly formats and then proceed with any type of analysis you plan for the research, debriefing session, and assessment activities described in chapters 7, 9, and 10.

Instructions for Participants

Feedback from students, as simulation participants, is crucial for the success of the simulation overview. To implement your feedback plan you have to instruct your students and explain feedback requirements in detail so they can fulfill their part of the overview activity properly. This section includes guidelines for feedback that are summarized briefly in table 8.7. You can duplicate the table as a handout in class, upload it on the simulation website, post it on the social network, or send it by e-mail. The tasks suggested in the table are common to face-to-face and cyber simulations alike. They require participants to get familiar with the nature and requirements of the feedback process, to study by revisiting the simulation events, to complete the feedback form, and to follow instructions.

Get Familiar

To complete the feedback activity properly students need to read all instructions carefully and understand the difference between information and evaluation. They must know that all feedback is a personal reflection submitted on an individual basis. An awareness of schedule requirements makes it possible for students to complete the requested feedback activity on time.

TABLE 8.7. Instructions for Participants on Feedback

Task	Details
Get familiar	Review feedback forms and read guidelines carefully
Study	Review your role and experiences from four perspectives: (1) an individual participant, (2) an assigned character, (3) part of an assigned team, (4) the simulation as a whole
Complete feedback forms	Answer feedback questions: provide information and evaluations, add explanations where requested
Follow instructions	Abide by guidelines and schedule Submit forms on time

Study

To provide accurate feedback, students should look back and study what happened in the simulation. Some of the feedback questions are informative, like questions on students' academic institution or role in simulation, and can be filled out immediately. Other queries, like evaluation of achievements, require time for thought, study, and reflections before replying. Make sure your students understand that to address the questions in the different forms they need to look at the simulation activities from four different perspectives: (1) as an individual participant, (2) as an assigned character (3) as part of an assigned team, and (4) through an objective overview on the simulation as a whole. Students should investigate the different perspectives and reply after revising the relevant issue. By carefully differentiating between these perspectives, students can clarify the larger and more complex picture of the simulation as a whole.

Complete Feedback Form

Feedback is a solitary activity. To avoid being affected by groupthink on individual responses, each student must submit feedback individually and on time. This requires students to select the most appropriate option in multiple-choice questions and provide a short and reasoned response in the open text questions. Students should answer all required questions and might find it interesting to address optional questions as well. They need to bring feedback forms to class on time or submit them online, depending on the method and date the educator chooses.

Follow Instructions

All academic courses and the ones that include simulations in particular require order so students must abide by preset rules and follow instructions. The same is true with feedback. Schedule restrictions and instructions for filling and submitting forms affect the quality of all feedback activities; questions are repeated from one form to the other, and many of them are later compared over time by the educator to detect changes and progress. All participants must be aware of timing and deadlines. With use of paper forms in class the lecture slot imposes strict time limits. Online procedures also impose restrictions since you can lock these systems after a specific date and time so that forms submitted late are rejected. Careful attention to all guidelines lets your students benefit the most from their feedback activity and increase the quality of the debriefing process, described in chapter 9.

Summary

Feedback is part of the simulation overview, which transforms the simulation from a theatrical stage where interactions occur to a serious teaching tool and an innovative analytical device to study world politics.

Feedback focuses on how the participants see the simulation. It is an essential student activity that sums up informative data on the participants and their simulation experience and provides evaluations of the learning progress, from their individual perspective. The chapter deals with the feedback plan you prepare, by looking at matters of focus, method, and schedule. Then it outlines procedures that translate the plan into an operational tool for implementation: prepare questions, create and distribute forms, back up and analyze data. The chapter ends with instructions for participants designed as a brief synopsis of the steps students need to take to fulfill feedback activities properly.

CHAPTER 9

Debriefing

*D*ebriefing is defined as a joint interactive session for discussions between students and the educator to reach a comprehensive overview of and a critical outlook on core topics, experiences, and study efficiency. The stretch of debriefing time is short and concentrated, much less than that of feedback and assessment. Debriefing sessions are important activities in all simulations. They can take place on campus or unfold synchronously on a cyber platform of your choice, such as a joint group on social networks as a "room" where all participants meet with the educator for brainstorming. So unless we mention specific tools for a physical or cyber platform, the discussion on the debriefing plan and procedures covers all types of simulations.

The Plan

Debriefing requires students and the educator to step outside role-play activities, move into an academic setting, and communicate with each other to revisit simulation gains and analyze drawbacks. Debriefing is a middle ground between formal learning with traditional lectures and informal learning with simulations. In debriefing, just as in traditional lectures, you are the primary driving force, and it is your prerogative and responsibility to decide on what, how, and when the students should take the lead. Yet the top-down hierarchy of traditional lectures is restructured. Students cease to be passive listeners and become active participants in discussions with you and their peers. Your role is to guide and conclude these discussions, but without motivated students who react,

argue, and brainstorm with you, no discussion would become a productive debriefing. As with feedback, to make debriefing an appealing and useful learning tool, careful planning of the debriefing focus, method, and schedule is needed.

Focus

Debriefing focus defines the leading contents of the discussion between you and your students. It often reflects the course curriculum and the learning goals you set in advance for the simulation. In your plan you sort out the most important implications of the simulation for your students to consider, learn, and retain. In particular, you can emphasize knowledge, practice of skills, and emotional experiences they have gained. When you choose highlights and introduce these cognitive, behavioral, and affective elements into the discussion, you lead your students through a comprehensive and balanced simulation overview.

An emphasis on *cognitive* contents in debriefing deals with knowledge-driven discussions on theoretical matters, such as the usefulness, applicability, robustness, validity, weaknesses, and possible adjustments of a chosen theory students have learned, such as realism, or a new rival theory such as liberalism, that you choose for debriefing. Empirical-driven discussions can focus on the simulation timeline, contextual background, core events, and turning points. In area studies, a review of the simulation reality compared with the real world is especially relevant, with discussions on regional dynamics and cultural-social complexities. In a methodology-driven debriefing, discussions evaluate simulation as a teaching and research tool and the relevance of the simulation to students' own research designs.

An emphasis on *behavioral* contents deals with the practice students gained when they step into the roles of decision-makers, participate in teamwork, and interact with other teams. For example, you can discuss the advantages and disadvantages of decision-making from an inner perspective with your students as practitioners who share their insights and critique. The debriefing can look at decision-making skills as ways to improve decision-making and reconcile the gap between decisions and implementation in the simulation compared with the real world.

In a similar vein you can discuss other skills students practice in the simulation, such as information processing, strategic planning, coercive diplomacy, negotiation, mediation, media management, and resolving ethical dilemmas. A possible caveat in the discussion on the behavioral element is that practice in a simulation may differ from activity in the real world. For example, being a journalist in a simulation does not transform the student into a journalist after the simulation ends, but it certainly familiarizes participants with problems that typify the relations between the media and politics in routine and crisis situations. During debriefing, the recognition of a gap between simulation conditions and live events helps students understand the importance of the skill practice they had acquired in the simulation as well as its limits.

An emphasis on *affective* content focuses on the emotional experience the students gain and its implications for learning as a social process. Though emotions are usually set aside in academe, they are a fundamental input and an inherent part of all learning, and it is wise to harness simulation-driven emotions to strengthen the knowledge gains of students. Experiences of fun and frustration, uncertainty and surprise, stress and patience, hostility and empathy, denial and identification, anger and happiness, as well as failure and success are all likely to remain in the memory of students long after the end of the simulation. It is important to address these emotions and discuss their impact on motivation and learning. It is also useful to acknowledge their effect on decisions, negotiation, media management, and simulation outcomes as insights for counterpart events in real situations of world politics. For example, identification and empathy toward others are crucial building blocks of peace, but they are often very difficult to develop. Prejudices are rarely confronted or put aside, values are usually sidestepped, and mirror images are hard to break. In the roles of a character on stage, students try to identify with an "other." During de-

briefing, when participants as an involved audience listen to one another, it is easier to visualize the costs of political blindness. Psychological inhibitions, together with political constraints, may have led to an impasse and frustrated students or forced them to feel the same disappointment as their enemies did. When this happens, students experience the meaning of empathy toward the other, a feeling that is a precondition for a fruitful dialogue and compromise in world politics. Affective elements like identification and empathy are not only valuable contributions to the outcomes of simulations, but the essential lessons to be derived from them.

The integration of cognitive, behavioral, and affective elements in the debriefing creates a spillover impact, strengthens learning, and makes debriefing a truly comprehensive overview of the simulation. An interactive discussion without cognitive, behavioral, and affective considerations addressed between you and your students is not much more than a formal lecture. Whatever weight you choose for each element, make sure to decide in advance on the most important contents of the debriefing and at least let your student have "a taste" of each of the three elements. When you encourage students to ask questions, argue, and debate, even at the expense of a partial shift from your preset plan, the debriefing fulfills its purpose and makes an impact. So within the plan, leave some room for flexibility and spontaneous developments to accommodate for inputs from active and motivated students.

Method

After setting your debriefing plan, you have to decide on a way to implement it. Method refers to the way you translate the debriefing plan into an operational session. It involves choices on how to (1) trigger, (2) conduct, and (3) conclude the debriefing. To trigger productive discussions you need to employ tools and procedures that attract students' attention, provoke their interest, stimulate their thinking, and call on them to react. We suggest you begin the debriefing by one of three perspectives: (1) yours, (2) the simulation teams, or (3) the heads of teams. Each option highlights a different perspective from the start and has advantages and shortcomings.

You, as the educator, may begin the session and trigger the discussion that follows. This option can contain highlights from the feedback findings. Students are usually very curious about the responses of their peers, and a discussion on what others think adds to the creation of a broad overview of the simulation project. If, for instance, you present feedback information on the media and show that, despite dozens of creative media products, only a few students regarded the media as an influential actor with a crucial impact on the policy and decisions of their team, you are likely to trigger discussions on the media-politics link. When you begin the debriefing with a presentation you created, you have maximum control of its contents and duration. But the danger is that the lead you take will overwhelm students and slip back to the traditional teaching structure, with the rewards of interactions within an active learning community diminished considerably.

Teams as collectives may open the session and draw most students into the debriefing. A team presentation is the result of joint work by all teammates, so it reflects the perspective of the group as a whole, not merely of its individual members. Even if only one student, like the head of team, presents this product at the beginning of the debriefing, others who were involved in its creation are equal partners. The format of a presentation enables teams to present pictures, videos, citations, and many other visuals, which can give the debriefing session an exciting, enjoyable, and attractive start. However, the time needed for each team to show and explain its presentation might well exceed the time you plan for a debriefing opening. If you stop the presentation, students might feel that most of their hard work was worthless. Limiting the time and length may be counterproductive if you want teams to be creative and prepare comprehensive presentations. Cyber tools help reduce these problems. You can request teams to send their presentations by e-mail in advance so you can help them focus on the most important slides for the debriefing opening. Later, you can upload the full version of their presentations on the simulation website or social network for access after the debriefing session.

Heads of teams as the first among equals may open the discussion by virtue of their position. They guided their teams during simulation, so it is natural to let them lead the opening of the debriefing. Heads of team are also expected to have a more comprehensive outlook on the simulation than others. When they share their insights and perspectives or reveal back-channels and secret deals, they provoke reactions from other students, and therefore add considerably to the discussion. But heads of team may emphasize topics you have not planned and some of them may gain too much attention at the expense of others. Motivated teammates might feel that heads of teams get too much credit, not only during the simulation but even after it ends. In face-to-face debriefing, some heads of teams may read their statement from paper, making it

hard for others to follow. To reduce these shortcomings, you can ask heads of teams to collaborate with teammates when they produce their opening statement and share it with you before the debriefing session begins.

The heart of the debriefing session is an interactive discussion between you and your students. You lead these discussions by asking questions and reacting to students' arguments. Students take an active part in the debate, address your questions, and raise ones of their own as they communicate and argue with you and other students. In planning this part of the debriefing, you should consider the centrality of your involvement in the process. One option is a more or less equal role for you and your students. As you get responses from students you move on to other topics following your preset plan. Another option is to let as many students as possible react and to emphasize their disagreements, to provoke discussions between them and summarize their debate before moving on to a different theme. The interactive brainstorming in the debriefing looks like a ping-pong match that involves an exchange of information, evaluations, insights, ideas, critiques, advice, and recommendations to improve future simulations.

The debriefing session ends with the conclusions and implications you raise. In your capacity as an educator you have the final word to summarize the simulation. It is crucial to plan a few major points that you want students take along with them from the debriefing and the simulation project as a whole. You may address the lessons you've learned from students and from the simulation, or suggest dilemmas with no clear-cut solutions as food for thought. This last part of the debriefing is relatively short, so it is useful to prepare some core points ahead of time, and add a few new ones that have emerged during the debriefing session.

Schedule

Debriefing is an interactive process that takes place during a preset and relatively short time. Schedule considerations for a debriefing plan involve (1) timing and (2) the duration of the debriefing sessions.

The timing for debriefing sessions should reflect themes you want to emphasize in the discussions. Table 9.1 outlines schedule options and points to the protracted nature of debriefing events. Periodical debriefing, first after policy formation and then after each round of world politics, ensures gradual learning. It requires an overview of the simulation as it evolves. As a result, you can integrate adaptations instantly as they are offered and debated, en-

TABLE 9.1. Debriefing Schedule

Attributes	Policy Formation	World Politics
Who	Educator and participants as individuals, heads of team, teammates, and collectively as a class	
When	After policy formation	After each round of world politics
What	Interactive discussions on policy formation, decision making, and initiatives, including exchange of information and evaluations, insights, critiques, and advice	Interactive discussions, insights, critiques, and advice on world politics and exchange of information and evaluations on media roles and products A dialogue on goal achievement, qualitative and quantitative data, and topics for research projects
Formats	Session includes (1) opening by educator, by heads of teams, or jointly by teams, (2) interactive brainstorming, (3) concluding remarks and implications by the educator	
Tools	Topics for aggregate summary of feedback data Theme questions for all participants Guidelines for team presentations Elements of opening statements for heads of teams	

abling your students to improve their performances and receive a huge motivation charge from you and from peer students. When stronger teams describe their intensive intrateam activity, they become role models for weaker teams to imitate. For instance, during a debriefing session after policy formation in the Palestinian statehood simulation, the *Global Crescent* media team disclosed that they had prepared some intriguing videos for release on Facebook once world politics negotiations begin. Two other media teams took this early notice as a challenge and decided to prepare quality media reports of their own. In this way debriefing after policy formation led to some competition and a higher quality of products prepared by all teams.

Debriefing after policy formation is also important for a revision of the decision-making process, students' participation, and teams' policy toward world politics. Yet devoting a separate lecture for the debriefing session in the midst of the simulation project, and then again after the simulation ends, may come at the expense of other lecture material you want to teach. In this case, you can considerably reduce the cost of multiple debriefing sessions by moving some of them to cyberspace, even when you run face-to-face simulations. You can schedule interactive discussions with students on social networks or by video conferences in the evenings or weekends, so that most students will be able to attend the online debriefing session. Discussions on social networks are automatically saved, and students that missed the live session can always keep up with the contents of the debriefing. Similarly, you can record a video conference and post the video on the simulation website or social network for convenient use by all students in the simulation.

In addition to debriefing throughout the simulation, a final debriefing session after the simulation ends is essential to summarize and gain an overview of the project as a whole. You may plan the concluding session immediately after interactions end or few days and weeks thereafter. The choice depends on your preferences, academic setting, and time constraints. In face-to-face simulations among participants from different courses, campuses, or states, it might be very difficult to arrange an additional joint meeting beyond the last round of world politics. In such cases, debriefing immediately as the simulation ends is an inevitable choice. In cyber simulations the physical constraint is not a factor, but it still requires you to find proper time for synchronous online debriefing that suits most participants, and immediate debriefing as the simulation ends might again be the solution. However, be aware that in face-to-face and cyber simulations alike, participants might find it very difficult to disconnect from the powerful experience they just had in a world politics meeting and focus primarily on the last encounter, rather than on the simulation as a whole. They may not be able to step off stage quick enough to look at developments from the standpoint of observers.

To ensure the benefits of debriefing, it is best to set your schedule for a few days after the simulation ends. This way you make it easier for your students to remove their character costume, rethink their activity as well as that of others, and overview the simulation in its totality. You also gain time to adjust the debriefing plan according to the last developments, prepare a summary of feedback results, post theme questions, and instruct leaders on the content of their concluding speech. Your students gain valuable time for preparations. Yet be aware that if you postpone the debriefing session for too long you may lose the momentum, the vividness of memories may fade, and the motivation to share experiences and learn from others may decline.

Procedures

The move from plan to procedures requires the translation of a strategic design for debriefing into operational measures and tools. These tools will guide your students in preparation for and participation in the debriefing session. Two verbs summarize your procedures for the debriefing session: *prepare* and *conduct*.

Prepare Tools

To set an in-depth debriefing discussion in motion and run efficient sessions, you need to prepare (1) topics for feedback summary, (2) theme questions for discussion, (3) guidelines for team presentation, (4) elements of wrap-up speeches, and (5) subjects for research projects.

The questions, themes, and elements that guide the debriefing preparations are individual tasks for each student as a solitary learning process, but some of them, as detailed below, require collective teamwork, so you have to make sure your students adhere to the debriefing schedule and have a way to get together and complete their joint tasks. For example, on their Facebook group, a team may decide how to allocate the responsibilities for their joint presentation. One teammate can focus on team goals, another on the team's achievements, and others may summarize aspects such as how the team was presented in the media, what the team's contributions to the simulation outcome were, or any other topic you request. With the aid of virtual platforms, your students, as a learning community, can share the products they create and comment on those of each other's so the final product is a well researched, carefully edited product that reflects the team's consensus as well as differences of opinion that emerged in the simulation.

Topics for Feedback Summary

A short list of core topics you want to include in a summary presentation on the feedback from students is useful in case you open the debriefing overview with an aggregate overview of findings. The feedback information is derived from the different forms described in chapter 8. It covers many aspects and provides you with a wealth of valuable information. At the overlap between feedback and debriefing, as illustrated in figure 7.2, you need to select from the feedback information a few aspects that can make a meaningful contribution to your debriefing event.

To create a good presentation that will shape an effective discussion, make sure to (1) choose the most interesting findings that will lead participants to join the dialogue; (2) add examples from events that occurred during the simulation to make it tangible and draw participants into the debate; (3) highlight the links between events in the simulation and what you teach in the course, to help students embed their acquired knowledge with the affective experiences and actual practice they went through; (4) challenge common assertions and show unexpected results to trigger a debate; and (5) be short and to the point, so you leave ample time for the brainstorming that follows. All in all, you must consider the weight of the presentation relative to other parts of the debriefing session and highlight topics that make a difference as far as the simulation project and the learning experience it produced are concerned.

Theme Questions

These questions focus on the main issues you want to include in the interactive part of the debriefing, mainly thought-provoking ones representing (1) problematic conceptual discontinuities, like how clash-of-civilizations explanations are used with no clear definition of a civilization or its members; (2) distressing value trade-offs, like how to strengthen democratic resolve against terror groups and prevent terror attacks without forsaking democratic freedoms; (3) disturbing empirical inconsistencies, like how a superpower could be confronted by revolutionary crowds who challenge the norms of diplomatic immunity and take the embassy staff hostage; (4) controversial behavioral paradoxes, like how a small number of extreme fanatics can challenge a large group of mighty nations and change their mode of conduct; and (5) salient ethical dilemmas, like should a nation release terrorists in return for hostages or engage in rescue operations against all odds.

To make the discussion well focused and practical, it is useful to choose themes that have some relevance to the values, goals, and plans considered during the policy formation process or to the events that took place during the world politics encounters. Whatever theme you choose, it should ignite a lively debate, so you may decide to use a normative starting point or a controversial position even from outside the range of your main curriculum. When you request students to cope with such theme questions in revisiting their simulation experience, you make them confront these issues, not only in the simulation, but beyond it.

Guidelines for Team Presentations

These instructions specify the essential information you want each team to address in the presentation. We suggest that students include (1) relevant data on the actor and its leading characters, (2) debates on team values, (3) debates on team goals, (4) debates on team policy plans, (5) media strategy, (6) main difficulties in each round of world politics, (7) main achievements in each round of world politics, (8) lessons learned from the simulation project, and (9) suggestions for improvements in the future.

The team presentations are a good way to motivate and guide students to accomplish a broad comparative overview across political and media teams. As an opening for a debriefing session or as a stand-alone assignment, it is a creative way to look back at all simulation events and focus on the highlights of the project.

Elements of Wrap-Up Speeches

These elements are the essential topics each head of team includes in a *wrap-up speech* to summarize the simulation and open the debriefing. Speeches should last approximately five minutes and contain some sound bites, that is, short sentences that are easy to remember and make an impact, like "we want change," "we are the winners," or "peace should prevail." In every speech each leader should provide (1) an eyewitness account of a personal encounter, (2) the most important gain of the team, (3) the main difficulty the team confronted, (4) the most important lesson teammates learned, and (5) inputs for change and practical adaptation to produce better simulations in the future.

Team leaders need to appraise their teamwork, their activities in world politics, and their achievements. Opening speeches add personal points of view of the team leaders and the encounters they went through. They encourage other students to share their feelings and perspectives with their peers. Opening speeches can also trigger a candid discussion about practical concerns related to all participants and ideas for modification in simulation conduct.

Subjects for Research Projects

Your curriculum and the contents of your course define the subjects for research. Simulation activities and products are another source for topics. Students should

be advised to build on their experiences as participants and blend them into their research projects. As a step to advance their research projects during debriefing, they should (1) choose a paradigm, theory, or model, (2) list its fundamental assumptions and check their relevance to the simulation scenarios, actors, and interactions, (3) decide on variables and hypotheses, and (4) conduct a brief literature review. After debriefing is over students can integrate insights and critiques with data generated during the simulation to test hypotheses in the simulated world. This can be done with or without other past, current, or fiction cases for comparison. Depending on the schedule you set, the full research project should be submitted on time with a summary of findings and a discussion on the use and contributions of simulations as a research tool.

Conduct Session

Debriefing sessions build on information and evaluation derived from the feedback stage and other simulation products as well as on the wealth of knowledge gained in the course. As noted, each debriefing session includes (1) an opening outline by the educator or by students as heads of team or as a joint team, (2) interactive brainstorming, and (3) concluding remarks and implications led primarily by the educator.

Opening Outline

The debriefing session begins with an *opening outline* that you or your students present. Since debriefing sessions may be planned for several points in time, as the simulation develops you may decide to open each debriefing with a different tool, as we did in the Palestinian statehood simulation summarized in the appendix. The debriefing meeting in class after policy formation began with speeches by heads of team on teamwork and achievements. The debriefing after a Facebook round of world politics began with *team presentations*. The last debriefing after the face-to-face world politics round on campus opened with our *presentation of feedback findings*. Together, the different debriefing sessions highlighted individual, team, and collective class perspectives, pointing to the multifaceted experience the simulation generated for all participants as an active learning community.

Interactive Discussion

The main thrust of an effective debriefing session involves brainstorming to examine, evaluate, and criticize within and between team activities and the simulation project in general. This dynamic introspective process is the longest and most important part of the debriefing event. It flows from the *theme questions* you provide all students ahead of time and from immediate reactions to the short opening overview. To reach fruitful insights and creative results during these interactions you may step aside and let your students engage in a *discussion*. Just make sure to let the different voices be heard and remain as open-minded and flexible as possible to allow for some deviations from your planned outline.

You may assign some students to take notes and record the debates and discussions in order to prepare draft outlines, draw comparative conclusions, and generate comprehensive summaries. You can post these products on a cyber platform so all students can add to revised documents and learn from them. We recommend that, when an improvised conversation flow occurs at some stage of the debate, you let it continue as it may lead the debriefing to unpredicted directions, air emotions that were aroused during the simulation, and bring to light insights for new research topics. These may include issues like the ability to see reality from the opponent's viewpoint, the importance of empathy and identification in politics, or the question of changing attitudes as a result of practice through simulation.

When you cooperate with colleagues, effective debriefing is a challenge in both face-to-face and cyber simulations. Without a joint physical location, such debriefing becomes possible on cyber platforms. One way is to exchange short written messages online in real time. Another is by video conferences that provide a much richer experience, as a close surrogate to a face-to-face on-campus meeting. An effective session is dependent on the availability of high-speed broadband connections, a well-structured plan, and closely monitored interactions. The collective brainstorming between colleagues and students from afar is a unique opportunity to reveal cultural differences, shared frustrations, new understandings, and ultimately a need for closer ties across our global village.

Concluding Remarks and Implications

Your leading role as an educator is essential during the last part of the debriefing encounter. Your task is to summarize the results of the brainstorming discussion and to highlight the most important implications of the simulation project for the learning experience. At this point you may decide to pay special attention to mishaps and unplanned occurrences and comment on adjustments and

changes offered by your students. Don't forget to keep the records of all debriefing sessions for rigorous research in the future based on comparative insights, practical adaptations, and a comprehensive analysis of several simulations.

In our courses we have made many changes as a consequence of debriefing sessions, regarding the content of feedback forms, the choice of cyber platform, ways to overcome Facebook deficiencies, backup information, and the analysis of data. We started our initial shift to a cyber platform with online talks and negotiation using free e-mail systems for transactions and later moved to popular social networks like Facebook that allowed us utilize the advantages of the Web 2.0 at its best. Our advice to use cyber tools, even as you conduct face-to-face simulations, stems from the way students already operate. It is their habits and recommendations that drew us to the conclusion that hybrid learning should occur daily, not only in distance learning courses but also during most traditional ones. Our student body has already relocated to the virtual environment, even when they are physically in class, making it reasonable for us to join them to ensure that the learning process we lead does not lose its audience and active participants.

Instructions for Participants

As in earlier chapters, this section on instructions for participants concisely summarizes the main points described in the chapter till now. It is designed as a quick summary you can present to your students, with table 9.2 as a handout in class, a file sent by e-mail, or uploaded on the simulation website and social network platform. The brief explanations provided in this section assume that the reader is familiar with the details and analysis provided in this chapter.

Get Familiar

Debriefing involves interactions, which differ from students' solitary work on simulation questionnaires, surveys, and forms. To get ready for the debriefing and participate effectively in discussions, students must get familiar with subjects and topics of the debriefing, theme questions, the schedule, and the opening mode. They should understand your expectations for the debriefing meeting as early as you provide guidelines on the simulation website, social network, or during your lectures. When students review

TABLE 9.2. Instructions for Participants on Debriefing

Task	Details
Get familiar	Review schedule and theme questions
Study	Review your role and experiences from four perspectives: (1) an individual participant, (2) an assigned character, (3) part of an assigned team, (4) the simulation as a whole
Participate in the debriefing session	Listen and learn from others Share insights Raise questions Be critical and creative Suggest changes and improvements Integrate the different aspects into a comprehensive outlook Consider relevant inputs and ideas for preparation of final assignments and research projects
Follow instructions	Abide by the debriefing guidelines and schedule Prepare your contributions for the discussion on time

the schedule and theme questions they know what to prepare and can begin their individual and team study to increase the quality of the debriefing sessions.

Study

For a meaningful debriefing, students should revisit the simulation project thoroughly. In doing so they refresh their memories about experiences they have had, prepare better products for the debriefing session if requested, and come with new insights in retrospect. Study toward debriefing requires students to review their role and activities from four perspectives: (1) as an individual participant, (2) as an assigned character, (3) as part of a collective representing a political or media team, and (4) from an objective outlook on the simulation as a progressive experience. To be able to do so efficiently, students have to assemble all the material they have created during the simulation, classify and analyze it before the debriefing discussions begin, and compare it with products generated by others. This can be done by each student alone, or jointly with teammates to reduce individual workload and increase the quality of brainstorming with peers. The sources students need to review for debriefing involve all relevant products created beforehand, such as (1) individual assignments, for example, the character's biography; (2) collective team material, for example, records of intrateam dialogue, the joint actor portfolio, values, goals, and policy plans; (3) interaction logs and contributions from all participants, for example, posts on the social network platform and records of the interactions in the world politics including statements and speeches, negotiation summaries, drafts of documents, agreements,

treaties, or documents of disagreement; and (4) media products, for example, documents on media strategy and products like newspapers, photos, and video clips. After students revisit and summarize all these sources they have produced earlier with their peers as political characters and media professionals, they can contribute to a lively and productive discussion as observers in retrospect.

Participate in Debriefing

Participation requires attendance in a classroom session that you may even broadcast live by video conference to bring together students from afar or in one conducted on social networks. During the session, students should listen and think, react to the arguments and inquiries, share insights, raise critical questions, express creative ideas, and suggest changes and improvements for simulations in the future. Students that are naturally good speakers should be reminded that they need to be attentive to other students, let others express their opinions, and even encourage students to share their own perspective. Debriefing is an exchange of personal experiences with no "right" or "wrong" ideas, so every student can participate in the discussion and contribute to the collective overview of the simulation project.

Follow Instructions

Coordination between students and educators affects the success of an interactive discussion. Students must follow instructions to prepare for, contribute to, and learn from the debriefing. Students that disregard instructions spoil the learning experience of all others. For example, if students come late to the session or leave early, especially in face-to-face debriefing, they distract peers and educator and might find it difficult to catch up with an ongoing dialogue. They also miss the opening speeches or concluding remarks. So, all students must prepare their contributions for the discussion on time, abide by the debriefing guidelines, and take part in the meeting from beginning to end.

Summary

Debriefing is part of the simulation overview. It focuses on the plan and procedures for interactive sessions between the educator and the students to discuss cumulative data produced during the simulation, exchange ideas, provide insights, and offer critiques of the simulation project from different perspectives, as individuals, team members, heads of teams, and as a group of students who look back at the simulation events as an audience from outside. The chapter deals with the debriefing plan by looking at options for focus, method, and schedule. Then it outlines the procedures that translate the plan into an operational tool for implementation in face-to-face and cyber simulations, with details on how to open the session to trigger an effective discussion, conduct the brainstorming exchanges with flexibility, and lead the conclusion of the session to highlight the most salient issues, meaningful critiques, practical advice, and core implications. The chapter ends with a summary of instructions for participants to make the interactive debriefing session successful.

CHAPTER 10

Assessment

Assessment is an activity in which the educator revisits simulation goals, grades students, and appraises the simulation project in terms of its study efficiency. When you are done with the simulation and your course is almost over you have to grade your students. We all do so year after year. When it comes to the assessment of the simulation project itself, the task is often set aside. Scholars who run simulations usually believe in the tool they employ and enjoy. It is important to look back at the simulations you have run and ask: Is the project worth the costs? Does the simulation fulfill expectations? Is the simulation an effective mode of teaching in this digital information age?

Unfortunately, rigorous tools for assessment of simulation projects are still awaiting further development. Probably the best advice we have at present is to plan your simulation carefully in advance and assess it as it progresses in the most systematic and critical manner possible, to improve results over time. Though most of your assessment occurs after the simulation ends, it requires observations as the simulation evolves, inputs from students' feedback, and insights from interactive debriefing sessions. Assessment is important in face-to-face and cyber simulations alike, so unless we mention specific details, the discussion covers all types of simulations.[1]

The Plan

Assessment requires a twofold plan to (1) grade students and (2) appraise the simulation. Grading students is characteristic of all academic courses, programs, and projects where students earn credit for their study. In a simulation it is more difficult to grade students because the component of active participation is much more extensive than in traditional courses. We recommend that you plan and upload your grading rubric on the cyber platform of your choice and explain it in your introduction lectures so that students will not be surprised or disappointed at the end of the simulation project.

Appraisal of a simulation requires your consideration of simulation goals and achievements. Simulations can make study enjoyable, enable practice, and deepen students' knowledge, but they demand more work on your behalf than traditional lectures. A full assessment of the simulation is essential to identify major changes needed for long-term restructuring of the educational tool you use. But from a practical point of view, it is valuable in the short run as well, for the immediate introduction of adaptations during an ongoing simulation.

From time to time it is important to step aside and revisit the payoffs gained by the simulation. The plan for appraising simulations involves concerns of focus, method, and schedule for the assessment.

Focus

Assessment focus refers to the elements you choose to emphasize in grading students and appraising the simulation. Table 10.1 presents grading rubrics with alternative weight options for different components of student contributions, and table 10.2 offers appraising options for a simulation project in retrospect.

A plan on how to *grade students* takes into account (1) assignments, (2) participation in policy formation and

TABLE 10.1. Grading Options

Contents	Weights (%)		
	Option A Assignment driven	Option B Participation driven	Option C Overview driven
Assignments			
Preparation for the simulation	30	10	10
Postsimulation research	40	none	10
Participation			
Activities as an assigned character	10	20	10
Contribution to teamwork		20	10
Contribution to world politics		20	10
Contribution to simulation outcome		20	10
Overview activity			
Feedback	10	5	20
Debriefing	10	5	20
Total	100	100	100

world politics, and (3) participation in feedback and debriefing. The assessment plan involves difficult dilemmas and recognition of trade-offs. For instance, you have to measure solitary work versus teamwork, calculate the quality of written assignments versus active participation, and decide how to grade shy students correctly and how to reward heads of teams or other very motivated students.

An emphasis on students' *assignments* is described in option A of table 10.1. In simulations that aim primarily at the acquisition of knowledge you may follow the usual practice in traditional courses with written assignments as the main inputs for a final grade. In this option, products like actor portfolio, values, goals, and plans handed in before the simulation or postsimulation research projects receive the highest weight in the grading rubric. But participation and overview activity get less credit and may affect students' motivation to invest in active communications within and among teams and in the practice of major skills like coping, teamwork, critical thinking, empathy, and leadership.

An emphasis on students' *participation*, illustrated in option B of table 10.1, looks at the multifaceted contributions of each student. When you underline participation, you motivate students to take more active part in simulation and therefore maximize their gains from the simulation exercise as a learning tool. But such grading requires interpretive methods and tools beyond the ones employed in traditional courses, as discussed in the method section below.

An emphasis on *overview activity*, detailed in option C of table 10.1, focuses on each student's contributions to feedback and debriefing. This option is especially recommended for graduate courses that seek methodological gains and explore the balance sheet of simulations as an emerging social science lab. Feedback and debriefing are protracted activities that cover the simulation from beginning to end, so they require your ongoing observation along with continuous student participation. The advantages and problems of grading overview activities are similar to those of grading participation.

You can assign more or less equal importance to preparation, assignments, participation, and simulation overview, thus motivating your students to fulfill all assignments and participate in all activities including those of the overview. This choice frees you from trade-off decisions and integrates traditional formal grades with interpretive ones on activities, befitting the use of innovative tools in formal learning environments.

When it comes to a plan for *appraising of the simulation*, you have several options, summarized in table 10.2. Each option highlights different aspects and has an impact on the overall score a simulation gets.

Option A emphasizes *knowledge gains* as the primary goal. It involves cognitive learning and the achievements your students make, detailed in items 34 to 37 of table 8.6 and explained in the procedures section below. This type of plan is most common for simulations run as a complementary tool in traditional courses that advance

TABLE 10.2. Appraising Options for the Simulation Project

Students' Learning Gains	Weights (%)		
	Option A Knowledge driven	Option B Practice driven	Option C Methodology driven
Cognitive: knowledge base			
On a case, period, and region	30	10	none
Theory	30	10	none
Methodology	5	none	60
Behavioral: practice			
Policy formation	15	20	10
World politics		20	10
Skills		20	10
Affective: emotional experience			
One's own	none	10	10
One's team	10	5	none
Others: allies and rivals	10	5	none
Total	100	100	100

knowledge attainment and retention. Other benefits of active learning with simulations are considered as secondary gains that may supplement and strengthen knowledge development.

Option B emphasizes *skill practice*. While skills are a gift students bring with them, they may also develop by observation of others, imitation, and practice of individual participation, leadership, and teamwork throughout the simulation.[2] When you plan to highlight skill attainment, you can concentrate on abilities to cope with analytical dilemmas and emotional challenges, as outlined in items 38 to 46 in table 8.6.

Option C emphasizes *methodology* considerations for use in courses designed mostly for graduate-level research design and simulation programs. It is the closest you can get to the use of simulations as a research lab in its dual role of (1) testing hypotheses in a deductive manner and (2) creating a database of simulation-generated products that can be used for a variety of research purposes. To appraise simulations designed to advance methodology and test theory, you can use the quality of research proposals, reports, and full research projects as a gauge, based on traditional ways to grade academic assignments. There are many other options for an appraisal of simulation projects, like illuminating moral dilemmas, problems of identification, or empathy with others in conflict situations. These and other topics of your choice can be integrated as core goals that you aim to promote. Your views

on the results of the simulation, compared with feedback responses students provide and insights raised during the debriefing sessions, provide a good starting point for a thorough assessment of the simulation project. As long as you stay open-minded, the inputs you gain from simulation participants should serve as a core indicator of goal attainment, coupled and at times contrasted with your own assessment on these matters.

Method

After setting your assessment plan you have to decide on a way to implement it. *Method* refers to the way you translate a plan into operational tools to grade students and appraise the simulation. Most grading concerns of assignments are common to all academic courses so we look at methods to assess participation as a special requirement in simulations. Then we offer a method to appraise simulations that blends qualitative and quantitative tools and integrates feedback from students with interpretive inputs of your own.

To grade participation you can choose between quantitative, qualitative, or combined methods. With a quantitative method you can explore the *breadth of participation*. To calculate the ratio of individual involvement compared with total activity in an objective way, you need to track the volume and timing of each and all students' contributions in policy formation, world politics, feedback, and debriefing. Grading of participation in policy formation and world politics interactions, for example, should take into account whether a student attended a team meeting and participated in each of the world politics rounds and in the breaking news session. But assessment also requires qualitative considerations of content.

To explore the *depth of participation* you should take the quality of student's contributions into account. Students who suggest creative and innovative ideas, demonstrate understanding of theory and empirical knowledge, adhere to simulation rules, share tasks with others, and lead with initiatives of their own should receive a higher grade.

Grading also involves assessment of contributions in terms of theoretical and empirical contents that demonstrate personal knowledge and advance the dialogue between peers. You can make a list of core concepts and data as essential content to look for in written or oral messages in order to systematically appraise the content. But make sure to leave room for second thoughts about your interpretations, because the difference between regular and excellent messages is neither easy to determine nor easy to apply in a systematic manner across all participants.

Part of the work within teams in policy formation and among teams during world politics interactions is done individually by students while performing their role in the simulation. While heads of team may invest more time and efforts than others, creative initiatives may come from all students. Even the shy ones may feel confident to propose ideas within their team. So, *collective teamwork* is another important input to your assessment of simulation activities, to be added to the grade of all members of each team.

In face-to-face simulations it may be hard to record participation and revisit it for the purpose of grading. To overcome this deficiency you may need to keep a log of simulation activities, but you can only be in one place at any point in time, and you always miss activities that occurred elsewhere, in other rooms, or even other parts of the same room. Still, it is extremely difficult to quantify conversations and accurately measure the volume of students' contributions, unless you employ sophisticated recording devices. Protocols of discussions may be useful, but they shed light on main themes, not on the details. Full recording of all proceedings may solve this problem, but it is a costly solution.

In simulations on social networks all conversations are automatically recorded and saved as a robust database for quantitative assessment of participation. Social networks are an ideal solution as they instantly back up all activities and media products, enable teams to upload and share documents, links, photos, and video clips. All these are available for your examination so that you can summarize the number and quality of messages, both by individual participant and by teams. By using two consecutive rounds, one on a cyber platform and the other as a face-to-face meeting, you gain the best of all worlds and can integrate quantitative data on the former with qualitative assessments from the latter.

As detailed in table 10.5, the assessment of simulations involves (1) student inputs, (2) educator views, (3) weights that are a result of your choice of simulation goals and the promotion of topics you have planned to focus on. We suggest a combined qualitative and quantitative method that integrates students' perspectives with your own judgments.

The *inputs from students' feedback* involve both methods. When you resort to multiple-choice questions with prefixed answers, feedback is mainly quantitative. Open questions provide qualitative comments. Both are a rich data source on the achievement of simulation goals from the participants' perspective. As you plan the feedback forms, explained in chapter 8, keep in mind that you are also advancing the task of performing a rigorous simulation appraisal.

Beyond the students' outlook, assessment concerns your own views as a core input. Remember that you must be your own "devil's advocate" as you look critically at the exercise you have just completed. To reach a somewhat objective assessment, we suggest that you use both methods, although the bulk of the process is qualitative. Quantitative inputs to your *decisions on goal attainment* may be formal, such as attendance in class or average grades and their increase as the simulation proceeds. If you want other quantitative tools, you need to develop indicators to measure each of the goals summarized in table 10.5. Some help is provided by cooperation with colleagues in a joint simulation project. A mutual plan for the simulation requires compromises on topics, schedule, and assignments, as detailed in chapters 4, 5, and 6, but it ensures that at least two educators will take part in the critical postsimulation analysis.

Most assessments of goal attainment used nowadays, raised often in the simulation literature and addressed in chapter 3, are based on qualitative interpretations. Beyond these assessments, a more rigorous measure of *educators' inputs* should be developed through an ongoing dialogue between simulation users. In the absence of formal appraisal scales, the most useful approach is to compare each simulation you ran with other exercises from the past, and with simulations other educators have conducted. A comparative perspective is productive since it can illuminate common and persistent problems, as well as successful adaptations and helpful solutions. The future task should be to generate a pool of accepted criteria and operational measures, as discussed in chapters 7 and 11.

An additional task in the quest for a comprehensive simulation assessment is the analysis of differences in estimates of goal attainment between students' perspectives and that of the educator. When no gaps are evident, the implications are straightforward. As a result of joint student-educator inputs you should continue your project with minor or major revisions. But what if you find meaningful discrepancies in assessment between your own observations and that of your students? For a start, as hard as it may be, remember not to overlook meaningful critiques from students that come despite a reasonable tendency to conform and add positive comments in order to gain good grades. An effective solution in such circumstances is awaiting methods that may emerge from constructive deliberations and joint research by colleagues who use simulations as an active learning tool.

Schedule

Considerations for assessment of a simulation over time involve the identification of a few turning points where intermediate assessment is necessary, but the bulk of it takes place at the end of simulation. Important turning points in this process are (1) after policy formation, as you assess students' performance during intrateam activities; (2) between world politics rounds; and especially (3) after the simulation ends, as you appraise interteam activities. Providing students with grades on their assignments and participation as the simulation unfolds lets them integrate your comments and improve their performance as a gradual learning experience. It also gives you an idea of students' progress so you can adjust lecture and simulation contents and pace accordingly. The comprehensive assessment of the simulation project as a whole requires examination of the full learning cycle. That becomes possible after the simulation ends, taking into consideration your own insights without forsaking critical feedback provided in a systematic manner by simulation participants.

Procedures

For an in-depth assessment of student achievements and goal attainment you can apply seven procedures: (1) grade assignments, (2) assess individual participation and joint teamwork, (3) integrate the participants' perspectives and compare them with your own, (4) review skill development, (5) calculate final grades for students, (6) figure the balance sheet for the simulation project, and (7) consider adjustments for future simulations.

Once you complete all these procedures you will have a comprehensive simulation overview in hand. Make sure to back up all this information, analysis, and conclusions. They are likely to serve you well in the future, for a comparative examination of the simulations you conduct and for research purposes.

Grade Assignments

Table 10.3 builds on the assignments listed in table 4.3 and serves as a matrix for grading each individual student. You can adjust it according to the assignments you choose to include in your course and their weights. You can then transform it into an Excel sheet if you are used to database formats, or fill it in on a sheet of paper and back it up as a digital file. A database format for the grading scheme, preferably digital, on a cyber platform is useful as it allows for easy storage and backup and is accessible for research purposes as you run simulations over the years.

Summarize Individual Participation and Collective Teamwork

Simulation as a teaching tool provides incentives for students, as individuals and as members of teams, to participate in activities and to generate working papers, documents, and other products. In the section on method we suggest quantitative and qualitative measures to assess participation and point to the dilemma of interpretation as a basis for assessing the quality of activities. When you deal with procedures, you need to apply the methods and indicators of quality you have chosen in a systematic manner and summarize the results in a grade rubric similar to the prototype suggested in table 10.3.

Integrate Participants' Perspective

Table 10.5 serves as a rubric for assessing the simulation project as a whole. The first step is to take a look at aggregate findings from the feedback provided by your students in the simulation and after it ends. You may find that students see things in a different way than you do and that the students themselves are not a uniform group. So we advise that you address the students' written remarks and

TABLE 10.3. Grading Scheme

Learning Cycle	Task	When	Weight (%)	Grade
Preparation	Actor portfolio for states, international organizations, nonstate, and media teams	Before policy formation		
	Character biography			
	Actor and character values and ideology			
Policy formation and world politics for political teams	Team's goals, policy plan, and alternative moves	Before world politics		
	Participation in intrateam policy formation	Before and during world politics		
	Operational proposals, agreements, interviews with the media, and policy briefings for the media			
	Participation in world politics interactions among teams	During world politics		
Policy formation and world politics for media	Network orientation, values, and goals	Before world politics		
	Plans for products and division of labor			
	Media products: text, photos, video clips, news flashes, and newspapers	Before and during world politics		
Feedback, debriefing, and research	Feedback activities on an individual basis Participation in debriefing sessions Contribution to the collective discussion as a dynamic process	Mainly after world politics ends		
	Research proposals, reports, and complete research projects	Optional after the simulation ends		

evaluations and observe the main trends, as well as anomalies, carefully. While written remarks represent the cumulative experience of an individual participant, the main trends may indicate repetitive problems and lead you to think about solutions and avoid pitfalls, thereby making the simulation a better tool for all participants.

Review Skill Development

Beyond knowledge accumulation and retention, simulations are an ideal tool to help students acquire and practice many skills they need as professional citizens of the global village in the 21st century. These skills are covered in the registration form, detailed in table 8.2, as expectations students have. They also appear in follow-up reflections of students on skill development in many feedback questions, like items 38–46 in table 8.6. While the grades students get on a final exam may gauge the success of your simulation as a teaching tool, they do not indicate whether core skills were advanced.

With respect to grades, top students who are capable and motivated will usually get the highest grades, with or without simulations. Those that are at the very bottom may unfortunately stay there, regardless of all your ef-

forts and coaching. From our experience we have learned that simulations can improve the grades of students at the middle of the curve, providing them with a way to elevate their studies and advance their skills. But skill development is more than grades in a final exam. The plan for simulations and the procedures we offer are designed to promote the development of various skills and a genuine love of learning, as summarized in table 10.4.

Participation in the simulation project touches upon cognitive, behavioral, and affective skills that include analytical reasoning, critical thinking, expression, patience, coping with workload, stress, frustration, failure, empathy, creativity, and humor, both on an individual basis and during collective teamwork, while contributing to one another, being helped, and helping others. The development of cognitive skills occurs when students confront a gradual increase in difficulties, complexity, and scope of knowledge as they look for information in the process of learning and apply the knowledge they gained during the simulation. Behavioral skills are practiced during activities within and among teams.

The simulation overview offers a chance for advanced use of acquired knowledge and further skill development, with a special emphasis on putting the pieces of the puzzle

TABLE 10.4. Simulation Procedures for Skill Development

When	Procedure	Result
Throughout the simulation project	Progressive, consecutive preparation of assignments and feedback forms	Confront increased difficulty, complexity, and scope of knowledge
Policy formation	Discuss and decide policy by use of values, goals, and plans	Individual and collective use and practice of knowledge gained and skills like analytical reasoning, critical thinking, patience, teamwork, coping with workload, stress, frustration, failure, empathy, creativity, being helped, and helping others
	Create a collective team document by use of individual actor portfolio assignments	
Policy formation and world politics	Learn by activity and practice	
	Actors are represented by teams, not individuals	
	Media teams interact with political teams	
	Change and gradual increase in complexity, challenge, and uncertainty from (1) initial to opening scenario and ad-hoc events, (2) policy formation to world politics, (3) preparation for feedback and participation in debriefing, (4) preparation of research projects	
	Coaching by educator and peers	
	Use of social networks for activities within and among teams	
Feedback	Progressive feedback activities	Advanced use of acquired knowledge and skills to form a comprehensive overview and evaluate gains from diverse elements and personal experiences
Debriefing	Provocative theme questions for the debriefing session	
	Analytical overview and eyewitness experience in team presentations and opening speeches	
	Comparison of real and simulated worlds	

together and reconciling differences between one's own views, those of one's team, and of others, allies and especially rivals.

The results of the simulation in terms of skill achievement can be assessed qualitatively based on performance and quantitatively based on feedback from students. Together they indicate the contribution of your simulation project as a valuable study tool.

Calculate Final Grades

Table 10.3 presented above summarizes a rubric for producing the overall grade students get in your course, taking all elements of the simulation project into account. To solve core dilemmas of final grading we integrate many items in the prototype rubric, with slots to calculate separate achievements into the full account based on the weights you plan for each one of them in the final assessment. With careful integration of all relevant criteria and weights you can apply a progressive and systematic grading process. We recommend that you grade students as early as possible after they complete their assignments

during the simulation. This will provide them with information on their achievements so that they can make progress as the simulation unfolds.

Appraise the Simulation Project Balance Sheet

Table 10.5 summarizes the elements for producing the overall simulation project balance sheet. We believe that simulations should generate a comprehensive experience for individuals and teams, based on a meaningful engagement and multilevel study accomplishments. Together, these include cognitive, behavioral, and affective aspects summarized in table 1.2 on the framework of world politics simulation. To reflect the diverse issues that make simulations an effective study tool, we integrate many items into the balance sheet, with slots to appraise separate achievements into an overall account. We also leave separate slots for weights in the final assessment.

By applying table 10.5 at different points in time, as the simulation progresses and after the course ends, you can blend in data from feedback forms to reflect students' views. Then you can combine quantitative information

TABLE 10.5. Appraising Scheme for the Simulation Project

Learning	Goal Achievement	Feedback Inputs	Educator's View	Weight (%)	Total
Cognitive: knowledge base	Make the study more tangible so theories of international relations, political studies, social sciences, history, or media come to life				
	Apply paradigms and theories to complex situations				
	Expose underlying processes and causal mechanisms				
	Enrich learning by linking simulation developments to real events				
Behavioral: practice and skills	Combine systematic, flexible, and varied methods of study at individual and team levels				
	Serve as a laboratory for practical training and research on decision-making, negotiations, and journalism				
	Allow informal learning between educators and students				
	Expose diversity of cultural, ethical, and religious issues, value judgments, prejudice, and subjective points of view				
	Manage information and retain it longer				
	Develop critical thinking and analytical skills				
	Elevate civic culture and rhetoric skills				
	Encourage peer-based collaborative teamwork				
	Increase the number of students reached by the educator				
Affective: emotional experience	Complement and enhance traditional study by increasing motivation and encouraging an attentive and active learning process				
	Add creativity and improvisation to make learning emotional, intensive, and enjoyable				
	Facilitate sympathy, empathy, identification, and attitude modifications				

with qualitative estimates of "high" and "low" to capture participants' responses and your own interpretations. The final score takes your view into account, together with that of your students, and requires a decision on how to reconcile differences, explain them, and cope with their implications. We regard the task of how to calculate the grand total as an open issue that still awaits future solutions to ensure progress toward the development of more rigorous simulation assessment tools.

Consider Adjustments for Future Simulations

After reading the feedback comments from your students, addressing the aggregate feedback data, and conducting debriefing sessions, you probably have some ideas for adjustments, adaptations, and revisions of the course curriculum and the simulation project. For example, you can

start with a change in (1) topic, to conduct simulations on new empirical cases or on theories and paradigms you have not yet tested; (2) teams and roles, to emphasize regional powers or superpowers, nonstate actors you might have overlooked, or the role of public opinion in democratic and nondemocratic regimes; and (3) scenario formats, from a formal invitation as detailed in chapters 5 and 6, to a newspaper to highlight the role of the media in publicizing information and the difficulties of validating the uncertainties related to this type of source. You can also (4) implement a policy formation debate within all teams after running a simulation with world politics rounds alone; (5) shift from individual role-play to teamwork, highlighting the effects of group dynamics and domestic constraints on policy formation; (6) apply different schedules, change the duration of the project and its rounds to validate the impact of time and gradual practice on the quality of simulations you run; (7) move beyond traditional face-to face simulations by intensive reliance on cyber tools or the coupling of two rounds, one on a cyber platform, the other face-to-face; or (8) run a simulation with colleagues from afar to offer your students an exciting intercultural experience.

Each of these changes builds upon the experiences you have gained in the past and provides you with new challenges, some difficulties, and many rewards. The most important thing is that by using different tools, readjusting old plans, and creating new story lines, you start afresh and prevent teaching stagnation.

By the introduction of change you also get an opportunity to compare different simulations you run and gain insights about the relative advantages of each one of them. This way, over time you can reach the best-fit prototype for your teaching requirements. Based on your experience, you can also allow for flexibility within a simulation plan you run, react to problems as they appear, and cope with unexpected occurrences in a smooth manner.

Summary

Like feedback and debriefing, this chapter on assessment is part of the simulation overview. It focuses on educator activities to summarize the individual learning achievements of each student and the effectiveness of the entire simulation project as a teaching tool.

The chapter begins with a plan for dual assessment of students and the simulation project and then details the procedures designed to implement the plan. For an assessment of student achievements and goal attainment, you can apply seven procedures: grade assignments, assess individual participation and joint teamwork, integrate participants' perspectives and compare it with your own, review skill development, calculate final grades for students, appraise the balance sheet for the simulation project, and consider adjustments for future simulations.

To accomplish proper grading, a detailed assessment rubric is suggested with the various assignments addressed in chapter 4 and other inputs such as participation and expressions of core skills, which are harder to quantify. To assess the value of simulations as a teaching tool we suggest that you blend your own judgments with feedback from participants. The goals set in advance and costs incurred throughout the simulation are revised during the assessment process, making it possible for adjustments to be introduced as an incremental development for perfecting your simulations.

PART IV

Conclusion

CHAPTER 11

The Future of World Politics Simulations

This chapter highlights the core themes that drive a successful integration of simulations into hybrid learning to create an exciting pedagogical experience for students and educators. Simulations of all types can considerably enhance learning efficiency. Without forsaking the human touch, cyber applications in general and social networks in particular can contribute to even better results. Let us recall and draw together the major ideas that we believe will shape the evolution of simulations in coming years.

The theoretical part of the book argues that simulations as a subset of hybrid learning leads to a positive change in teaching and learning and to the emergence of a sense of community among students and educators. It offers a new typology of simulation genres that emphasizes the importance of technological innovations. This typology illuminates an overview of simulations over time to show how pioneering scholars integrated new technologies to improve modes of study, to test theories, and to provide a more comprehensive explanation of world politics. It is the cumulative work of these previous generations that led to the present state of affairs, in which successful simulations of the past, like face-to-face ones, maintain relevance along with the emergence of new cyber genres. However, it is surprising to find that in the midst of the second decade of the 21st century, after Facebook has become a core icon of the digital age, the integration of virtual platforms and especially social networks into world politics simulations is still rather limited.

Back to the Future

We intend this book to be a helpful companion and step by step guide for the implementation of simulations in hybrid learning. It provides explanations on why modifications of older traditions are necessary for you to plan and run exciting simulation projects. The hands-on description of how to conduct a successful diplomatic exercise details the choices you have and procedures you can adopt. Each recommendation relates to the goals and benefits of the simulation plan and its procedures, specifies the difficulties you may encounter, and suggests practical tips on how to overcome them.

Major Themes

Organized in a modular format, this book encompasses major themes that emphasize the multifaceted, comprehensive, and appealing character of simulations in the digital age and reflect the value of simulations for the study of world politics. Running through its different chapters, the themes we discuss are (1) face-to-face and cyber simulations, (2) past and present simulations in the literature with some prospects for future developments, (3) along a full cycle from preparation to debriefing and research, (4) with detailed explanations on plans and procedures, (5) from the outlook of the educator and that of students, (6) by focusing on learning and teaching, (7) designed for experienced users and newcomers, (8) in undergraduate and graduate programs, (9) on diverse topics that fit a wide array of course subjects, (10) in many fields of humanities and social sciences, (11) with an emphasis on interdisciplinary cooperation among colleagues and joint enrichment, (12) bringing together teams that represent political actors and media organs, (13) for a protracted learning and gradual practice, (14) from decision-making during policy formation, (15) to the implementation of policies in world politics interactions, (16) including considerations for policy revision and adaptation.

A 2014 simulation of Israeli-Palestinian negotiations on the establishment of a Palestinian state brought to bear the core themes summarized above. Since it was a training exercise for ISA members, preparation was limited and relied on the expertise of the participants. The simulation started with policy formation on Facebook where, at their convenience, teammates from different parts of the world discussed the initial simulation scenario and reached consensus as to their team's values, goals, and policy plans. After several weeks of within-team dialogue, participants representing the European Union, Israel, Jordan, the Palestinians, Saudi Arabia, the United States, and the media, met online at a scheduled time for a round of negotiations. To trigger immediate interactions among teams, we released an updated scenario in the form of a Saudi peace plan and asked all parties to discuss its clauses in an effort to reach an agreement. Intensive negotiations took place for two and a half hours, with a media break midsession. News flashes with salient headlines accompanied by photographs added authenticity to the Facebook atmosphere. Despite the geographic distance among participants and the difference in time zones, the social network successfully enabled policy formation and multilateral negotiations. But just like in the real world, the Israeli and Palestinian teams were unable to agree on whether Hamas should have a role in the talks, which ended in deadlock.

The cyber platform was indispensable for making the simulation project a protracted and gradual practice, which lasted for more than two months before participants met during the annual ISA convention in Toronto. Most participants had never met before in person, but their joint experience on Facebook brought an immediate air of familiarity to the face-to-face encounter. After a brief meeting for policy revision within teams, the simulation continued from the point where the online negotiations had ended. Not surprisingly, face-to-face negotiations on the peace plan stalled almost immediately, as the parties strongly disagreed on who should sit where at the negotiation table and whether Hamas should be included as part of a unified Palestinian leadership. These fundamental disagreements remained intact even during an informal diplomatic "Falafel party" in the midst of the simulation, when the Israeli team refused to attend an event with Hamas. Negotiations ended in stalemate, demonstrating the complexities of a search for a solution to the Israeli-Palestinian conflict. Postsimulation debriefing discussions focused on the advantages of face-to-face and cyber simulations as an effective teaching tool. Those who had never taken part in a simulation before, as well as experienced users, eagerly agreed that it is important to try out innovative teaching modes and to consider how the experience feels from a student's perspective. Many of them compared our ISA simulation with other simulations they had used previously in their classes, on diverse subject areas and in different disciplines, such as history, communications, international relations, environment, comparative public policy, and area studies. Most participants expressed their willingness to take part in similar faculty simulations in the future and suggested cross-continental simulations for graduate and undergraduate students in the United States, the Middle East, Europe, and other regions.

Obstacles and Recommendations for Change

This conclusion sets an agenda for future use of world politics simulations. Tables 11.1 to 11.4 summarize common obstacles related to simulations and provide recommendations for how to overcome them. Many of the obstacles derive from the first part of the book on the theory, while the suggestions for change are drawn mainly from the second part on implementation.

The review of obstacles and recommendations covers the entire learning cycle, from solitary preparation to a full simulation overview, with feedback, debriefing, and assessment, as detailed in part III of the book on analysis. The simulation overview is about looking at the project as a whole, from hindsight. It is not a part of the interactive process in which participants step into assigned roles as decision-makers or media professionals and follow the story lines of simulation scenarios. As a dynamic element some of the inputs to this overview take place while the simulation unfolds. The students who provide intermediate feedback and partake in the debriefing look back at their encounters, from the outside, to gain insights and improve their understanding of world politics. The full overview of the simulation as a whole takes into account both student and educator perspectives to ensure that the interactive experiences are translated into an effective study cycle.

We hope simulations gain mainstream status and become a regular component of higher education for the coming generations of students. We confess our bias: a belief that simulations are an indispensable educational experience that should be gradually integrated into major academic programs in the humanities and social sciences. At the same time, we are aware of the obstacles and costs related to simulations. Close and continuous dialogue among simulation users can make the tool we all use a better one. We regard this book as a step forward and invite you to join us and enrich the field, based on your own experiences, insights, critiques, and advice. With a long tradition of face-to-face simulations and the recent developments in cyber ones, the ongoing mission of improving simulations as a mode of study in the digital information age will continue to evolve. As part of hybrid learning and innovative teaching, the future use of simulations will undoubtedly be based on trial and error exercises to develop and systematically apply rigorous tools that measure study efficiency and improve simulations.

A best-fit simulation depends on your personal inclinations and on the opportunities and constraints of your academic setting, namely the subject you teach, the type of course you conduct and its duration, the size of your class, and the extent of cooperation you plan with other colleagues.

The framework of simulation attributes presented in chapter 1 is used herein to guide the summary of core obstacles and recommendations related to platforms, boundaries, interactions, and study efficiency. Beyond this brief summary you can always return to the relevant chapters of the book for an in-depth analysis on how to run simulations and improve them.

Platform Choice

Platforms characterize the physical infrastructure and virtual environments of learning in general and of the simulation in particular. They involve a wide range of settings, from a lecture hall or conference room for face-to-face meetings to virtual "rooms" for interactions on social networks. The use of various platforms for simulations requires fundamental changes in the ways we teach world politics and promote the essential skills students need. Table 11.1 summarizes the main obstacles related to platform selection and highlights the recommendations to overcome them.

The study cycle suggested in this book, from preparation, via participation in policy formation and world politics, to debriefing, redesigns the curriculum, transforms solitary learning, expands traditional resources, and replaces passive learning with active participation. It leads to the emergence of a learning community among peer students and a meaningful partnership between students and educator that advances the success of the simulation project and study in general.

Cyber tools of the digital age overcome many obstacles related to simulations. As technology advances, it be-

comes easier to run simulations. An entire simulation or part of it can take place online, parallel to regular class meetings. Various educators' tasks and students' assignments can be performed in cyberspace. The real change introduced by the digital era is not one of platform, but of the broad spectrum of choices you have in creating a simulation that fits your specific academic setting and teaching goals. You can assemble any combination of simulation elements and decide which part of the project will evolve in class, on social networks, or in a combination of both platforms. For instance, you may begin with introductory lectures on the simulation project in class or via distance learning tools, move on to policy formation on social networks, and culminate the learning experience with an international politics conference conducted face-to-face on campus. For the simulation overview, you may post feedback forms online in order to collect, review, and summarize cumulative data from the participants' perspective and then organize a debriefing session in class. Alternatively, you may use video conference applications, such as Skype, to bring together participants from distant locations and instantly broadcast their products to one another. Such proxy face-to-face tools maximize the benefits of both the human and virtual worlds.

It is this great variation of traditional and cyber tools, as major or supplementary platforms, that makes teaching and learning with simulations enjoyable and rewarding. Competition between campuses and prudent selection of academic programs by students make it necessary to create an exciting and challenging curriculum. Simulations are a good choice for drawing academic institutions into the "outside" world and meeting growing student demand for practical knowledge and skills.

Boundaries Choice

The spatial and temporal boundaries encompass core attributes of topics, participants, teams, and time frame that shape the contents of a simulation and affect interactions within and among teams. Table 11.2 pulls together the common difficulties with regards to boundaries and suggests solutions.

Online features can considerably expand the spatial and temporal boundaries of a simulation. When you use cyberspace in your course, more places emerge for students to look for information, to upload individually prepared assignments, and to interact with their teammates or the class as a whole. The web is a boundless source of information. Whatever topic you choose for the simulation, your students will be able to find, read, listen, watch,

TABLE 11.1. Change in Simulation Platform

Obstacles
• *A genuine learning experience requires dedicated educators:* a full learning cycle builds on the central role and major impact of ongoing contacts with an educator on an individual and group basis.
• *Traditional learning environments no longer suffice:* varied digital stimuli, a wealth of resources, and multiple cyber tools are available on the Internet. All these have become a central part of daily life but a core element in only some academic institutions.
• *Distance learning has proliferated:* competition among academic institutions that offer online courses has increased considerably, and quality programs with exciting and practical elements are in demand.
• *The human touch in learning is indispensable:* through centuries of human evolution, eye contact, speech intonations, nonverbal communication, and charisma have become an integral part of learning heuristics. But it is still hard to include these elements in cyber communications.

Recommendations
• *Integrate social networks and other web platforms as teaching aids:* online features have already become a familiar mode of communication among students, so it is useful to incorporate them into the learning environment.
• *Keep the human touch intact:* couple physical and virtual platforms and add cyber tools, like Skype and YouTube, as supplementary or major platforms for simulations that retain a human dimension.
• *Create a theatrical setting:* add physical and digital accessories to enhance the authentic atmosphere of the simulated world. Use products created by media teams to enrich the simulation and help participants step into the story and roles they play.
• *Stay tuned and integrate new cyber applications:* add novel alternatives and improvements for the simulations you run as they become available and popular.
• *Reduce simulation costs:* recycle, adjust, and archive forms, scenarios, assignments, instructions for participants, and theatrical accessories you create for use from one simulation to another.
• *Secure privacy:* create closed groups on social networks for educational purposes, with your students as the only authorized members.

learn, and communicate easily about it online, whenever they want. This enables you to move part of the study to the virtual realm, beyond the classroom. For instance, when you explain the simulation in class, you may focus on a few core attributes of an event and encourage students to deepen their familiarity with that event and its historical background on their own via the web. This also gives your students a sense of partnership in the creation of a joint knowledge base, while letting you devote more attention to specific points you want to address in your lectures.

Cyber tools enable the use of digital formats for assignments. The actor portfolio, for example, can be enriched by a wealth of online sources, such as interactive maps, historical documents, photos, video clips, and relevant information from governmental and other websites. Students can create their own video clips and post them on YouTube, publish newspapers and media breaking news alerts, perform video interviews through Skype, and submit digital surveys, such as the feedback form, online.

With online features you can extend the academic level of participants in your simulation. While it is difficult to bring students from different courses to a single meeting

room, cyberspace is an accessible and convenient alternative to a physical meeting place on a campus. When most communication takes place online, graduate and undergraduate students from different courses and disciplines can join the same simulation.

Spatial extension also means cooperation across the global village. The Internet transcends physical boundaries among states and enables people around the world to communicate instantly on cyberspace. Cyber tools are useful for promoting collaboration with colleagues worldwide for a joint simulation project. This reduces simulation costs because the division of labor with other instructors lets everyone contribute to the shared enterprise. For your students, a simulation with peers from other regions across the globe provides a unique multicultural event.

When it comes to the temporal boundaries, online features allow the simulation to extend beyond lecture times and office hours. Many simulation activities, especially time-consuming ones, can be moved to the web, leaving classroom time for the tasks that require your direct, face-to-face coaching. Policy formation within political and media teams, for example, is a continuous process that usually requires less intervention on your side, so most

TABLE 11.2. Change in Simulation Boundaries

Obstacles
• *World politics realities and theories mismatch*: complexity, uncertainty, and transitions in the real world challenge the simplicity of traditional concepts, models, and theories.
• *A conflict of pace*: slow and passive traditional teaching lags behind the rapid changes in the realities of political life in the global village.
• *A restless student generation with a low attention span*: study plans should include excitement and the opportunity for skill development through practice.
• *Scarcity of free time*: students must be highly motivated to allocate extracurricular time for academic activities.
• *The multicultural reality of world politics*: extension of spatial boundaries requires cooperation among colleagues and peer students, beyond a single course, campus, state, or region.
Recommendations
• *Take the academic setting into account*: course length, topics, student attributes, and cooperation with colleagues should shape the simulation schedule, number of rounds, and their duration.
• *Choose simulation topics carefully*: create a scheme to fit the orientation of your course, highlighting its empirical contents, theory, area study, or methodology.
• *Simulation schedule*: plan, publicize, and explain the timetable for the simulation project and all study assignments.
• *Extend the temporal boundaries*: (1) use asynchronous interactions to increase time for calculated reactions; (2) incorporate consecutive rounds for practice; (3) add cyber sessions to prolong activities beyond class time; (4) allocate sufficient time for preparation, breaking news sessions, intrateam reassessment, feedback, and debriefing; (5) build on daily habits of digital natives to increase and intensify learning.
• *Extend the spatial boundaries*: (1) bring together students from different courses and academic levels; (2) cooperate beyond state boundaries and across the globe; (3) incorporate both political and media teams; (4) assign decision-maker roles as well as those of opposition members and public opinion representatives; (5) couple the world politics rounds among teams with preparatory policy formation processes within teams.
• *Rules*: define, clarify, and enforce rules to maintain order in the simulation.
• *Be flexible and responsive*: solve problems as they arise to minimize frustration and detachment from the simulation project.
• *Adjust and recycle materials to offset costs*: application of similar schemes, like rules, instructions, websites, and scenarios for policy formation and world politics, make the first project easier to implement and facilitate subsequent runs.
• *Remember the nuances*: not all students are alike, and the appeal of simulations varies, so follow participants closely and adjust your attention to their individual needs.

of it can be performed on a social network. In this case, the temporal boundaries are extended even farther: you can observe full discussions of all teams in real time or access them later, a feature that is missing in face-to-face meetings. But, remember that participants, unlike computers and the web, have overload time limits. Students can work very intensively around the clock for a short time. If you request that level of attention for weeks or months you will get pushback. Be cautious about expecting too much of your students' time. The simulation is probably not your students' only class. They are likely to have other projects, extracurricular activities, jobs. If you demand too much of them, they can become resentful, reducing the fun of the simulation project.

Some of your coaching can take the advantage of the web. Instant communication with your students, by e-mail or through a social network, increases students' motivation and keeps them constantly engaged in the learning process. With cyber tools, the learning process is extended to flexible social interaction times. Asynchronous communications on social networks enable each student to log in and post messages at her or his convenience, making study an integral part of daily life. Role-playing through instant communication with peers on social networks makes learning an informal and enjoyable practice.

Online features can also considerably expand the length of a simulation, from a single event that lasts a few hours to a semester or even a yearlong process. When a simulation goes on for several weeks or months and takes place online, parallel to the regular classes, it may serve as a useful readily available and familiar case for implementation of course material. There is also enough time for full application of all parts of the simulation cycle, with intermediate breaks between them for reassessment and

TABLE 11.3. Change in Simulation Interactions

Obstacles
• *Policy formation and world politics:* the theoretical separation between internal and foreign politics ignores their interconnectedness in a global village and in the simulated world.
• *A learning community:* active learning is hard to implement in a formal classroom setting and in distance learning.
• *Skill development:* progressive practice, individual leadership, and cooperative teamwork are often missing in academic study.
Recommendations
• *Couple policy formation and world politics:* (1) instruct participants to define, rank, discuss, and decide their joint actor portfolio, values, goals, policy plans, and core elements of a coherent policy; (2) highlight links between policy formation and its implementation.
• *Reveal simulation story lines gradually:* (1) trigger policy formation within teams with a specific initial scenario; (2) trigger world politics interactions among teams through an acute opening scenario.
• *Plan your simulation pace:* (1) build up interactions slowly and gradually speed them up; (2) insert ad-hoc events, especially when deadlock looms or when teams are willing to compromise too quickly.
• *Combine asynchronous and synchronous interactions for:* (1) quick updates with simulation developments; (2) progressive practice; and (3) adjustments and gradual improvements in participation and learning.
• *Provide opportunities for skill development:* (1) individual commitment, leadership, initiatives, creativity, critical thinking, expression, coping and persistence, goal evaluation and adjustments; (2) collective teamwork to discuss and decide on interdependent policy matters.
• *Coach and supervise:* (1) provide feedback to motivate participation and promote excellence, (2) encourage peer-student coaching by matching motivated peers with hesitant ones, (3) detect and deter free riders as early as possible, (4) monitor simulation activities in an invisible manner, so participants feel ownership for events as the simulation proceeds.
• *Combine face-to-face and cyber tools for step-by-step learning:* (1) policy formation is a basis for world politics interactions; (2) each round of world politics prepares for the next round; (3) cyber rounds lay the groundwork for face-to-face encounters; (4) feedback precedes and enriches debriefing; (5) completed assignments generate lively debriefing and creative research projects.
• *Ensure the centrality of diplomacy:* (1) end simulations by an agreement or a summary of disagreements; (2) if teams resort to violence, switch to the "day after" time frame to highlight the need for negotiations and compromise.
• *Allocate prime time for the media:* use a breaking-news session in the midst of world politics encounters to make all participants aware of the links between media and politics.

adjustments. When most activities take place online and simulation is free from lecture time, as well as space constraints, you have greater freedom to choose the simulation boundaries that suit your goals and academic setting.

Together, spatial and temporal boundaries create variations in the simulations, so it is easy to adjust and adopt materials you have created in previous simulations for use in future ones. This also includes a recycling of website contents and social network groups, so the costs of preparation for each run can be considerably reduced. Careful awareness of boundary concerns promotes the simulation's goals and helps make the interaction process within and among teams more focused.

Interactions Choice

Interactions are the essence of the simulation experience. Encounters among political and media teams tell the story of the simulation and embody the complex patterns of planned and unplanned developments. Diplomatic offers, negotiations, mediation, and political outcomes may involve up-front speeches and interactive discussions on campus, exchanges on virtual platforms at flexible and fixed login times, or a combination of both. When students step into the shoes of decision-makers or media professionals and must react to major dilemmas of world politics, they learn by practice. They express themselves and improve their skills. They share their knowledge and gain new insights. Table 11.3 encapsulates the core hurdles related to interactions and how to resolve them.

Cyber tools enable a full process of policy formation before world politics interactions start and the continuation of policy adjustments parallel to the world politics rounds. This is true on both face-to-face and social network platforms. In the former, interactions involve on-campus negotiations among political teams, with media observing, covering, and sometimes manipulating the course of events. During face-to-face interactions, repre-

TABLE 11.4. Change in Study Efficiency

Obstacles
• *Simulation types:* simulations of all genres and creative cyber tools are not yet common in the academic mainstream.
• *The study cycle:* active learning programs need better correspondence among plans, assignments, implementation procedures, feedback, debriefing, grading rubrics, and assessment schemes for the simulation project.
• *Active learning tools:* simulation analysis lacks (1) conceptualization and rigorous measures for comprehensive overview; (2) integration of complex topics for teaching world politics in a global village; (3) skill assessment.

Recommendations
• *Indicate where simulation and reality intersect:* help students step out of the academic setting and enter a past, current, or fictional reality.
• *Highlight subjective perspectives:* (1) incorporate major dilemmas real leaders face; (2) confront students with the prejudices and mind-sets of others; (3) practice empathy; (4) demonstrate deception, failures, and compromise as indispensable aspects of politics; (5) reveal the contents of policy formation after the simulation ends and let students use all simulation products to discuss and reconsider world politics interactions from the perspective of others.
• *Break the dull routine:* (1) advertise the simulation project as an exciting pedagogical experiment in the course description and elsewhere; (2) transform the learning process into an entertaining, attractive, and fun experience.
• *Replace the rigid top-down structure of teaching:* facilitate the creation of a motivated learning community by the use of simulations to partner with students in creating the simulation world, its products, and its outcomes.
• *Know your destination from the beginning and pace the study cycle accordingly:* ensure a comprehensive outlook by adopting procedures that fit your plan, incorporate practical techniques, and guide participants.
• *Progress gradually:* (1) explain new teaching methods; (2) move from abstract and strategic planning, via alternatives and choice, to overview and revision; (3) coordinate and synchronize progress throughout the learning cycle between students and the educator; (4) disclose assignments with clear deadlines; (5) build up information for practice of complex realities; (6) plan increases in time pressure, stress, and intensity of interactions and learning.
• *Plan compelling story lines:* (1) employ multiple modes to publicize the scenario and ad-hoc events; (2) apply guidelines for an effective narrative; (3) use creative formats; (4) provide exciting triggers to set policy formation and world politics in motion.
• *Use media and political teams:* (1) explain the crucial role of the media in politics; (2) encourage insights from multiple perspectives; (3) add authenticity to the atmosphere through media products.

sentatives of all teams are supposed to follow their team policy plans, but they often act autonomously until the formal break, when intrateam policy reassessment becomes possible. Moreover, face-to-face interactions make covert and informal negotiations harder to perform than in the cyberspace.

When the world politics meetings take place on social networks, more options emerge for interactions among and within teams, including covert back-channel talks via cyber communications. Such occurrences are visible only to you as the administrator of the secret group on the social network and to the few leaders who interact in that group. Secret contacts that take place out of sight of other teams may produce a true surprise if a breakthrough occurs. The activity of media teams can intensify as reporters contact political leaders directly on the web without interrupting the flow of negotiations. Media teams can extend their exposure beyond the media break and repeatedly publish reports and news

flashes during negotiations. Intrateam reassessment during world politics negotiations becomes much easier when interactions take place on the web, as participants can communicate simultaneously on multiple social network groups with representatives of other teams and with their own teammates. The coupling of policy formation and world politics enriches the knowledge in both fields and improves the understanding of the complex linkages between them.

But student interactions are not only about the advancement of knowledge. Rather, they are closely related to the gradual practice of skills and the development of good habits for solitary study and teamwork. Interactions are the core component in active learning with simulations. Practice of negotiations, team management, media manipulation, leadership, coaching of peer students, coping with crisis situations, and making decisions are among the many skills reinforced when students learn by doing.

The current generation of digital natives has endless opportunities and myriad choices for learning in cyberspace. Our student body already consists of active information pursuers who are used to doing many things simultaneously and quickly. The traditional way of conveying knowledge, with students as passive listeners who need to summarize what they remember in the final exam, has increasingly become unattractive. To succeed in a globalized online world, students need to develop and practice many skills beyond memory, like critical thinking, creativity, leadership, teamwork, and coping with complexity and frustration.

Implications for Study Efficiency

Study efficiency captures the core function of simulations as an innovative method of teaching. Simulations trigger creative initiatives, increased motivation, and a wider array of experiences beyond the traditional modes of classroom teaching. Personal and team activity creates an interplay between cognitive, behavioral, and emotional stimuli encountered in the simulation and makes the overall learning impact much greater than the sum of its separate effects. By actual participation and repeated practice, students are able to reach an understanding of abstract paradigms, theories, and concepts. Such results are frequently stated in written feedback and during the debriefing session after the simulation ends. Table 11.4 presents the problems associated with study efficiency and offers measures to move beyond them.

Simulations enable students, as players on a stage, to add to the story line you initiate and to cope with the details without losing sight of the big picture. This is achieved as they dissect the study elements to reveal the building blocks, such as the team's values, goals, and policy plans, that help solve complex problems. Then participants reassemble the different parts of the interaction process to achieve a comprehensive view of (1) the developments that evolved from the initial and opening scenarios, (2) the links between policy formation and world politics, (3) interactions among teams and simulation outcomes, and (4) personal feedback in conjunction with collective debriefing and critique. Participants report that such advanced knowledge and broader comprehension of world politics is often accompanied by memories of intense, exciting simulation episodes that endure beyond final exams.

Simulations in the 21st Century: What's Next

Ten years from now, what will future simulations be like? Will face-to-face simulations take the lead? Could cyber ones become the preferable choice? The decisions that you and your colleagues make, regarding which kind of simulations to use, will shape future trends. Meanwhile, traversing a time tunnel to the future, we sketch two likely competing options at the opposing ends of the simulation spectrum: continued face-to-face dominance and extensive cyber ascendance. Then we point to the hybrid simulation as a synthesis practice.

Continued Face-to-Face Dominance

Face-to-face simulations have maintained their lead from the beginning. They set the stage for a group of people, at any physical location, to communicate and practice world politics by performing the roles of political leaders and media professionals. As long as campuses remain the primary meeting place for academic study, face-to-face simulations are likely to be a regular choice for educators in the coming years. But face-to-face simulations will nonetheless change to befit the era. Simulations completely detached from the Internet and high-tech means of communication will become rare events confined to brief role-play exercises.

Future refinements and innovations in cyber tools are likely to supplement and enrich face-to-face simulations, increasing the appeal and effectiveness of the hybrid kind. Readily available cyber aids will be integrated throughout the study cycle. During preparation for a face-to-face simulation, online information on the simulation topic, states, nonstate actors, and decision-makers will be a basic source, instantly retrieved with a click of a mouse. YouTube clips, photos, and historical documents from digital archives will be a natural choice, in class, during solitary learning, and for discussion between peer students on the social network. Policy formation during a face-to-face simulation is likely to involve interactions within teams in cyberspace to enable a full-fledged decision process that is not at the expense of lecture time. The world politics exchanges in face-to-face simulations are likely to include online features to publicize the opening scenario and ad-hoc events online, to host breaking news sessions on the social network, and to open back-channel groups for leaders who want to hold secret negotiations in the midst of open face-to-face contacts. Teammates will communicate on the social network to coordinate their moves during face-to-face interactions with other teams and to follow media products. Such cyber tools in conjunction with face-to-face contacts are a natural way of conduct for digital natives, nowadays, and even more so for those of the future. To make the postsimulation analysis a more rigorous and central part of the learning experience, feedback, debriefing, and assessment of face-to-face simulations is also likely to integrate supplementary cyber tools, like online feedback forms, digital surveys, questions for the debriefing sessions, and a detailed rubric for grading simulation assignments and assessing the development of essential skills.

Social networks have already entered the classroom, through the backdoor. Many students surf the web during lectures and communicate on social networks, to socialize and stay connected with peers. But the educator remains largely outside of all these interactions. Face-to-face simulations in the coming years must open up to new technologically driven options in order to strengthen their appeal and keep their lead in the digital age.

Extensive Cyber Ascendance

Cyber simulations emerged at the beginning of the 21st century and have been used ever since as an active learning tool on campus and in some programs of online study. The increased popularity and rapid proliferation of distance learning may trigger the further integration of simulations on cyberspace, leading eventually to an extensive ascendance of cyber simulations, parallel to or as a replacement for face-to-face ones.

The use of cyber simulations as a mainstream tool may vary considerably. First, they might supplement on-campus courses and enable cooperation among multiple academic institutions in one state, across regions, or in distant locations across the globe. This will increase the multicultural experience for students and educators and help offset the many costs of running a simulation, by a division of labor among colleagues. Second, they will bring together students of online courses with participants in on-campus classes. In this case, the advantages of a face-to-face experience practiced by the latter are likely to spill over to the students who are linked to the project only via the Internet. Third, they can also add and advance a novel type of interactive communications in fully online courses. By running a simulation, the educator will be able to transform a group of strangers that have never met in person into active partners, better motivated students, and a cohesive learning community.

All these variations are likely to increase the popularity

of cyber simulations and even make them an attractive alternative to strictly face-to-face ones. World politics interactions in cyber simulations of all three variants are likely to move from the classroom to the web and from face-to-face contacts to communications behind computer screens.

But, a reliance on the Internet alone might diminish much of the magic atmosphere that occurs with costumes, body language, facial expressions, intonations, and other verbal and nonverbal communications when parties are in the same room. Since the human touch is indispensable in learning, cyber ascendance will be dependent on the effective integration of proxy personal encounters on cyberspace. In preparation for a cyber simulation, educators should allow for a human dimension to excite students and motivate them to invest extensive time in the project. Perhaps they could record and upload video clips with gradual instructions and invitations for video conferences. During policy formation, video conferences in addition to written messages on social networks will be used by teammates to plan policy and by educators to coach students and help them get ready for world politics interactions. With further high-tech innovations and improved hardware and software quality, cyber simulations with online video conferences of world politics will eventually become common surrogates for face-to-face encounters. Smart phones and tablets and the many applications they offer, like FaceTime, Instagram, Twitter, or WhatsApp, may introduce new cyber tools for face-to-face simulations or even change the choice of future platforms for running simulations and conducting postsimulation analysis. Feedback, debriefing, and assessment of cyber simulations are also likely to integrate proxy face-to-face tools to make the postsimulation analysis a more rigorous and central part of the learning experience. In this process, the educator is likely to record video messages with questions for feedback and upload digital surveys. Debriefing will easily be held through video conferences, and assessment will include digital databases of many simulations with text, photos, audio, and video materials.

If participants will not meet in person, an effective integration of proxy face-to-face tools in cyber simulations can overcome the lack of direct human interactions. This can happen on social networks with video applications or any other future web developments that enable participants to communicate with one another from distant places, beyond the exchange of written messages. Over time, technology is likely to revolutionize synchronous face-to-face communications through screens in multiple locations. When that happens, an even more extensive ascendance of cyber simulations in academe will become possible.

Synthesis: Hybrid Simulations as Common Practice

Hybrid simulations involve extensive reliance on two platforms of coequal importance, each in its own round of world politics negotiations. This multiround practice provides the most meaningful simulation experience and the likelihood of extensive learning that couples the benefits of both worlds. Yet, hybrid simulations are also the most costly to create and manage, so we have generally refrained from promoting the hybrid simulation as the ultimate choice. The best model for you to adopt is the one that fits your particular needs, resources, and constraints.

We believe, however, that through practice and habit, hybrid simulations are likely to become the default mode of the future, albeit with variations in "degrees of hybridity." Cyber tools are ubiquitous in many aspects of daily life and are already penetrating academe. By enhancing face-to-face simulations with online components or complementing cyber simulations with a proxy human touch, hybrid simulations will likely proliferate as a regular component of higher education. As more educators embrace simulations as a pedagogical practice and then increasingly integrate online features into face-to-face encounters, cyber elements will become the dominant platform in at least one of the rounds. Similarly, as cyber simulations include progressively more effective proxy face-to-face meetings, they too are apt to evolve into hybrid forms. Both roads will eventually lead to creative, vigorous, and highly rewarding cross-cultural engagements among colleagues and peer students on far-flung campuses around the world.

Your students already live in cyberspace. Chances are you rely upon the Internet for accomplishing many of the tasks in your own life, as well. For generations educators have integrated the innovations of their times into the classroom, from chalkboards to overhead projectors to YouTube. By designing courses that incorporate cutting-edge world politics simulations as a critical element of the learning process, you are pursuing the timeless goals of teachers: introducing your students to fresh perspectives, inspiring them to expand their knowledge base, challenging them to hone their skills in critical thinking, analysis, expression, reading, and research, and arousing in them a love of learning. Cyber-infused simulations allow students to expand their horizons in a space where horizons are open like never before. All this will make your classes the ones they remember for years to come.

APPENDIX: SIMULATION SUMMARIES

This appendix describes three simulations from different genres as prototypes of face-to-face, cyber, and hybrid simulations. For each simulation we provide a detailed summary and a table with basic data for easy comparison across genres.

Gulf Nuclear Face-to-Face Simulation

The Gulf nuclear simulation was held during half a day in 2012, for students of an executive program at Tel Aviv University as the final stage of a summer semester.

The simulation covered the Israeli-Palestinian conflict and the Iranian nuclear development, but it was focused mainly on the Iranian issue, which was the most salient subject that summer in Israel after Israeli leaders and U.S. president Barack Obama announced they will do everything to prevent Iran from reaching nuclear military capability.

To conduct the face-to-face simulation we used one of the faculty conference rooms on campus, equipped with a round table and electronic teaching devices including Wi-Fi connections to access cyber resources using laptops and smart phones. Regular classrooms in the same building were also used by the teams as a home base for intrateam consultations.

The students were divided into ten teams with 3–5 players per team including the United States as a superpower, Russia as a great power, Egypt, Iran, Israel, and Jordan as regional states, the Palestinians as a nonstate actor, and three media networks: the *Global Crescent* as an Arab media organ, the *Global Times* as

an American media organ, and *Our Israel* as an Israeli media organ.

Preparations in class before the simulation were short and included an analysis of the Osirak 1981 crisis as a historical analogy and a brief within-team discussion on policy formation.

The simulation started as a UN General Assembly meeting on the Gulf nuclear issue with opening speeches by the heads of team that were prepared ahead of time and lasted half an hour. The media teams attended the session as observers.

Multilateral negotiations took place after the official gathering for 45 minutes in two alternative Gulf nuclear and Palestinian working groups. Each group had to prepare a short document of agreement on three major points we set in the opening scenario. The goal of reaching an agreement, despite the gaps in national interests and under time pressure, was designed to capture crisis decision-making in world politics.

The synchronous face-to-face interactions involved bilateral-secret talks behind the scenes and formal-multilateral negotiations open to the media. During these world politics interactions the Israeli prime minister got information from the media about an Iranian plan to strike first through the diversionary use of a nonstate actor.

Both the Iranian and the Israeli leaders requested permission to use military force, according to simulation rules. They did so almost simultaneously, and we approved their requests after the multilateral negotiation efforts had failed. Our consent shifted the topic of activities to "the day after" diplomacy, an unplanned turning point in the simulation. But the media teams had anticipated

TABLE A1. The Gulf Nuclear Face-to-Face Simulation

Attributes	Details
Topic	Current affairs in the Middle East and the Gulf focusing mainly on Iran's nuclear program
Educator goals	To capture the essence of crisis decision-making in world politics and reach an agreement under time pressure, despite gaps in national interests
Date	September 14, 2012
Participants	45 graduate students in a summer semester of an executive program at Tel Aviv University
Platform	A face-to-face event in a conference room for all teams together, with access to cyber resources using Wi-Fi connection for laptops and smart phones Additional classrooms for separate teams
Rounds	One round with four sessions
Political teams	Seven teams: Egypt, Iran, Israel, Jordan as regional states, the Palestinians as a nonstate actor, the U.S. as a superpower, and Russia as a great power. The UN as an international organization was represented during the last session by one of the students.
Media teams	Three teams: American, Arab, Israeli media organs
Feedback	Registration form, world politics feedback form, university administered course evaluation form and final research assignments
Debriefing	In class discussions
Assessment	Student grading Appraisal of the project with adjustments in future simulations

the outbreak of violence and recorded video clips that blended well with these developments. So, the third session of the world politics began with the announcements of military strikes by the Israeli and Iranian teams. It was followed by breaking news clips and interviews the media teams had prepared.

An emergency UN Security Council meeting opened the last session to meet the challenge of adjusting positions to the new poststrike reality. The UN secretary-general played a decisive role by offering creative suggestions to sidestep deadlocks, urging the teams to negotiate a provisional UN resolution. Formal rhetoric, decisive intonations, determined facial expressions, and restrained body language set the atmosphere for strenuous bargaining leading to a vote on the "day after" resolution. The Palestinian team remained aloof during the discussion, frustrated that their core interests were set aside due to the violent escalation between Israel and Iran. Though the Jordanian and Egyptian teams condemned all violence, they were subjected to intensive U.S. coercive diplomacy and decided to support the U.S.-led resolution. The simulation ended with a short debriefing of what it meant to the stability of a poststrike Middle East.

Middle East Cyber Simulation

The simulation covered current affairs in the Arab-Israel conflict with two topics and designated working groups: (1) statehood for the Palestinians and (2) nonproliferation in the Gulf by preventing Iran from gaining the status of a nuclear power.

Its participants were International Studies Association members who interacted during a protracted period of eight months, from the official announcement and registration starting in September 2011, through a one-month intensive Facebook round on February, and a face-to-face debriefing on April at the 2012 ISA conference in San Diego.

The use of Facebook made this global multicultural project possible, bridging distances and diverse player locations. As a voluntary simulation, the time investment during preparation was limited to a few deliberations in teams on Facebook. Given the different time zones from which participants came throughout the world, some coordination was essential. The Facebook platform provided an additional contribution since all activities were automatically saved.

Before the simulation began, participants were requested to fill out a questionnaire specifying their geographic location, area of expertise, previous experience

TABLE A2. Middle East Cyber Simulation

Attributes	Details
Topic	Current affairs in the Middle East and the Gulf, including the Iranian quest for nuclear status and the Palestinian quest for statehood
Educator goals	Bridging across distances and diverse participants' locations, by interacting on Facebook Making the entire process and all its information instantly available, backed up and retrievable for study and research
Dates	*Eight months in total* September 2011: registration announcement February 7, 2012: two-hour cyber round on Facebook February 27, 2012: two-hour cyber round on Facebook April 2, 2012: face-to-face debriefing at the ISA San Diego conference
Participants	ISA members from across the globe, all on a voluntary basis 100 applicants, 59 registered members, 20 active players came to the ISA panel
Platform	Full cyber simulation with an intensive face-to-face debriefing session at the ISA conference. The cyber simulation was conducted on Facebook, and supplemented by a designated website, e-mails in early preparations and various applications like YouTube, Skype and Google Drive throughout the simulation
Rounds	Two rounds of world politics with two sessions each, a short reassessment break within each round and a longer interim break between them
Political teams	Planned for twelve teams, reduced to four: Iran and Israel as regional states, the Palestinians as a nonstate actor, the U.S. as a superpower 5 participants per team
Media teams	One team: *The Global Crescent* network
Feedback	Registration and world politics forms
Debriefing	An innovative panel at the ISA San Diego conference
Assessment	Appraisal of the project with adjustments included and tested in the 2014 and 2015 simulation runs between ISA scholars Research papers by simulation coordinators and collaborators on modes of assessment

with simulations, and preferences for team and role. While the registration process took place, a Facebook group was created to host the world politics encounters, and separate groups were set up for each team. All participants were divided into four political teams: Iran and Israel as regional states, the Palestinians as a nonstate actor, the United States as a superpower, and one media team: the *Global Crescent*. Each team had 3–5 participants.

The schedule included two synchronous rounds of negotiations among teams with reassessment breaks in each and a two-week interim period between them. The interactions were activated by a scenario with activity triggers for all teams and relevant information on both the Iranian and the Palestinian issues.

In the first round on the Gulf nuclear topic the situation mirrored real-world affairs between these adversaries and events developed along the path we planned for the simulation. However, during the interim break between synchronous rounds on Facebook, the political leaders in Iran debated the strategy of direct contacts with Israel, decided to propose secret negotiations to the Israeli foreign min-

ister, and indicated that they were willing to make serious compromises, which eventually led to a breakthrough in the second round of world politics. Israel reciprocated with a risky decision of its own and agreed to join the back-channel we opened on Facebook to host these secret negotiations. So, while the media professionals were actively building up a "clash of civilizations" agenda between Israel and Iran, top decision-makers behind closed doors were bridging gaps. After the agreement was nailed down, we requested the teams not to rush to the press, as they had originally wanted to do, but to hold off on publication of the accord, and a personal handshake, for the San Diego meeting. This delay triggered genuine surprise and the agreement was one of the most exciting points in the face-to-face gathering at the panel.

At the same time the negotiations on the Palestinian statehood issue gradually advanced along the two-state solution path. Major developments followed the track paved by the scenario, although the topics of agreement and the specifics of the actual document were a result of heated confrontations and nerve-wracking efforts to bypass critical stumbling blocks. Since both the Israeli and the Palestinian teams had built-in opposition players, the road to compromise was not an easy one to travel. Despite near collapse of the entire process, Israel and the Palestinians agreed on a four-point plan that contained the principles of the agreement and left the disagreements open for later negotiations.

The Global Crescent was the only media actor, designed as an equivalent to *Aljazeera.* Its reporters produced "Arab-centric" video clips, newspapers, and short breaking news during two synchronous rounds. Yet, despite the considerable efforts of the media representatives and their creative contributions, the political teams found it hard to follow the news in real time.

The simulation participants met face-to-face six weeks after the cyber interactions at the 2012 ISA conference in San Diego. The first gathering was an informal social event followed by a formal innovative panel of the ISA conference on the next day. It combined a short face-to-face encounter to conclude the simulation and reveal the back-channel between Israel and Iran, surprising all other participants and mainly the media. The second part of the panel was used as an in-depth debriefing on the use of cyber simulations and to plan future joint work and research.

Palestinian Statehood Hybrid Simulation

The Palestinian statehood hybrid simulation focused on the establishment of a Palestinian state. Participants included 25 undergraduate communication students from Sapir College in Israel and 35 graduate political studies and communication students from Bar-Ilan University in Israel, as part of their whole-year academic courses.

The simulation covered a period of eight months in total, two months of preparation and within team interactions, two intensive synchronous cyber rounds of world politics in January and May, a half day face-to-face round in May, and a final month of studies and debriefing.

Before the courses started we set up a joint Facebook group for world politics activities and separate groups for each political and media team. We also prepared registration and feedback forms on the Google Forms platform. In the introductory meetings of both courses the students were told about the Palestinian statehood simulation and asked to complete the online registration form indicating their team and role preferences. The face-to-face meetings in class triggered a sense of belonging to a coherent

team. Intrateam discussions continued in closed Facebook groups for several weeks to discuss values, goals, and plans. At the same time, regular classes continued and some ad-hoc meetings took place during the breaks before or after class.

On the simulation website, we first posted a detailed schedule and later uploaded the opening scenario. It described contacts between Israeli and Palestinian leaders, talks between the United States and Israel, developments regarding Palestinian prisoners held by Israel, and a news flash about a missing Israel soldier held in Gaza, all published in the format of news items. All interactions and communications were posted on the joint Facebook "wall" according to five relevant topics—terror, regional cooperation, Palestinian elections, mutual Israeli and Palestinian recognition, and public opinion debate—so that interactions were easy to follow and could proceed in a systematic manner.

Intensive negotiations took place especially between Israel and Palestinian teams with the United States active during all rounds in an attempt to promote the Middle East Reform, proposed by the U.S. president for the region. The plan made the U.S. team a major actor and important mediator in the simulation. This role continued and intensified later, in the face-to-face round, during the secret tripartite international summit. While the Americans demonstrated creativity, the Israeli and Palestinians teams were somewhat less flexible and found it hard to initiate moves beyond their traditional positions.

The face-to-face interactions at Bar-Ilan University included an up-front opening ceremony for all participants, in which a representative of each team delivered a policy statement from the podium. After the short 15-minute opening it was natural to continue intensive negotiations like the ones that took place earlier during the Facebook interactions. Signs, flags, and costumes added to the decor and atmosphere, and a simulation cocktail for diplomats and media professionals was offered during the break between sessions. Some high-tech touches were also added to this typical face-to-face setting, like links to YouTube clips that were prepared by the media and continuous within group contacts on Facebook during world politics negotiations.

Three media organs were active during the cyber and face-to-face rounds: the *Global Times,* an international newspaper with a *CNN* ideology; *Our Israel,* an Israeli newspaper with a strong Jewish perspective and ethnocentric views; and the *Global Crescent,* an Arab news organization inspired by the *Aljazeera* network. They competed to publish exclusive items and at the same time to keep in touch with the political leaders and interview

TABLE A3. Palestinian Statehood Hybrid Simulation

Attributes	Details
Topic	Current affairs in the Arab-Israel conflict focusing on statehood for the Palestinians with four working groups on borders, security, Jerusalem and terror in the first round and bilateral ones between U.S.-Israel, U.S.-Palestinians and Israel-Palestinians, in the second round
Educator goals	Experimental practice with use of a cyber platform for simulations that bridge intercampus distances Allow students to experience current regional events
Dates	January 3, 2012: one-hour cyber round on Facebook January 4, 2012: one-hour cyber round on Facebook May 6, 2012: one-hour cyber round on Facebook May 8, 2012: one-hour cyber round on Facebook May 18, 2012: half day face-to-face round
Participants	60 students 25 Undergraduate Communication students, Sapir College 35 Graduate Political Studies and Communication students, Bar-Ilan University
Platform	In-class face-to-face preparations Four cyber rounds on Facebook One half day face-to-face round with Wi-Fi connections for instant use of Facebook and YouTube
Rounds	Four cyber rounds of world politics One face-to-face round
Political teams	Three teams: the U.S. as a superpower, Israel as a regional state, the Palestinians as a nonstate actor 5 to 17 participants per team. The Palestinian team contained Hamas as an opposition group; the Israeli team with 17 players contained opposition leaders and public opinion representatives
Media teams	Three teams: Arab, International, Israeli media organs
Feedback	Registration and world politics forms and research projects submitted by students
Debriefing	In class debriefing, separately in each campus
Assessment	Student grading Joint appraisal of the project by cooperating educators with adjustments in future simulations

them. The media teams quickly discovered they were unable to gain attention at the height of the negotiation process. To prevent frustration, we dedicated a special time slot for a media conference with "live" news, video clips, and other media products.

In light of an American brokered agreement, the Palestinians, with tacit American approval, surprised Israel and declared statehood. When the plenary conference was over, the Israeli prime minister claimed he had been deceived, not knowing that the U.S. president had supported the Palestinian move. This led to heated debate and ended the simulation with a burst of misunderstandings and mutual accusations. The drama at the end of the face-to-face round indicated the depth of the learning process, which allowed the Palestinian team, played by Israeli students, to overcame major prejudices, express a better understanding of the other, and show some empathy when the Palestinian leader declared statehood. The simulation ended with concluding speeches by team leaders.

NOTES

Chapter 1

1. On hybrid or blended learning in education and social sciences, see Caillier and Riordan (2009); Garrison and Kanuka (2004); Ginns and Ellis (2007); Greenhow, Robelia, and Hughes (2009); Hall and Davison (2007); Holley and Oliver (2010); Johnson (2002); Kirk (2004); Köse (2010); LeNoue, Hall, and Eighmy (2011); Lewis and Harrison (2012); Lindsay (2004); López-Pérez, Pérez-López, and Rodriguez-Ariza (2011); Moskal, Dzuiban, and Hartman (2013); Ross and Rosenbloom (2011); Siemens (2004, 2009); Senior (2010); Sims et al. (2008); Singer (2008); Tuckman (2002); Vaughan and Garrison (2005); Willson (2008); Yeh, Yeh, and Chen (2012); Yen and Lee (2011).

2. See chapter 3 for a detailed typology of simulations and the appendix for examples of face-to-face, cyber, and hybrid simulations.

3. Consistently throughout the book when we refer to conceptual matters and practical instructions, we use "social networks" as a generic term. When we discuss examples from actual simulations, we refer to Facebook, the cyber platform we commonly use.

4. For some background on the complexities of the Arab-Israel conflict, see Ben-Yehuda and Sandler (2002); Brecher with Geist (1980); Eisenberg and Caplan (2010); Karsch (2010); Maoz (2006); Miller (1997); Morris (2004, 2008).

5. Such narratives are used to teach world politics like Ruane and James (2012) and can easily be adapted as scenarios for simulations.

6. See *The World Factbook, Central Intelligence Agency* under websites in references.

7. See links to websites under the references for the following: the Correlates of War (COW) Project, the Militarized Interstate Disputes (MID) Data Collection, the International Crisis Behavior (ICB) Project, UCDP/PRIO Armed Conflict Dataset, and the Minorities at Risk (MAR) Project.

8. See Ashby (1954, 1957) for the basic concepts of systems analysis. For a review of their application in political science and international relations, see Brecher and Ben-Yehuda (1985) and Haas (1970).

9. See Brecher and Ben-Yehuda (1985, 17) for definitions of structure and process.

10. On simulation goals related to platform, see, for example: Asal (2005); Asal and Blake (2006); Boyer, Trumbore, and Fricke (2006); Boyer et al. (2009); Brynen (2010); Butcher (2012); Crossley-Frolick (2010); Darling and Foster (2012); DeGarmo (2006); Enterline and Jepsen (2009); Glazier (2011); Kanner (2007); Kelle (2008); McMahon and Miller (2012); Mintz, Redd, and Vedlitz (2006); Obendorf and Randerson (2012); Parmentier (2013); Rothman (2012); Schnurr, Santo, and Craig (2013); Simpson and Kaussler (2009); Weir and Baranowski (2011); Zaino and Mulligan (2009). See also *Peace-Maker* and *Statecraft* under websites in references.

11. On simulation goals related to spatial and temporal boundaries, see, for example: Asal (2005); Asal and Blake (2006); Blum and Scherer (2007); Brynen (2010); Corbeil and Laveault (2011); Crossley-Frolick (2010); Enterline and Jepsen (2009); Fowler (2009); Fowler and Pusch (2010); Glazier (2011); Lay and Smarick (2006); Smolinski and Kesting (2012); Stover (2007); Weir and Baranowski (2011).

12. On simulation goals related to interactions, see, for example: Asal and Blake (2006); Asal and Schulzke (2012); Boyer, Trumbore, and Fricke (2006); Boyer et al. (2009); Brynen (2010); Cioffi-Revilla and Rouleau (2010); DeGarmo (2006); Dexter and Guittet (2014); Earnest (2008); Enterline and Jepsen (2009); Glazier (2011); Kanner (2007); Korosteleva (2010); Lay and Smarick (2006); Parmentier (2013); Simpson and Kaussler (2009); Smolinski and Kesting (2012); Stoll (2011); Zaino and Mulligan (2009).

13. Altschull (1995); Lambeth (1995); Merrill (1974); Siebert, Peterson, and Schramm (1956).

14. Atkinson (2011); Hermida (2010); Keith (2004); Seib (2007); Zelizer (1993).

15. Cook (1998); Gaber (2000); Gergen (1991); Kurtz (1998); Paletz (1998); Pfetsch (1998).

16. On simulation goals related to the media, see, for example: Asal and Blake (2006); Mintz (2004); Mintz, Redd, and Vedlitz (2006); Zaino and Mulligan (2009). See also *Peace-Maker* under websites in references.

Chapter 2

1. *Hybrid learning*, as defined in chapter 1, brings together traditional and modern technology-based teaching procedures to achieve in-depth learning.

2. *Agenda setting* theory focuses on the mode by which media organs emphasize and highlight specific topics, disregard others, and create a unique news scheme. It involves the content of press coverage and its structural attributes that affect the exposure an event receives and demarcates the choice of news made by the media. See Ben-Yehuda, Naveh, and Levin-Banchik (2013a, 2013c); Cohen (1963); Cottle and Mugdha (2008); Iyengar and Simon (1994); McCombs (1981); McQuail (1994, 2007); Rogers and Dearing (2007); Soroka (2003); Weaver (2007); Weaver, McCombs, and Shaw (2004); Zelizer, Park, and Gudelunas (2002). Studies on the "CNN effect" may also be considered as part of the agenda setting approach. See Livingston (2011); P. Robinson (2011). *Framing* transforms events through "formats" that filter and reflect images of reality in world politics. This process involves a struggle over interpretive frames, ideological or value perspectives, story lines, symbols, and relevant stereotypes. See Druckman (2001); Entman (1991, 2007); Hallahan (1999); Iyengar and Simon (1994); Kolmer and Semetko (2009); Norris, Kern, and Just (2003); Roeh and Nir (1993); Scheufele (1999); Scheufele and Tewksbury (2007); Wolfsfeld (1997, 2011).

3. On the democratic response and retaliations against terror, see, for example, Ben-Yehuda and Levin-Banchik (2014).

4. See Bartels, McCown, and Wilkie (2013) for an example of how simulations can be used for methodology concerns like the choice of levels of analysis and their impact on scenario construction and role specification.

Chapter 3

1. If the policy formation process gains a similar weight to that of world politics encounters it can develop in the future to a round in itself. Then a new form of hybrid simulations may emerge with policy formation on a cyber platform and face-to-face world politics encounters, or vice versa.

2. See also Aldrich (2009) for an in-depth overview of simulations and the progress over time from Johannes Gutenberg to Google.

3. In this article Brody presents a rich survey of what we call first-generation simulations. Similar works are provided by Shubik (1960) and North (1963).

4. See also Shubik (1958, 1959).

5. See, for example, Benson (1961); Bloomfield and Padelford (1959); De Sola Pool and Abelson (1961); Milbrath (1958).

6. See, for example, Guetzkow (1959); Harrison and Lee (1960); Howard (1961); Kaplan, Burns, and Quandt (1960).

7. Crookall and Wilkenfeld (1985); Kraus et al. (1992); Starkey, Boyer, and Wilkenfeld (1999); Starkey and Wilkenfeld (1996); Wilkenfeld and Kaufman (1993).

8. On the progress of cyber interactions, from a small interuniversity mode of communication to the Internet and the development of the World Wide Web and social networks, see Gore (2013), Shih (2011); Zittrain (2008).

9. For a detailed description of these developments, see Zittrain (2008), part 1.

10. See National Model United Nations (NMUN) and ICONS Project under websites in references.

11. See *PeaceMaker* under websites in references.

12. See *Statecraft* under websites in references.

13. On these changes, their meaning and consequences, see Gore (2013); Shih (2011); Yang et al. (2011).

14. Carpenter and Drezner (2010). On web developments during this period, see Cohen-Almagor (2011); Yang et al. (2011); Zittrain (2008).

15. A volume of *International Studies Perspectives* (vol. 15, no. 4) focusing on simulations was published in November 2014, when the manuscript for this book was already finished. Beyond the survey discussed herein, new articles add valuable contributions to the analysis of simulations in world politics. In particular, see Asal, Griffith, and Schulzke (2014); Bridge and Radford (2014); Carvalho (2014); Cuhadar and Kampf (2014); DiCicco (2014); Elias (2014); Glasgow (2014); Hatipoglu, Müftüler-Baç, and Murphy (2014); Hodson and Hill (2014); Kempston and Thomas (2014); Pettenger, West, and Young (2014).

16. For literature reviews on simulations, see Boyer (2011); Brynen and Milante (2013); Carpenter and Drezner (2010); Guilhot (2011); Hudson and Butler (2010); Kachuyevski and Jones (2011); Kee (2011); Kikkawa and Crookall (2011); Mayer (2009); McDermott (2011); Mintz, Yang, and McDermott (2011); Parmentier (2013); Pepinsky (2005); Rothman (2012); Shubik (2009); Smith (2010); Van Ments (2011); Wilson et al. (2009). Several additional sources for our literature review were derived from these articles.

17. Studies on war and peace simulations appeared in a special issue of *Simulation & Gaming*, vol. 44, issue 1. Many of them are a valuable source on simulations research, like Crookall (2013), but do not fit the inclusion criteria of our literature review.

18. See Brynania.net Peacebuilding Simulation and the PaxSims Blog under websites in references.

19. The use of virtual environments is also common in other fields beyond world politics simulations, but there too social networks are not yet common. See, for example, Douglas and Johnson (2008); Ebner et al. (2009); Ebner, Coben, and Honeyman (2012).

20. For a discussion of the potential for use of video games for politically related educational purposes, see Powers (2014); Wortley (2013).

21. A brief update past the 2013 cutoff date shows that most articles in other fields, such as business (Aertsen, Jaspaert, and Van Gorp 2013; Jeong and Bozkurt 2014; Palmunen et al. 2013), education (Dieker et al. 2014), law (Donohue 2013), or health care (Clapper 2014), report on the use of face-to-face simulations; a few studies use board games, like Greco, Baldissin, and Nonino (2013), while some others, like Squazzoni, Jager, and Edmonds (2014), or Joseph et al. (2014), Neumann (2014), Yukawa, Yoshimoto, and Yamakage (2014) in political science, continue the tradition of computer-based simulation modeling. Publications in other fields that emphasize the use of simulations for skill development, like Lopes et al. (2013), can be useful for application in world politics on leadership and teamwork.

22. See, for example, Shih (2011); Zittrain (2008).

23. On simulation costs, see for example: Asal (2005); Asal and Blake (2006); Blum and Scherer (2007); Brynen (2010); Darling and Foster (2012); Lay and Smarick (2006); Obendorf and Randerson (2012); Parmentier (2013); Raymond and Sorensen (2008); Rothman (2012); Rousseau and Van der Veen (2005); Schnurr, Santo, and Craig (2013); Smolinski and Kesting (2012); Stoll (2011); Taylor (2013); Taylor, Backlund, and Niklasson (2012); Zaino and Mulligan (2009). See also *Peace-Maker* and *Statecraft* under websites in references.

Chapter 5

1. For some examples of simulations on domestic affairs, see Ansoms (2013); Herrmann (2014); Jozwiak (2013); Landwehr et al. (2013); Pace (2013); Schreiber (2014).

2. For terror-driven international crises, see Ben-Yehuda and Levin-Banchik (2011).

3. In figures 5.7 and 5.8, to protect the privacy of our players we have reproduced their posts under our user names.

4. For a definition and list of values, see Bardi and Schwartz (2003, 1208); Schwartz et al. (2001, 521); Schwartz and Boehnke (2004, 239).

Chapter 7

1. See, for example, Asal and Blake (2006); Beck (2010); Boin, Kofman-Bos, and Overdijk (2004); Boyer, Trumbore, and Fricke (2006); Butcher (2012); Chin, Dukes, and Gamson (2009); Christopher (1999); Crookall (2010, 2013); DeGarmo

(2006); Dormans (2011); Dorn (1989); Duran (1998); Flynn (2000); Garris, Ahlers, and Driskell (2002); Gilboa (1979); Golich (2000); Goon (2011); Kelle (2008); Lederman (1992); McMahon and Miller (2012); Petranek (2000); Petranek, Corey, and Black (1992); Rothman (2012); Schnurr, De Santo, and Craig (2013); Shaw (2010); Shellman and Turan (2006); Smith and Boyer (1996); Taylor, Backlund, and Niklasson (2012); Taylor (2013); Vavrina (2006); Vincent and Shepherd (1998); Williams and Williams (2010).

2. See, for example, Dormans (2011, 626); Flynn (2000, 53); Garris, Ahlers, and Driskell (2002, 454); Golich (2000, 22); Parmentier (2013, 7); Petranek (2000, 65).

3. See, for example, Crookall (2010, 907; 2013, 21); Lederman (1992, 146).

4. See, for example, Beck (2010, 280); Chin, Dukes, and Gamson (2009, 562); DeGarmo (2006, 10); Duran (1998, 224); Golich (2000, 22–23); Goon (2011, 264); Rothman (2012, 444); McMahon and Miller (2012, 2–3); Vincent and Shepherd (1998, 13).

5. To share information among members, the ISA website has a section with information on scholars who run simulations and a description of each project. See http://www.isanet.org/Programs/PRC/Teaching/Simulations.

Chapter 10

1. See Ben-Yehuda et al. (2014).

2. On the development of creativity and leadership as an expression of collective interactions within a social context, see Haslam (2004); Haslam, Adarves-Yorno, and Postmes (2011, 2014); John-Steiner (2000).

REFERENCES

Abt, Clark C. 1961. *Design for a Strategic Model*. Waltham: Raytheon Co.

Aertsen, Tamara, Koen Jaspaert, and Baldwin Van Gorp. 2013. From Theory to Practice: A Crisis Simulation Exercise. *Business Communication Quarterly* 76 (3): 322–38.

Aldrich, Clark. 2009. *The Complete Guide to Simulations and Serious Games: How the Most Valuable Content Will Be Created in the Age beyond Gutenberg to Google*. San Francisco: Pfeiffer.

Alhabash, Saleem, and Kevin Wise. 2014. Playing Their Game: Changing Stereotypes of Palestinians and Israelis through Videogame Play. *New Media Society*, accessed June 26, 2014. DOI: 10.1177/1461444814525010.

Altschull, Herbert J. 1995. *Agents of Power: The Media and Public Policy*. 2nd ed. White Plains, NY: Longman.

Ansoms, An. 2013. Negotiating on Poverty: A Participatory Poverty Assessment Simulation Game. *Simulation & Gaming* 44 (4): 586–601.

Ansoms, An, and Sara Geenen. 2012. Development Monopoly: A Simulation Game on Poverty and Inequality. *Simulation & Gaming* 43 (6): 853–62.

Asal, Victor. 2005. Playing Games with International Relations. *International Studies Perspectives* 6 (3): 359–73.

Asal, Victor, and Elizabeth L. Blake. 2006. Creating Simulations for Political Science Education. *Journal of Political Science Education* 2 (1): 1–18.

Asal, Victor, Lewis Griffith, and Marcus Schulzke. 2014. The Dalig and Vadan Exercise: Teaching Students about Strategy and the Challenges of Friction and Fog. *International Studies Perspectives* 15 (4): 477–90.

Asal, Victor, and Marcus Schulzke. 2012. A Shot Not Taken: Teaching about the Ethics of Political Violence. *International Studies Perspectives* 13 (4): 408–22.

Ashby, Ross W. 1954. *Design for a Brain*. New York: Wiley.

Ashby, Ross W. 1957. *An Introduction to Cybernetics*. London: Chapman & Hall.

Atkinson, Joe. 2011. Performance Journalism: A Three-Template Model of Television News. *International Journal of Press/Politics* 16 (1): 102–29.

Bachen, Christine M., Pedro F. Hernandez-Ramos, and Chad Raphael. 2012. Simulating REAL LIVES: Promoting Global Empathy and Interest in Learning through Simulation Games. *Simulation & Gaming* 43 (4): 437–60.

Bardi, Anat, and Shalom H. Schwartz. 2003. Values and Behavior: Strength and Structure of Relations. *Personal and Social Psychology Bulletin* 29 (10): 1207–20.

Bartels, Elizabeth, Margaret McCown, and Timothy Wilkie. 2013. Designing Peace and Conflict Exercises: Level of Analysis, Scenario, and Role Specification. *Simulation & Gaming* 44 (1): 36–50.

Beck, Robert J. 2010. Teaching International Law as a Partially Online Course. *International Studies Perspectives* 11 (3): 273–90.

Benson, Oliver. 1961. A Simple Diplomatic Game. In *International Politics and Foreign Policy: A Reader in Research and Theory*, edited by James N. Rosenau, 504–11. New York: Free Press.

Ben-Yehuda, Hemda, and Luba Levin-Banchik. 2011. The Dangers of Terror in World Politics: International Terror Crises, 1918–2006. *Studies in Conflict and Terrorism* 34 (1): 31–46.

Ben-Yehuda, Hemda, and Luba Levin-Banchik. 2014. Regime and Power in International Terror Crises: Strong Democracies Fight Back Hard. *Terrorism and Political Violence* 26 (3): 504–22.

Ben-Yehuda, Hemda, Chanan Naveh, and Luba Levin-Banchik. 2013a. Crises Press Coverage: Local and Foreign Reporting on the Arab-Israel Conflict. *Studies in Media and Communication* 1 (2): 35–46.

Ben-Yehuda, Hemda, Chanan Naveh, and Luba Levin-Banchik. 2013b. From Virtual to Real: Simulating Conflict Dynamics in a Global Information Age. Paper presented at the Annual Convention of the International Studies Association, San Francisco, April 3–6.

Ben-Yehuda, Hemda, Chanan Naveh, and Luba Levin-Banchik. 2013c. When Media and World Politics Meet: Crisis Press Coverage in the Arab-Israel and East-West Conflicts. *Media, War & Conflict* 6 (1): 71–92.

Ben-Yehuda, Hemda, Chanan Naveh, Luba Levin-Banchik,

and Mary Jane Parmentier. 2014. Assessing Less Tangible Simulation Aspects: International Collaborations on Facebook. Paper presented at the ISA Annual Convention of the International Studies Association, Toronto, Canada, March 26–29.

Ben-Yehuda, Hemda, and Shmuel Sandler. 2002. *The Arab-Israeli Conflict Transformed: Fifty Years of Interstate and Ethnic Crises*. Albany: State University of New York Press.

Blair, Bruce, Victor Esin, Matthew McKinzie, Valery Yarynich, and Pavel Zolotarev. 2010. Smaller and Safer: New Plan for Nuclear Postures. *Foreign Affairs* 89 (5): 9–16.

Bloomfield, Lincoln P., and Robert Beattie. 1971. Computers and Policy-Making: The CASCON Experiment. *Journal of Conflict Resolution* 15 (1): 33–46.

Bloomfield, Lincoln P., and Norman J. Padelford. 1959. Three Experiments in Political Gaming. *American Political Science Review* 53 (4): 1105–15.

Blum, Andrew, and Audrey Scherer. 2007. What Creates Engagement? An Analysis of Student Participation in ICONS Simulations. Paper presented at the American Political Science Association Teaching and Learning Conference, Charlotte, NC, February 9–11.

Boin, Arjen, Celesta Kofman-Bos, and Werner Overdijk. 2004. Crisis Simulations: Exploring Tomorrow's Vulnerabilities and Threats. *Simulation & Gaming* 35 (3): 378–93.

Bos, Nathan D., Sadat N. Shami, and Sara Naab. 2006. A Globalization Simulation to Teach Corporate Social Responsibility: Design Features and Analysis of Student Reasoning. *Simulation & Gaming* 37 (1): 56–72.

Boyer, Mark A. 2011. Simulation in International Studies. *Simulation & Gaming* 42 (6): 685–89.

Boyer, Mark A., Peter Trumbore, and David O. Fricke. 2006. Teaching Theories of International Political Economy from the Pit: A Simple In-Class Simulation. *International Studies Perspectives* 7 (1): 67–76.

Boyer, Mark A., Brian Urlacher, Natalie Florea Hudson, Anat Niv-Solomon, Laura L. Janik, Michael J. Butler, Scott W. Brown, and Andri Ioannou. 2009. Gender and Negotiation: Some Experimental Findings from an International Negotiation Simulation. *International Studies Quarterly* 53 (1): 23–47.

Brecher, Michael, and Hemda Ben-Yehuda. 1985. System and Crisis in International Politics. *Review of International Studies* 11 (1): 17–36.

Brecher, Michael, with Benjamin Geist. 1980. *Decisions in Crisis: Israel 1967 and 1973*. Berkeley: University of California Press.

Bremer, Stuart A. 1977. *Simulated Worlds: A Computer Model of National Decision-Making*. Princeton: Princeton University Press.

Bridge, Dave, and Simon Radford. 2014. Teaching Diplomacy by Other Means: Using an Outside-of-Class Simulation to Teach International Relations Theory. *International Studies Perspectives* 15 (4): 423–37.

Brody, Richard A. 1963. Some Systemic Effects of the Spread of Nuclear Weapons Technology: A Study through Simulation of a Multi-Nuclear Future. *Journal of Conflict Resolution* 7 (4): 663–753.

Brynen, Rex. 2010. (Ending) Civil War in the Classroom: A Peacebuilding Simulation. *PS: Political Science & Politics* 43 (1): 145–49.

Brynen, Rex, and Gary Milante. 2013. Peacebuilding with Games and Simulations. *Simulation & Gaming* 44 (1): 27–35.

Butcher, Charity. 2012. Teaching Foreign Policy Decision-Making Processes Using Role-Playing Simulations: The Case of US-Iranian Relations. *International Studies Perspectives* 13 (2): 176–94.

Caers, Ralf, Tim De Feyter, Marijke De Couck, Talia Stough, Claudia Vigna, and Cind Du Bois. 2013. Facebook: A Literature Review. *New Media & Society* 15 (6): 982–1002.

Caillier, Stacey L., and Robert C. Riordan. 2009. Teacher Education for the Schools We Need. *Journal of Teacher Education* 60 (5): 489–96.

Carpenter, Charli, and Daniel W. Drezner. 2010. International Relations 2.0: The Implications of New Media for an Old Profession. *International Studies Perspectives* 11 (3): 255–72.

Carvalho, Gustavo. 2014. Virtual Worlds Can Be Dangerous: Using Ready-Made Computer Simulations for Teaching International Relations. *International Studies Perspectives* 15 (4): 538–57.

Chasek, Pamela S. 2005. Power Politics, Diplomacy, and Role-Playing: Simulating the UN Security Council's Response to Terrorism. *International Studies Perspectives* 6 (1): 1–19.

Chin, Jeffrey, Richard Dukes, and William Gamson. 2009. Assessment in Simulation and Gaming: A Review of the Last 40 Years. *Simulation & Gaming* 40 (4): 553–68.

Christopher, Elizabeth M. 1999. Simulations and Games as Subversive Activities. *Simulation & Gaming* 30 (4): 441–55.

Cioffi-Revilla, Claudio, and Mark Rouleau. 2010. MASON RebeLand: An Agent-Based Model of Politics, Environment, and Insurgency. *International Studies Review* 12 (1): 31–52.

Clapper, Timothy C. 2014. Situational Interest and Instructional Design: A Guide for Simulation Facilitators. *Simulation & Gaming* 45 (2): 167–82.

Cohen, Bernard C. 1963. *The Press and Foreign Policy*. Princeton: Princeton University Press.

Cohen-Almagor, Raphael. 2011. Internet History. *International Journal of Technoethics* 2 (2): 45–64.

Cook, Timothy. 1998. *Governing with the News: The News Media as a Political Institution*. Chicago: University of Chicago Press.

Coplin, William D. 1970. The State System Exercise: A Teaching Note. *International Studies Quarterly* 14 (4): 412–26.

Corbeil, Pierre, and Dany Laveault. 2011. Validity of a Simulation Game as a Method for History Teaching. *Simulation & Gaming* 42 (4): 462–75.

Cottle, Simon, and Rai Mugdha. 2008. Global 24/7 News Providers: Emissaries of Global Dominance or Global Public Sphere? *Global Media and Communication* 4 (2): 157–81.

Crookall, David. 2010. Serious Games, Debriefing, and Simulation/Gaming as a Discipline. *Simulation & Gaming* 41 (6): 898–920.

Crookall, David. 2013. Peace, Violence, and Simulation/Gaming. *Simulation & Gaming* 44 (1): 7–26.

Crookall, David, and Jonathan Wilkenfeld. 1985. ICONS: Communications Technologies and International Relations. *System* 13 (3): 253–58.

Crossley-Frolick, Katy A. 2010. Beyond Model UN: Simulating Multi-Level, Multi-Actor Diplomacy Using the Millennium Development Goals. *International Studies Perspectives* 11 (2): 184–201.

Cuhadar, Esra, and Ronit Kampf. 2014. Learning about Conflict and Negotiations through Computer Simulations: The Case of PeaceMaker. *International Studies Perspectives* 15 (4): 509–24.

Darling, Juanita, and Mira Foster. 2012. Preparing Students to Join the Global Public Sphere. *International Studies Perspectives* 13 (4): 423–36.

DeGarmo, Denise. 2006. ICONS and 'Resistant Populations': Assessing the Impact of the International Communication and Negotiation Simulations Project on Student Learning at SIUE. Paper Presented at the American Political Science Association Conference on Teaching and Learning in Political Science, Washington, DC, February 18–20.

De Sola Pool, Ithiel, and Robert Abelson. 1961. The Simulmatics Project. *Public Opinion Quarterly* 25 (2): 167–83.

De Sola Pool, Ithiel, and Allan Kessler. 1965. The Kaiser, the Tsar, and the Computer: Information Processing in a Crisis. *American Behavioral Scientist* 8 (9): 31–38.

Dexter, Helen, and Emmanuel-Pierre Guittet. 2014. Teaching (Something about) Terrorism: Ethical and Methodological Problems, Pedagogical Suggestions. *International Studies Perspectives* 15 (4): 374–93.

DiCicco, Jonathan M. 2014. National Security Council: Simulating Decision-Making Dilemmas in Real Time. *International Studies Perspectives* 15 (4): 438–58.

Dieker, Lisa A., Jacqueline A. Rodriguez, Benjamin Lignugaris-Kraft, Michael C. Hynes, and Charles E. Hughes. 2014. The Potential of Simulated Environments in Teacher Education: Current and Future Possibilities. *Teacher Education and Special Education: The Journal of the Teacher Education Division of the Council for Exceptional Children* 37 (1): 21–33.

Donohue, Laura K. 2013. National Security Law Pedagogy and the Role of Simulations. *Journal of National Security Law & Policy* 6 (2): 489–547.

Dormans, Joris. 2011. Beyond Iconic Simulation. *Simulation & Gaming* 42 (5): 610–31.

Dorn, Dean S. 1989. Simulation Games: One More Tool on the Pedagogical Shelf. *Teaching Sociology* 17 (1): 1–18.

Douglas, Kathy, and Belinda Johnson. 2008. The Online Mediation Fishbowl: Learning about Gender and Power in Mediation. *Journal of the Australasian Law Teachers Association* 1 (1–2): 95–107.

Druckman, James N. 2001. On the Limits of Framing Effects: Who Can Frame? *Journal of Politics* 63 (4): 1041–66.

Duran, Richard P. 1998. Learning and Technology: Implications for Culturally Responsive Instructional Activity and Models of Achievements. *Journal of Negro Education* 67 (3): 220–27.

Earnest, David C. 2008. Coordination in Large Numbers: An Agent-Based Model of International Negotiations. *International Studies Quarterly* 52 (2): 363–82.

Earnest, David C. 2009. Growing a Virtual Insurgency: Using Massively Parallel Gaming to Simulate Insurgent Behavior. *Journal of Defense Modeling and Simulation: Applications, Methodology, Technology* 6 (2): 55–67.

Ebner, Noam, Anita D. Bhappu, Jennifer Gerarda Brown, Kimberlee K. Kovach, and Andrea Kupfer Schneider. 2009. You've Got Agreement: Negoti@ting via Email. In *Rethinking Negotiation Teaching: Innovations for Context and Culture*, edited by Christopher Honeyman, James Coben, and Giuseppe De Palo, 89–114. St. Paul, MN: Hameline University School of Law, DRI Press.

Ebner, Noam, James Coben, and Christopher Honeyman, eds.. 2012. *Assessing Our Students, Assessing Ourselves*. St. Paul, MN: Hameline University, DRI Press.

Ebner, Noam, and Yifat Winkler. 2009. PASTA WARS: A Prisoner's Dilemma Simulation-Game. *Simulation & Gaming* 40 (1): 134–46.

Eisenberg, Laura Zittrain, and Neil Caplan. 2010. *Negotiating Arab-Israeli Peace: Patterns, Problems, Possibilities*. 2nd ed. Bloomington: Indiana University Press.

Elias, Anwen. 2014. Simulating the European Union: Reflections on Module Design. *International Studies Perspectives* 15 (4): 407–22.

Enterline, Andrew J., and Eric M. Jepsen. 2009. Chinazambia and Boliviafranca: A Simulation of Domestic Politics and Foreign Policy. *International Studies Perspectives* 10 (1): 49–59.

Entman, Robert M. 1991. Framing US Coverage of International News. *Journal of Communication* 41 (4): 6–27.

Entman, Robert M. 2007. Framing Bias: Media in the Distribution of Power. *Journal of Communication* 57 (1): 163–73.

Flynn, Stephen. 2000. Drug Trafficking, the International System, and Decision-Making Constraints: A Policy-Making Simulation. *International Studies Perspectives* 1 (1): 45–55.

Fowler, Michael R. 2009. Culture and Negotiation: The Pedagogical Dispute Regarding Cross-Cultural Simulations. *International Studies Perspectives* 10 (3): 341–59.

Fowler, Sandra M., and Margaret D. Pusch. 2010. Intercultural Simulation Games: A Review (of the United States and Beyond). *Simulation & Gaming* 41 (1): 94–115.

Gaber, Ivor. 2000. Government by Spin: An Analysis of the Process. *Media, Culture & Society* 22 (4): 507–18.

Garris, Rosemary, Robert Ahlers, and James E. Driskell. 2002. Games, Motivation, and Learning: A Research and Practice Model. *Simulation & Gaming* 33 (4): 441–67.

Garrison, Randy D., and Heather Kanuka. 2004. Blended Learning: Uncovering Its Transformative Potential in Higher Education. *Internet and Higher Education* 7 (2): 95–105.

Geller, Armando, and Shah Jamal Alam. 2010. A Socio-Political and-Cultural Model of the War in Afghanistan. *International Studies Review* 12 (1): 8–30.

Gergen, David. 1991. Diplomacy in a Television Age: The Dangers of Teledemocracy. In *The Media and Foreign Policy*, edited by Simon Serfaty, 47–63. New York: St. Martin's Press.

Gilboa, Eytan. 1979. Educating Israeli Officers in the Processes of Peacemaking in the Middle East Conflict. *Journal of Peace Research* 16 (2): 155–62.

Ginns, Paul, and Robert Ellis. 2007. Quality in Blended Learning: Exploring the Relationships between On-Line and Face-to-Face Teaching and Learning. *Internet and Higher Education* 10 (1): 53–64.

Glasgow, Sara M. 2014. Stimulating Learning by Simulating Politics: Teaching Simulation Design in the Undergraduate Context. *International Studies Perspectives* 15 (4): 525–37.

Glazier, Rebecca A. 2011. Running Simulations without Ruining Your Life: Simple Ways to Incorporate Active Learning into Your Teaching. *Journal of Political Science Education* 7 (4): 375–93.

Goldhamer, Herbert, and Hans Speier. 1959. Some Observations on Political Gaming. *World Politics* 12 (1): 71–83.

Golich, Vicki L. 2000. The ABCs of Case Teaching. *International Studies Perspectives* 1 (1): 11–29.

Gonzalez, Cleotilde, Lelyn D. Saner, and Laurie Z. Eisenberg. 2013. Learning to Stand in the Other's Shoes: A Computer Video Game Experience of the Israeli-Palestinian Conflict. *Social Science Computer Review* 31 (2): 236–43.

Goon, Michael. 2011. Peacekeeping the Game. *International Studies Perspectives* 12 (3): 250–72.

Gopnik, Allison. 2012. Why Play Is Serious. *Smithsonian* 43:13–14.

Gore, Al. 2013. *The Future: Six Drivers of Global Change.* New York: Random House.

Greco, Marco, Nicola Baldissin, and Fabio Nonino. 2013. An Exploratory Taxonomy of Business Games. *Simulation & Gaming* 44 (5): 645–82.

Greenhow, Christine, Beth Robelia, and Joan E. Hughes. 2009. Learning, Teaching, and Scholarship in a Digital Age: Web 2.0 and Classroom Research: What Path Should We Take Now? *Educational Researcher* 38 (4): 246–59.

Guetzkow, Harold. 1959. A Use of Simulation in the Study of Inter-Nation Relations. *Behavioral Science* 4 (3): 183–91.

Guetzkow, Harold, ed. 1962. *Simulation in Social Sciences: Readings.* Englewood Cliffs, NJ: Prentice-Hall.

Guetzkow, Harold, Chadwick F. Alger, Richard A. Brody, Robert C. Noel, and Richard C. Snyder. 1963. *Simulation in International Relations: Developments for Research and Teaching.* Englewood Cliffs, NJ: Prentice-Hall.

Guetzkow, Harold, and Lloyd Jensen. 1966. Research Activities on Simulated International Processes. *Background* 9 (4): 261–74.

Guilhot, Nicolas. 2011. Cyborg Pantocrator: International Relations Theory from Decisionism to Rational Choice. *Journal of the History of the Behavioral Sciences* 47 (3): 279–301.

Haas, Michael. 1970. International Subsystems: Stability and Polarity. *American Political Science Review* 64 (1): 98–123.

Hall, Hazel, and Brian Davison. 2007. Social Software as Support in Hybrid Learning Environments: The Value of the Blog as a Tool for Reflective Learning and Peer Support. *Library & Information Science Research* 29 (2): 163–87.

Hallahan, Kirk. 1999. Seven Models of Framing: Implications for Public Relations. *Journal of Public Relations Research* 11 (3): 205–42.

Hallin, Daniel C., and Paolo Mancini. 2004. *Comparing Media Systems: Three Models of Media and Politics.* Cambridge: Cambridge University Press.

Harding, Tucker B., and Mark A. Whitlock. 2013. Leveraging Web-Based Environments for Mass Atrocity Prevention. *Simulation & Gaming* 44 (1): 94–117.

Harrison, Joseph O., and Edward M. Lee. 1960. *The Stratspiel Pilot Model.* Bethesda, MD: Operations Research Office, Johns Hopkins University.

Haslam, Alexander S. 2004. *Psychology in Organizations: The Social Identity Approach.* Los Angeles: Sage.

Haslam, Alexander S., Inmaculada Adarves-Yorno, and Tom Postmes. 2014. Creative Communities Are Key to Innovation. *Scientific American Mind* 25 (4), accessed June 22, 2014. http://www.scientificamerican.com/article/creative-communities-are-key-to-innovation/.

Haslam, Alexander S., Stephen D. Reicher, and Michael J. Platow. 2011. *The New Psychology of Leadership: Identity, Influence, and Power.* New York: Psychology Press.

Hatipoglu, Emre, Meltem Müftüler-Baç, and Teri Murphy. 2014. Simulation Games in Teaching International Relations: Insights from a Multi-Day, Multi-Stage, Multi-Issue Simulation on Cyprus. *International Studies Perspectives* 15 (4): 394–406.

Helmer, Olaf, and Nicholas Rescher. 1959. On the Epistemology of the Inexact Science. *Management Science* 6:25–53.

Hermann, Charles F. 1965. *Crises in Foreign Policy Making: A Simulation in International Politics.* China Lake, CA: Project Michelson, Naval Ordnance Test Station.

Hermann, Charles F., and Margaret G. Hermann. 1962. *The Potential Use of Historical Data for Validation Studies of the Inter-Nation Simulation: The Outbreak of World War I as an Illustration.* Chicago: Northwestern University Program on International Relations.

Hermann, Charles F., and Margaret G. Hermann 1967. An Attempt to Simulate the Outbreak of World War I. *American Political Science Review* 61 (2): 400–416.

Hermann, Charles F., Margaret G. Hermann, and Robert A. Cantor. 1974. Counterattack or Delay: Characteristics Influencing Decision Makers' Responses to the Simulation of an Unidentified Attack. *Journal of Conflict Resolution* 18 (1): 75–106.

Hermida, Alfred. 2010. New Challenges for Journalism in the 21st Century. In *The New Journalist: Roles, Skills, and Critical Thinking,* edited by Paul Benedetti, Timothy Currie, and Kim Kierans, 9–21. Toronto: Emond Montgomery Publications.

Herrmann, Michael. 2014. Polls, Coalitions and Strategic Voting under Proportional Representation. *Journal of Theoretical Politics* 26 (3): 442–67.

Hodson, Douglas D., and Raymond R. Hill. 2014. The Art and Science of Live, Virtual, and Constructive Simulation for Test and Analysis. *Journal of Defense Modeling and Simulation: Applications, Methodology, Technology* 11 (2): 77–89.

Holley, Debbie, and Martin Oliver. 2010. Student Engagement and Blended Learning: Portraits of Risk. *Computers & Education* 54 (3): 693–700.

Howard, Warren Dee. 1961. The Computer Simulation of a Colonial Socio-Economic System. General Motors Corporation, Defense Systems Division. Paper presented at the Western Joint IRE-AIEE-ACM Computer Conference, New York, May 9–11.

Hudson, Natalie Florea, and Michael J. Butler. 2010. The State of Experimental Research in IR: An Analytical Survey. *International Studies Review* 12 (2): 165–92.

Iyengar, Shanto, and Adam Simon. 1994. News Coverage of the Gulf Crisis and Public Opinion. In *Taken by Storm: The Media, Public Opinion, and U.S. Foreign Policy in the Gulf War,* edited by Lance W. Bennett and David L. Paletz, 167–84. Chicago: University of Chicago Press.

Jeong, Ki-Young, and Ipek Bozkurt. 2014. Evaluating a Project Management Simulation Training Exercise. *Simulation & Gaming* 45 (2): 183–203.

John-Steiner, Vera. 2000. *Creative Collaboration*. Oxford: Oxford University Press.

Joseph, Kenneth, Geoffrey P. Morgan, Michael K. Martin, and Kathleen M. Carley. 2014. On the Coevolution of Stereotype, Culture, and Social Relationships: An Agent-Based Model. *Social Science Computer Review* 32 (3): 295–311.

Jozwiak, Joseph. 2013. "Vegelate" and Greece: Teaching the EU through Simulations. *European Political Science* 12 (2): 215–30.

Kachuyevski, Angela, and Sandra F. Jones. 2011. Bringing Theory to Life through Field Study. *International Studies Perspectives* 12 (4): 447–56.

Kaehler, Richard. C. 1961. *A Systems Engineering Approach to the Problems of International Conflict*. General Motors Corporation, Defense Systems Division. Unpublished manuscript.

Kanner, Michael D. 2007. War and Peace: Simulating Security Decision Making in the Classroom. *PS: Political Science & Politics* 40 (4): 795–800.

Kaplan, Morton A., Arthur Lee Burns, and Richard Quandt. 1960. Theoretical Analysis of the Balance of Power. *Behavioral Science* 5 (3): 240–52.

Karsch, Efraim. 2010. *Palestine Betrayed*. New Haven: Yale University Press.

Kaufman, Joyce P. 1998. Using Simulation as a Tool to Teach about International Negotiation. *International Negotiation* 3 (1): 59–75.

Kee, Kevin. 2011. Computerized History Games: Narrative Options. *Simulation & Gaming* 42 (4): 423–40.

Keith, Michael C. 2004. *The Radio Station: Broadcast, Satellite, and Internet*. 6th ed. Boston: Focal Press.

Kelle, Alexander. 2008. Experiential Learning in an Arms Control Simulation. *PS: Political Science & Politics* 41 (2): 379–85.

Kempston, Tanya, and Nicholas Thomas. 2014. The Drama of International Relations: A South China Sea Simulation. *International Studies Perspectives* 15 (4): 459–76.

Kikkawa, Toshiko, and David Crookall. 2011. Biography and Discipline: Key Players in Simulation/Gaming. *Simulation & Gaming* 42 (3): 281–88.

Kirk, James J. 2004. The Making of a Gaming-Simulation Course: A Personal Tale. *Simulation & Gaming* 35 (1): 85–93.

Kleinrock, Leonard. 2008. History of the Internet and Its Flexible Future. *IEEE Wireless Communications* 15 (1): 8–18.

Kolmer, Christian, and Holli A. Semetko. 2009. Framing the Iraq War: Perspectives from American, U.K., Czech, German, South African, and Al-Jazeera News. *American Behavioral Scientist* 52 (5): 643–56.

Korosteleva, Elena A. 2010. Threshold Concepts through Enactive Learning: How Effective Are They in the Study of European Politics? *International Studies Perspectives* 11 (1): 37–50.

Köse, Utku. 2010. A Blended Learning Model Supported with Web 2.0 Technologies. *Procedia—Social and Behavioral Sciences* 2 (2): 2794–2802.

Kraus, Sarit, Jonathan Wilkenfeld, Michael A. Harris, and Elizabeth Blake. 1992. The Hostage Crisis Simulation. *Simulation & Gaming* 23 (4): 398–416.

Kuperman, Ranan D. 2010. Analyzing Conflict Dynamics with the Aid of an Interactive Microworld Simulator of a Fishing Dispute. *Simulation & Gaming* 41 (3): 293–315.

Kurtz, Howard. 1998. *Spin Cycle: How the White House and the Media Manipulate the News*. New York: Touchstone.

Lambeth, Edmund B. 1995. Global Media Philosophies. In *Global Journalism: Survey of International Communication*, 3rd ed., edited by John C. Merrill, 3–18. New York: Longman.

Landwehr, Peter, Marc Spraragen, Balki Ranganathan, Kathleen M. Carley, and Michael Zyda. 2013. Games, Social Simulations, and Data—Integration for Policy Decisions: The SUDAN Game. *Simulation & Gaming* 44 (1): 151–77.

Lay, Celeste J., and Kathleen J. Smarick. 2006. Simulating a Senate Office: The Impact on Student Knowledge and Attitudes. *Journal of Political Science Education* 2 (2): 131–46.

Lederman, Linda Costigan. 1992. Debriefing: Toward a Systematic Assessment of Theory and Practice. *Simulation & Gaming* 23 (2): 145–60.

LeNoue, Marvin, Tom Hall, and Myron A. Eighmy. 2011. Adult Education and the Social Media Revolution. *Adult Learning* 22 (2): 4–12.

Lewis, J. Scott, and Marissa A. Harrison. 2012. Online Delivery as a Course Adjunct Promotes Active Learning and Student Success. *Teaching of Psychology* 39 (1): 72–76.

Limor, Yehiel. 2003. Mass Media in Israel. In *Trends in Israeli Society* [in Hebrew], vol. 2, edited by Ephraim Yaar and Zeev Shavit, 1017–1103. Tel Aviv: Open University of Israel.

Lindsay, Elizabeth Blakesley. 2004. The Best of Both Worlds: Teaching a Hybrid Course. *Academic Exchange Quarterly* 8 (4), accessed February 15, 2014. http://rapidintellect.com/AEQweb/cho2738z4.htm.

Lisk, Timothy C., Ugur T. Kaplancali, and Ronald E. Riggio. 2012. Leadership in Multiplayer Online Gaming Environments. *Simulation & Gaming* 43 (1): 133–49.

Livingston, Steven. 2011. The CNN Effect Reconsidered (Again): Problematizing ICT and Global Governance in the CNN Effect Research Agenda. *Media, War & Conflict* 4 (1): 20–36.

Loggins, Julie A. 2009. Simulating the Foreign Policy Decision-Making Process in the Undergraduate Classroom. *PS: Political Science & Politics* 42 (2): 401–7.

Lopes, Mauricio Capobianco, Francisco A. P. Fialho, Cristiano J. C. A. Cunha, and Sofia Inés Niveiros. 2013. Business Games for Leadership Development: A Systematic Review. *Simulation & Gaming* 44 (4): 523–43.

López-Pérez, M. Victoria, Carmen M. Pérez-López, and Lázaro Rodríguez-Ariza. 2011. Blended Learning in Higher Education: Students' Perceptions and Their Relation to Outcomes. *Computers & Education* 56 (3): 818–26.

Luce, Duncan R., and Howard Raiffa. 1957. *Games and Decisions: Introduction and Critical Survey*. New York: John Wiley.

Maoz, Zeev. 2006. *Defending the Holy Land: A Critical Analysis of Israel's National Security and Foreign Policy*. Ann Arbor: University of Michigan Press.

Mason, Roger, and Eric Patterson. 2013. War Gaming Peace Operations. *Simulation & Gaming* 44 (1): 118–33.

Mayer, Igor S. 2009. The Gaming of Policy and the Politics of Gaming: A Review. *Simulation & Gaming* 40 (6): 825–62.

McCombs, Maxwell. E. 1981. The Agenda Setting Approach. In *Handbook of Political Communication*, edited by Dan D. Nimmo and Keith R. Sanders, 121–40. London: Sage.

McDermott, Rose. 2011. New Directions for Experimental Work in International Relations. *International Studies Quarterly* 55 (2): 503–20.

McMahon, Sean F., and Chris Miller. 2012. Simulating the Camp David Negotiations: A Problem-Solving Tool in Critical Pedagogy. *Simulation & Gaming* 44 (1): 134–50.

McQuail, Denis. 1994. *Mass Communication Theory*. 3rd ed. London: Sage.

McQuail, Denis. 2007. The Influence and Effects of Mass Media. In *Media Power in Politics*, 5th ed., edited by Doris A. Graber, 19–36. Washington, DC: CQ Press.

Merrill, John C. 1974. *The Imperative of Freedom: A Philosophy of Journalistic Autonomy*. New York: Hastings House.

Milbrath, Lester W. 1958. Predispositions toward Voting Decisions. *American Behavioral Scientist* 1 (5): 26–29.

Miller, Benjamin. 1997. The Great Powers and Regional Peacemaking: Patterns in the Middle East and Beyond. *Journal of Strategic Studies* 20 (1): 103–42.

Mintz, Alex. 2004. Foreign Policy Decision Making in Familiar and Unfamiliar Settings: An Experimental Study of High-Ranking Military Officers. *Journal of Conflict Resolution* 48 (1): 91–104.

Mintz, Alex, Steven B. Redd, and Arnold Vedlitz. 2006. Can We Generalize from Student Experiments to the Real World in Political Science, Military Affairs, and International Relations? *Journal of Conflict Resolution* 50 (5): 757–76.

Mintz, Alex, Yi Yang, and Rose McDermott. 2011. Experimental Approaches to International Relations. *International Studies Quarterly* 55 (2): 493–501.

Morell, Virginia. 2013. *Animal Wise: The Thoughts and Emotions of Our Fellow Creatures*. New York: Random House.

Morey, Daniel S. 2011. When War Brings Peace: A Dynamic Model of the Rivalry Process. *American Journal of Political Science* 55 (2): 263–75.

Morris, Benny. 2004. *The Birth of the Palestinian Refugee Problem Revisited*. Cambridge: Cambridge University Press

Morris, Benny. 2008. *1948: A History of the First Arab-Israeli War*. New Haven: Yale University Press.

Moskal, Patsy, Charles Dziuban, and Joel Hartman. 2013. Blended Learning: A Dangerous Idea? *Internet and Higher Education* 18:15–23.

Nannini, Christopher J., Jeffrey A. Appleget, and Alejandro S. Hernandez. 2013. Game for Peace: Progressive Education in Peace Operations. *Journal of Defense Modeling and Simulation: Applications, Methodology, Technology* 10 (3): 283–96.

Naveh, Chanan. 2001. *Teachers Guide (Simulations), Neighbors on the Web Project. Geopolitics of the Middle East* [in Hebrew]. Jerusalem: Mushinski Center for R&D, ORT, and Snunit Association.

Naveh, Chanan. 2002. The Role of the Media in Foreign Policy Decision Making: A Theoretical Framework. *Conflict & Communication Online* 1 (2), accessed June 15, 2014. http://www.cco.regener-online.de/2002_2/pdf_2002_2/naveh.pdf.

Neumann, Martin. 2014. The Escalation of Ethnonationalist Radicalization: Simulating the Effectiveness of Nationalist Ideologies. *Social Science Computer Review* 32 (3): 312–33.

Norris, Pippa, Montague Kern, and Marion Just, eds. 2003. *Framing Terrorism: The News Media, the Government and the Public*. London: Taylor & Francis.

North, Robert C. 1963. International Relations: Putting the Pieces Together. *Background* 7 (3): 119–30.

Obendorf, Simon, and Claire Randerson. 2012. *The Model United Nations Simulation and the Student as Producer Agenda*. Heslington, York: Higher Education Academy.

Pace, Dale K. 2013. Comprehensive Consideration of Uncertainty in Simulation Use. *Journal of Defense Modeling and Simulation: Applications, Methodology, Technology* 10 (4): 367–80.

Paletz, David. 1998. *The Media in American Politics: Contents and Consequences*. New York: Longman

Palmunen, Lauri-Matti, Elina Pelto, Anni Paalumäki, and Timo Lainema. 2013. Formation of Novice Business Students' Mental Models through Simulation Gaming. *Simulation & Gaming* 44 (6): 846–68.

Parmentier, Mary Jane C. 2013. Simulating in Cyberspace: Designing and Assessing Simple Role-Playing Activities for Online Regional Studies Courses. *International Studies Perspectives* 14 (2): 121–33.

Pepinsky, Thomas B. 2005. From Agents to Outcomes: Simulation in International Relations. *European Journal of International Relations* 11 (3): 367–94.

Petranek, Charles F. 2000. Written Debriefing: The Next Vital Step in Learning with Simulations. *Simulation & Gaming* 31 (1): 108–18.

Petranek, Charles F., Susan Corey, and Rebecca Black. 1992. Three Levels of Learning in Simulations: Participating, Debriefing, and Journal Writing. *Simulation & Gaming* 23 (2): 174–85.

Pettenger, Mary, Douglas West, and Niki Young. 2014. Assessing the Impact of Role-Play Simulations on Learning in Canadian and US Classrooms. *International Studies Perspectives* 15 (4): 491–508.

Pfetsch, Barbara. 1998. Government News Management. In *The Politics of News, the News of Politics*, edited by Doris Graber, Denis McQuail, and Pippa Norris, 70–93. Thousand Oaks, CA: CQ Press.

Pollins, Brian M. 1985. Breaking Trade Dependency: A Global Simulation of Third World Proposals for Alternative Trade Regimes. *International Studies Quarterly* 29 (3): 287–312.

Power, Marcus. 2007. Digitized Virtuosity: Video War Games and Post-9.11 Cyber-Deterrence. *Security Dialogue* 38 (2): 271–88.

Powers, Richard B. 2014. How I Became Addicted to Simulations and Games. *Simulation & Gaming* 45 (1): 5–22.

Powers, Richard B., and Kat Kirkpatrick. 2013. Playing with Conflict: Teaching Conflict Resolution through Simulations and Games. *Simulation & Gaming* 44 (1): 51–72.

Prescott, Julie. 2014. Teaching Style and Attitudes towards Facebook as an Educational Tool. *Active Learning in Higher Education* 15 (2): 117–28.

Raymond, Chad. 2010. Do Role-Playing Simulations Generate Measurable and Meaningful Outcomes? A Simulation's Effect on Exam Scores and Teaching Evaluations. *International Studies Perspectives* 11 (1): 51–60.

Raymond, Chad, and Kerstin Sorensen. 2008. The Use of a Middle East Crisis Simulation in an International Relations Course. *PS: Political Science & Politics* 41 (1): 179–82.

Robinson, James A. 1963. Decision-Making and Coalition Building. *Journal of Conflict Resolution* 7 (4): 763–68.

Robinson, Piers. 2011. The CNN Effect Reconsidered: Mapping a Research Agenda for the Future. *Media, War & Conflict* 4 (1): 3–11.

Roeh, Itzhak, and Raphael Nir. 1993. Reporting the Intifada in the Israeli Press: How Mainstream Ideology Overrides "Quality" and "Melodrama." In *Framing the Intifada: People and Media*, edited by Akiva A. Cohen and Gadi Wolfsfeld, 176–91. Norwood, NJ: Ablex.

Rogers, Everett M., and James W. Dearing. 2007. Agenda Setting Research: Where Has It Been? Where Is It Going? In *Media Power in Politics*, 5th ed., edited by Doris A. Graber, 80–97. Washington, DC: CQ Press.

Ross, Douglas N., and Al Rosenbloom. 2011. Reflections on Building and Teaching an Undergraduate Strategic Management Course in a Blended Format. *Journal of Management Education* 35 (3): 351–76.

Rothman, Steven B. 2012. Developing and Adapting Simulations through Six Points of Variance: An Example of Reaching Applied Game Theory through International Negotiations. *International Studies Perspectives* 13 (4): 437–57.

Rousseau, David, and Maurits A. Van der Veen. 2005. The Emergence of a Shared Identity: An Agent-Based Computer Simulation of Idea Diffusion. *Journal of Conflict Resolution* 49 (5): 686–712.

Ruane, Abigail E., and Patrick James. 2012. *The International Relations of Middle-earth: Learning from* The Lord of the Rings. Ann Arbor: University of Michigan Press.

Sasley, Brent E. 2010. Teaching Students How to Fail: Simulations as Tools of Explanation. *International Studies Perspectives* 11 (1): 61–74.

Schelling, Thomas C. 1961. Experimental Games and Bargaining Theory. *World Politics* 14 (1): 47–68.

Scheufele, Dietram A. 1999. Framing as a Theory of Media Effects. *Journal of Communication* 49 (1): 103–22.

Scheufele, Dietram A., and David Tewksbury. 2007. Framing, Agenda Setting, and Priming: The Evolution of Three Media Effects Models. *Journal of Communication* 57 (1): 9–20.

Schnurr, Matthew A., Elizabeth Santo, and Rachael Craig. 2013. Using a Blended Learning Approach to Simulate the Negotiation of a Multilateral Environmental Agreement. *International Studies Perspectives* 14 (2): 109–20.

Schofield, Julian. 2013. Modeling Choices in Nuclear Warfighting: Two Classroom Simulations on Escalation and Retaliation. *Simulation & Gaming* 44 (1): 73–93.

Schreiber, Darren. 2014. The Emergence of Parties: An Agent-Based Simulation. *Political Research Quarterly* 67 (1): 136–51.

Schulzke, Marcus. 2013. Being a Terrorist: Video Game Simulations of the Other Side of the War on Terror. *Media, War & Conflict* 6 (3): 207–20.

Schut, Kevin. 2007. Strategic Simulations and Our Past: The Bias of Computer Games in the Presentation of History. *Games and Culture* 2 (3): 213–35.

Schwartz, Shalom H., and Klaus Boehnke. 2004. Evaluating the Structure of Human Values with Confirmatory Factor Analysis. *Journal of Research in Personality* 38 (3): 230–55.

Schwartz, Shalom H., Gila Melech, Arielle Lehmann, Steven Burgess, Mari Harris, and Vicki Owens. 2001. Extending the Cross-Cultural Validity of the Theory of Basic Human Values with a Different Method of Measurement. *Journal of Cross-Cultural Psychology* 32 (5): 519–42.

Seib, Philip, ed. 2007. *New Media and the New Middle East.* New York: Palgrave Macmillan.

Senior, Rose. 2010. Connectivity: A Framework for Understanding Effective Language Teaching in Face-to-Face and Online Learning Communities. *RELC Journal* 41 (2): 137–47.

Shaw, Carolyn M. 2004. Using Role-Play Scenarios in the IR Classroom: An Examination of Exercises on Peacekeeping Operations and Foreign Policy Decision Making. *International Studies Perspectives* 5 (1): 1–22.

Shaw, Carolyn M. 2010. Designing and Using Simulations and Role-Play Exercises. In *The International Studies Encyclopedia*, edited by Robert A. Denemark, Blackwell Publishing, Blackwell Reference Online. Accessed March 12, 2014. http://www.blackwellreference.com/public/book.html?id=g9781444336597_9781444336597.

Shellman, Stephen M., and Kürsad Turan. 2006. Ready-to-Use Simulation: CONFRONTING GLOBAL ISSUES: A Multipurpose IR Simulation. *Simulation & Gaming* 37 (1): 98–123.

Shih, Clara. 2011. *The Facebook Era: Tapping Online Social Networks to Market, Sell, and Innovate.* 2nd ed. Upper Saddle River, NJ: Prentice-Hall.

Shubik, Martin. 1958. Simulation, Its Uses and Potential, Part I. *Expository and Development Paper No. 2.* New York: General Electric Company.

Shubik, Martin. 1959. Simulation, Its Uses and Potential, Part II. *Expository and Development Paper No. 3.* New York: General Electric Company.

Shubik, Martin. 1960. Bibliography on Simulation, Gaming, Artificial Intelligence, and Allied Topics. *Journal of the American Statistical Association* 55 (292): 736–51.

Shubik, Martin. 1968. On the Study of Disarmament and Escalation. *Journal of Conflict Resolution* 12 (1): 83–101.

Shubik, Martin. 1972. On the Scope of Gaming. *Management Science* 18 (5): 20–36.

Shubik, Martin. 2009. It Is Not Just a Game! *Simulation & Gaming* 40 (5): 587–601.

Siebert, Fred S., Theodore Peterson, and Wilbur Schramm. 1956. *Four Theories of the Press: The Authoritarian, Libertarian, Social Responsibility, and Soviet Communist Concepts of What the Press Should Be and Do.* Urbana: University of Illinois Press.

Siegel, David A., and Joseph K. Young. 2009. Simulating Terrorism: Credible Commitment, Costly Signaling, and Strategic Behavior. *PS: Political Science & Politics* 42 (4): 765–71.

Siemens, George. 2004. Connectivism: A Learning Theory for the Digital Age. *Elearnspace*, accessed March 12, 2014. http://www.elearnspace.org/Articles/connectivism.htm.

Siemens, George. 2009. Struggling for a Metaphor for Change. *Connectivism: Networked and Social Learning*, accessed March 12, 2014. http://www.connectivism.ca.

Simpson, Archie W., and Bernd Kaussler. 2009. IR Teaching Reloaded: Using Films and Simulations in the Teaching of International Relations. *International Studies Perspectives* 10 (4): 413–27.

Sims, Dana E., Shawn C. Burke, David S. Metcalf, and Eduardo Salas. 2008. Research-Based Guidelines for Designing Blended Learning. *Ergonomics in Design: The Quarterly of Human Factors Applications* 16 (1): 23–29.

Singer, David J., and Hirohide Hinomoto. 1965. Inspecting for Weapons Production: A Modest Computer Simulation. *Journal of Peace Research* 2 (1): 18–38.

Singer, Jane B. 2008. Posting for Points: Edublogs in the JMC Curriculum. *Journalism & Mass Communication Educator* 63 (1): 10–27.

Smith, Elizabeth T., and Mark A. Boyer. 1996. Designing In-Class Simulations. *PS: Political Science and Politics* 29 (4): 690–94.

Smith, Roger. 2010. The Long History of Gaming in Military Training. *Simulation & Gaming* 41 (1): 6–19.

Smolinski, Remigiusz, and Peter Kesting. 2012. Transcending the Classroom: A Practical Guide to Remote Role-Plays in Teaching International Negotiation. *Negotiation Journal* 28 (4): 489–502.

Soroka, Stuart N. 2003. Media, Public Opinion, and Foreign Policy. *Harvard International Journal of Press/Politics* 8 (1): 27–48.

Squazzoni, Flaminio, Wander Jager, and Bruce Edmonds. 2014. Social Simulation in the Social Sciences: A Brief Overview. *Social Science Computer Review* 32 (3): 279–94.

Starkey, Brigid, Mark A. Boyer, and Jonathan Wilkenfeld. 1999. *Negotiating in a Complex World*. New York: Rowman and Littlefield.

Starkey, Brigid, and Jonathan Wilkenfeld. 1996. Project ICONS: Computer-Assisted Negotiations for the IR Classroom. *International Studies Notes* 21 (1): 25–29.

Stoll, Richard J. 2005. Civil Reality? Simulation Experiments on the Impact of Civil War in a Realist World. *Conflict Management and Peace Science* 22 (1): 19–38.

Stoll, Richard J. 2011. Civil Engineering: Does a Realist World Influence the Onset of Civil Wars? *Simulation & Gaming* 42 (6): 748–71.

Stover, William J. 2007. Simulating the Cuban Missile Crisis: Crossing Time and Space in Virtual Reality. *International Studies Perspectives* 8 (1): 111–20.

Strand, Jonathan R., and David P. Rapkin. 2011. Weighted Voting in the United Nations Security Council: A Simulation. *Simulation & Gaming* 42 (6): 772–802.

Switky, Bob. 2004. The Importance of Voting in International Organizations: Simulating the Case of the European Union. *International Studies Perspectives* 5 (1): 40–49.

Tansey, Patrick J., and Derick Unwin. 1969. Sources in Simulation and Academic Gaming: An Annotated Bibliography. *British Journal of Educational Studies* 17 (2): 193–208.

Taylor, Anna-Sofia A., Per Backlund, and Lars Niklasson. 2012. The Coaching Cycle: A Coaching-by-Gaming Approach in Serious Games. *Simulation & Gaming* 43 (5): 648–72.

Taylor, Kirsten. 2013. Simulations Inside and Outside the IR Classroom: A Comparative Analysis. *International Studies Perspectives* 14 (2): 134–49.

Terhune, Kenneth W., and Joseph M. Firestone. 1970. Global War, Limited War, and Peace: Hypotheses from Three Experimental Worlds. *International Studies Quarterly* 14 (2): 195–218.

Tuckman, Bruce W. 2002. Evaluating ADAPT: A Hybrid Instructional Model Combining Web-Based and Classroom Components. *Computers & Education* 39 (3): 261–69.

Van Ments, Morry. 2011. Just Running Around: Some Reminiscences of Early Simulation/Gaming in the United Kingdom. *Simulation & Gaming* 42 (3): 397–404.

Vaughan, Norman, and Randy D. Garrison. 2005. Creating Cognitive Presence in a Blended Faculty Development Community. *Internet and Higher Education* 8 (1): 1–12.

Vavrina, Vernon. 2006. An Old-Timer's Reflections on IP Simulations. Paper Presented at the American Political Science Association Conference on Teaching and Learning in Political Science, Washington, DC, February 18–20.

Vincent, Andrew, and John Shepherd. 1998. Experiences in Teaching Middle East Politics via Internet-Based Role-Play Simulations. *Journal of Interactive Media in Education* 1998 (3): 11, DOI: http://dx.doi.org/10.5334/1998-11.

Ward, Michael D., and Alex Mintz. 1987. Dynamics of Military Spending in Israel: A Computer Simulation. *Journal of Conflict Resolution* 31 (1): 86–105.

Weaver, David H. 2007. Thoughts on Agenda Setting, Framing, and Priming. *Journal of Communication* 57 (1): 142–47.

Weaver, David H., Maxwell McCombs, and Donald L. Shaw. 2004. Agenda-Setting Research: Issues, Attributes, and Influences. In *Handbook of Political Communication Research*, edited by Lynda L. Kaid, 257–82. Mahwah, NJ: Lawrence Erlbaum Associates.

Weir, Kimberly, and Michael Baranowski. 2011. Simulating History to Understand International Politics. *Simulation & Gaming* 42 (4): 441–61.

Wilkenfeld, Jonathan, and Joyce Kaufman. 1993. Political Science: Network Simulation in International Politics. *Social Science Computer Review* 11 (4): 464–76.

Williams, Alexander J., and Robert H. Williams. 2011. Multiple Identification Theory: Attitude and Behavior Change in a Simulated International Conflict. *Simulation & Gaming* 42 (6): 733–47.

Williams, Robert H., and Alexander J. Williams. 2007. In Pursuit of Peace: Attitudinal and Behavioral Change with Simulations and Multiple Identifications Theory. *Simulation & Gaming* 38 (4): 453–71.

Williams, Robert H., and Alexander J. Williams. 2010. One for All and All for One: Using Multiple Identification Theory Simulations to Build Cooperative Attitudes and Behaviors in a Middle Eastern Conflict Scenario. *Simulation & Gaming* 41 (2): 187–207.

Willson, Richard W. 2008. In-Class—Online Hybrid Methods of Teaching Planning Theory: Assessing Impacts on Discussion and Learning. *Journal of Planning Education and Research* 28 (2): 237–46.

Wilson, Katherine A., Wendy L. Bedwell, Elizabeth H. Lazzara, Eduardo Salas, Shawn C. Burke, Jamie L. Estock, Kara L. Orvis, and Curtis Conkey. 2009. Relationships between Game Attributes and Learning Outcomes: Review and Research Proposals. *Simulation & Gaming* 40 (2): 217–66.

Wilson, Robert E., Samuel D. Gosling, and Lindsay T. Graham.

2012. A Review of Facebook Research in the Social Sciences. *Perspectives on Psychological Science* 7 (3): 203–20.

Wolfe, Wojtek M. 2010. A Taiwan Strait Conflict Simulation Model. *Journal of International and Area Studies* 17 (1): 31–53.

Wolfsfeld, Gadi. 1997. *Media and Political Conflict: News from the Middle East.* Cambridge: Cambridge University Press.

Wolfsfeld, Gadi. 2011. *Making Sense of Media and Politics: Five Principles in Political Communication.* New York: Routledge.

Wortley, David. 2013. Immersive Technology Strategies. *Simulation & Gaming* 44 (6): 869–81.

Yang Yuqin, Qiyun Wang, Huay Lit Woo, and Choon Lang Quek. 2011. Using Facebook for Teaching and Learning: A Review of the Literature. *International Journal of Continuing Engineering Education and Life-Long Learning* 21 (1): 72–86.

Yeh, Yu-chu, Yi-ling Yeh, and Yu-Hua Chen. 2012. From Knowledge Sharing to Knowledge Creation: A Blended Knowledge-Management Model for Improving University Students' Creativity. *Thinking Skills and Creativity* 7 (3): 245–57.

Yen, Jung-Chuan, and Chun-Yi Lee. 2011. Exploring Problem-Solving Patterns and Their Impact on Learning Achievement in a Blended Learning Environment. *Computers & Education* 56 (1): 138–45.

Yilmaz, Levent. 2007. Toward Next-Generation, Simulation-Based Computational Tools for Conflict and Peace Studies. *Social Science Computer Review* 11 (4): 464–76.

Yilmaz, Levent, Tuncer I. Ören, and Nasser Ghasem-Aghaee. 2006. Simulation-Based Problem-Solving Environments for Conflict Studies. *Simulation & Gaming* 37 (4): 534–56.

Yukawa, Taku, Iku Yoshimoto, and Susumu Yamakage. 2014. International Policy Diffusion at the Systemic Level: Linking Micro Patterns to Macro Dynamism. *Journal of Theoretical Politics* 26 (2): 177–96.

Zaino, Jeanne S., and Tricia Mulligan. 2009. Learning Opportunities in a Department-Wide Crisis Simulation: Bridging the International/National Divide. *PS: Political Science & Politics* 42 (3): 537–42.

Zelizer, Barbie. 1993. Journalists as Interpretive Communities. *Critical Studies in Mass Communication* 10 (3): 219–37.

Zelizer, Barbie, David Park, and David Gudelunas. 2002. How Bias Shapes the News: Challenging the *New York Times*' Status as a Newspaper of Record on the Middle East. *Journalism* 3 (3): 283–307.

Zittrain, Jonathan. 2008. *The Future of the Internet and How to Stop It.* New Haven: Yale University Press.

Links to Websites

Brynania.net Peacebuilding Simulation. Accessed April 15, 2014.
brynania.mcgill.ca

Correlate of War (COW) Project. Accessed May 29, 2014.
www.correlatesofwar.org

ICONS Project. Accessed April 15, 2014.
www.icons.umd.edu

International Crisis Behavior (ICB) Project. Accessed May 29, 2014.
www.cidcm.umd.edu/icb

Militarized Interstate Disputes (MID) Data Collection. Accessed May 29, 2014.
www.correlatesofwar.org/COW2%20Data/MIDs/MID310.html

Minorities at Risk (MAR) Project. Accessed May 29, 2014.
www.cidcm.umd.edu/mar

National Model United Nations (NMUN). Accessed April 15, 2014.
www.nmun.org

PaxSims Blog. Accessed April 15, 2014.
paxsims.wordpress.com

PeaceMaker. Accessed April 15, 2014.
www.peacemakergame.com/index.php

Statecraft, an International Relations Simulation. Accessed April 15, 2014.
www.statecraftsim.com

UCDP/PRIO Armed Conflict Dataset. Accessed May 29, 2014.
www.prio.org/data/armed-conflict

The World Factbook, Central Intelligence Agency. Accessed May 29, 2014.
www.cia.gov/library/publications/the-world-factbook

INDEX

Note: A page number followed by "t" refers to a table while a page number followed by "f" refers to a figure.